The Gen X Series

MATHS OLYMPIAD 7

Useful for Maths Olympiads Conducted at School, National & International Levels

Author
Prasoon Kumar

Peer Reviewer
Jyotsna Gopikrishnan

Strictly According to the Latest Syllabus of Maths Olympiad

Published by:

F-2/16, Ansari road, Daryaganj, New Delhi-110002
☎ 23240026, 23240027 • *Fax:* 011-23240028
✉ info@vspublishers.com • 🌐 www.vspublishers.com

Online Brandstore: amazon.in/vspublishers

Regional Office : Hyderabad
5-1-707/1, Brij Bhawan (Beside Central Bank of India Lane)
Bank Street, Koti, Hyderabad - 500 095
☎ 040-24737290
✉ vspublishershyd@gmail.com

Follow us on:

BUY OUR BOOKS FROM: AMAZON FLIPKART

© Copyright: *V&S* PUBLISHERS
ISBN 978-93-579405-6-6
New Edition

DISCLAIMER

While every attempt has been made to provide accurate and timely information in this book, neither the author nor the publisher assumes any responsibility for errors, unintended omissions or commissions detected therein. The author and publisher makes no representation or warranty with respect to the comprehensiveness or completeness of the contents provided.

All matters included have been simplified under professional guidance for general information only, without any warranty for applicability on an individual. Any mention of an organization or a website in the book, by way of citation or as a source of additional information, doesn't imply the endorsement of the content either by the author or the publisher. It is possible that websites cited may have changed or removed between the time of editing and publishing the book.

Results from using the expert opinion in this book will be totally dependent on individual circumstances and factors beyond the control of the author and the publisher.

It makes sense to elicit advice from well informed sources before implementing the ideas given in the book. The reader assumes full responsibility for the consequences arising out from reading this book.

For proper guidance, it is advisable to read the book under the watchful eyes of parents/guardian. The buyer of this book assumes all responsibility for the use of given materials and information.

The copyright of the entire content of this book rests with the author/publisher. Any infringement/transmission of the cover design, text or illustrations, in any form, by any means, by any entity will invite legal action and be responsible for consequences thereon.

Publisher's Note

General Trade and Mass Appeal books across various genres have helped **V&S Publishers** to gain widespread popularity. In a short span of 10 years, we have successfully published more than 1000 titles across 9 languages in our 50 subject categories. Being into the publishing business for about 40 years, we have always been a dynamic publishing house, with a massive distribution network, across India; including E-commerce platforms.

Understanding the need of inculcating knowledge and developing a spirit of healthy competition amongst students to make them ready for the world outside schools and colleges; we created Olympiad Series under the **GEN X SERIES Imprint** which, owning to its rich content and unique representation became popular amongst students, in no time. The motivation is not to improve marks in terms of numbers, but is to make sure that the students are already prepared to face competitive environment with respect to college admissions and cracking various entrance examinations, while ensuring their conceptual clarity.

Published for classes 1-10 across subjects English, Mathematics, Science, Computers, General Knowledge, the books are unlike any other in the market and are written in a guidebook pattern and exhaustively include examples and Multiple-Choice Questions.

Here, we present the latest Edition of **MATHS OLYMPIAD CLASS 7.**

Unique Features of the book are as follows:

- Authored by Subject Matter Experts' and Peer reviewed by School Principals and HOD's for the respective subjects
- Books based on principles of Applied Psychology and Bloom's Taxonomy
- Suited for Olympiad Examinations held at School level, National level & International Level irrespective of organizing body.
- The only Olympiad Book in India written in Guidebook Pattern with Concise Theory, images and illustrations.
- Exhaustively include Examples, MCQs, Subjective Questions, and HOTS with Answer Keys & Solutions.
- Multiple Model Papers for thorough practice also given inside the book with solutions.
- OMR sheets appended at the end of the book for simulating exam environment.

Besides, we are also planning to launch an App very soon for the Olympiad preparation which further testifies our constant endeavor to keep up with student demands. We have made sure to closely follow syllabus patterns of not only Olympiad conducting bodies but also education boards & organizations like CBSE and NCERT, to make sure that our books prove useful to students; helping them to boost their academic performance in schools as well.

P.S. While every care has been taken to ensure the correctness of the content, if you come across any error, howsoever minor, do not hesitate to discuss with teachers while pointing that out to us in no uncertain terms.

We wish you All the Best!

DISTINCTIVE

WHY OLYMPIADS?
Olympiads are just like competitive exams; conducted by various bodies at national and international levels. The aim is to experience a competitive examination at the school level and also to help students to discover their interest acrss subjects like English, Mathematics, Science and General Knowledge.

WHY V&S OLYMPIADS?
We at V&S Publishers aim to build an avid-reading student audience. Hence, our resolve is to follow an innovative pedagogic pattern which would help students to navigate through the book with utmost ease and comfort. Crisp theory practical examples and illustrations keep our book interactive and comprehensive.

01 LEARNING OBJECTIVES
They list the whole chapter as subtopics, helping the teachers to guide children in a step-by-step manner.

02 DID YOU KNOW
Enhance your knowledge by getting acquainted with some amazing facts across various subjects like science, Mathematics and English.

03 MULTIPLE CHOICE QUESTIONS
MCQs act as an excellent learning aid, helping you to understand and work on your mistakes.

04 THINGS TO REMEMBER
A quick recap of the chapter in a summarized format helps in faster revision along with conceptual clarity.

05 HOTS
The High Order Thinking Questions aim to help the student to solve Application-based questions and gain practical understanding of the subject.

FEATURES

06 SUBJECTIVE QUESTIONS
Help to place the knowledge gained in orderly fashion by using **"WH"** questions, mostly in the form of bullet points.

07 ACHIEVER'S SECTION
Offers a quick revision of the book along with some new facts for the students to discover.

08 A SET OF OMR SHEETS
To allow the student to practice question in an exam-like format which would help them to get the "feel" of how Olympiad exams take place.

09 MODEL TEST PAPERS
Two model test papers are provided at the end of each book, which help the student to test the knowledge which they have gained after thorough reading of all chapters.

10 ANSWER KEY & SOLUTIONS
Detailed Answer Key along with explanations aid the pupil to indentify, understand the mistakes they make during the course of Olympiad preparation.

COMPLEMENT SCHOOL SYLLABI
The syllabi across all Olympiad examination closely follow the pattern of academic books. Hence, they not only provide a competitive examination experience, but also help to revise topics for school examinations as well, while strengthening conceptual precision.

ENHANCEMENT OF ANALYTICAL & LOGICAL REASONING
Practicing analytical ability questions, not only helps in developing intellectual ability but also plays a vital role in building critical thinking ability which helps an individual to think about a question or a crisis like situation in day to day life; from all aspects and directions.

Note to Parents

Dear Parents,

Olympiad examinations come with a plethora of advantages. First and foremost among such advantages is the application of knowledge studied, in the form of multiple-choice questions. It helps the child not only to step away from rote learning, but also helps them to exhibit their competencies across various subjects.

In addition to this, Olympiads help the student to understand the importance of revision and practice, and to imbibe upon these practices; which also prove useful in academic performance of the child.

The Olympiads are conducted across multiple subjects, and help the child to recognize their field of interest, thereby encouraging the students to make a career in the field where they can excel the most.

However, cognitive development of a child is not just limited to the four walls of classroom. Following steps can be encouraged by you, to ensure their ward is able to grasp various concepts with ease or lesser difficulty:

- **Eat a balanced diet:** Ensure intake of vitamins and minerals to keep you active. Include fruits and super foods like millet in your diet to ensure healthy functioning of organs. Huge intake of junk food should be avoided.
- **Indulge in outdoor activities:** Outdoor games break the monotony of life. Play your heart out in greenery to keep yourself alert, active and fit.
- **Sleep well:** A sound sleep of 7-8 hours refreshes the brain and makes it ready to understand new topics with more clarity. A sleep derived person faces difficulty in doing even the simplest tasks of day to day life.
- **Reduce your Screen time:** More screen time leads to not only weakening of eyesight but decreases concentration span. Regulated Screen time should be encouraged
- **Do not hesitate to raise a hand:** Having a doubt in class? Do not hesitate to ask your parents or teachers. This ensures more Conceptual Clarity and hence leads to Application based understanding of various subjects and topics.
- **Teach and Learn:** No need to do rote-learning. Once you understand a topic teach or explain it to your friends, siblings and parents. It brings clarity and ensures the child does his revision this way.
- **Keep smiling:** A positive attitude promotes a growth mindset and encourages the child to be more inquisitive and try to learn something new, everyday!

HAPPY LEARNING!

Contents

SECTION 1 : MATHEMATICAL REASONING

1. Integers — 9
2. Fractions and Decimals — 16
3. Rational Numbers — 23
4. Exponents and Powers — 30
5. Ratio and Percentage — 35
6. Profit and Loss — 40
7. Simple and Compound Interest — 47
8. Algebraic Expressions — 54
9. Linear Equations in One Variable — 60
10. Lines and Angles — 66
11. Triangles — 74
12. Data Handling — 81
13. Elementary Mensuration: Perimeter & Area — 89
14. Visualizing Solid Shapes — 97
15. Mathematical Reasoning — 105

SECTION 2 : LOGICAL REASONING

1. Pattern — 111
2. Number Series — 117
3. Alphabetical Series — 119
4. Odd One Out — 122
5. Coding Decoding — 126
6. Alphabet Test — 130
7. Blood Relation Test — 134
8. Direction Sense Test — 138
9. Number Ranking Test — 143
10. Odd One Out — 147
11. Dice — 151
12. Mirror Images — 156
13. Water Images — 160
14. Embedded Figures — 165
15. Venn Diagrams — 170

SECTION 3: ACHIEVER'S SECTION

Some Thoughtful Questions — 177
Model Test Paper–1 — 181
Model Test Paper–2 — 185

ANSWER KEYS (Access Content Online on Dropbox) — 189
APPENDIX — 197

SECTION 1
MATHEMATICAL REASONING

Integers

Learning Objectives: In this chapter, students will learn about:
- ✓ Types of numbers
- ✓ Operation on integers
- ✓ Properties of Integers

CHAPTER SUMMARY

Types of Numbers

Natural Numbers: 1, 2, 3, 4,... These numbers are also called counting numbers.

Whole Numbers: 0, 1, 2, 3, 4,... These numbers are natural numbers and zero. Fractions: -, -, -,... These numbers lie between two whole numbers.

Decimals: 0.1, 2.4, 5.9,... These numbers are made up of a whole part, decimal point and a decimal part. They also lie between two whole numbers.

Integers: ..., −4, −3, −2, −1, 0, 1, 2, 3, 4,... Whole numbers along with the negative numbers are called integers.

- Natural numbers are positive integers. For example, 1, 2, 3, etc.
- Numbers having negative sign are negative integers. For example, −1, −2, −3, etc.
- Zero is neither positive nor a negative integer.

Integers on Number Line

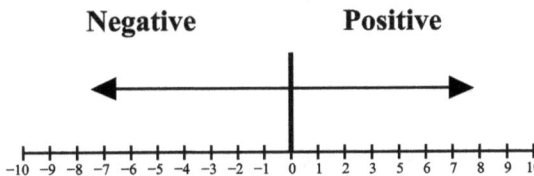

- Zero lies in the middle of positive and negative numbers.
- Every positive integer is greater than 0 and negative integers.
- Every negative integer is smaller than 0 and positive integers.
- Zero is less than every positive integer but greater than every negative integer.
- Out of any two integers on a number line, the integer on the left is always smaller than the integer on its right.

Operations on Integers

Addition and Subtraction

- If two positive or two negative integers are added, we add their values regardless of their signs and the sum has their common sign.

  Example: $(-7) + (-4) = -11$

- If a positive and a negative integer is added, we find the difference between their numerical values regardless of their signs and give the sign of the integer having greater numerical value to the difference.

  Example: $(-7) + 4 = -3$

Multiplication and Division

- If two integers with opposite signs are multiplied, we find the product of their numerical values regardless of their signs and give a negative sign to the product.

  Example: $(-3) \times 5 = -15$

- If two integers with the same sign are multiplied, we find the product of their numerical values and give a positive sign to the product.

  Example: $(-3) \times (-5) = 15$

- If two integers with opposite signs are divided, we find the quotient of their numerical values regardless of their signs and give a negative sign to the quotient.

  Example: $(-10) \div 2 = -5$

- If two integers with the same sign are divided, we find the quotient of their numerical values and give a positive sign to the quotient.

  Example: $(-10) \div (-2) = 5$

The numbers on opposite sides of a dice add up to seven.

Properties of Integers

Closure Property: If a and b are integers, then
- $a + b$, $a - b$, and $a \times b$ are always an integer.
- $a \div b$ need not be an integer.

Example: Let us take (-2) and 3. Then, $(-2) + 3 = 1$, $(-2) - 3 = -5$, $(-2) \times 3 = -6$ are integers but $(-2) \div 3$ is not an integer.

Commutative Property: If a and b are integers, then
- $a + b = b + a$
- $a \times b = b \times a$
- $a - b \neq b - a$
- $a \div b \neq b \div a$

Example: Let us take 2 and 3. Then,
(i) $2 + 3 = 3 + 2 = 5$
(ii) $2 - 3 = -1$ and $3 - 2 = 1$
  so $2 - 3 \neq 3 - 2$
(iii) $2 \times 3 = 3 \times 2 = 6$
(iv) $2 \div 3 = \frac{2}{3}$ and $3 \div 2 = \frac{3}{2}$
  so $2 \div 3 \neq 3 \div 2$

Associative Property: If a, b and c are integers, then
- $(a + b) + c = a + (b + c)$
- $(a - b) - c \neq a - (b - c)$
- $(a \times b) \times c = a \times (b \times c)$
- $(a \div b) \div c \neq a \div (b \div c)$

Example: Let us take 2, 3 and 4. Then,

(i) $(2 + 3) + 4 = 2 + (3 + 4) = 9$
(ii) $(2 - 3) - 4 = -5$ and $2 - (3 - 4) = 3$
  so $(2 - 3) - 4 \neq 2 - (3 - 4)$
(iii) $(2 \times 3) \times 4 = 2 \times (3 \times 4) = 24$
(iv) $(2 \div 3) \div 4 = \frac{1}{6}$ and $2 \div (3 \div 4) = \frac{8}{3}$
  so $(2 \div 3) \div 4 \neq 2 \div (3 \div 4)$

Identity: If a is an integer, then
- $a + 0 = 0 + a = a$, where 0 is called the additive identity of integers.
- $a \times 1 = 1 \times a = a$, where 1 is called the multiplicative identity of integers.

  Example: (i) $(-5) + 0 = 0 + (-5) = -5$ (ii) $(-8) \times 1 = 1 \times (-8) = -8$

Inverse: If a is an integer, then
- $a + (-a) = (-a) + a = 0$, where $-a$ is called the additive inverse of a.
- $a \times \frac{1}{a} = \frac{1}{a} \times a = 1$, where $\frac{1}{a}$ is called the multiplicative inverse of a.

  Example: (i) $6 + (-6) = (-6) + 6 = 0$
  (ii) $7 \times \frac{1}{7} = \frac{1}{7} \times 7 = 1$

Property of Zero: If a is an integer, then
- $a \times 0 = 0 \times a = 0$
- If $a \neq 0$, then $0 \div a = 0$ but $a \div 0$ is meaningless.

  Example: (i) $(-9) \times 0 = 0 \times (-9) = 0$
  (ii) $0 \div 3 = 0$
  (iii) $4 \div 0$ is meaningless

Property of One: If a is an integer and $a \neq 0$, then $a \div a = 1$ and $a \div 1 = a$.

Example: (i) $(-7) \div (-7) = 1$ (ii) $(-2) \div 1 = (-2)$

Distributive Property: If a, b and c are integers, then
- $a \times (b + c) = (a \times b) + (a \times c)$
- $a \times (b - c) = (a \times b) - (a \times c)$

  Example: Let us take 2, 3 and 4. Then,
  (i) $2 \times (3 + 4) = (2 \times 3) + (2 \times 4) = 14$
  (ii) $2 \times (3 - 4) = (2 \times 3) - (2 \times 4) = -2$

Absolute Value: The absolute value of an integer is its numerical value regardless of its sign.

Example: (i) $|-3| = 3$ (ii) $|7| = 7$

MUST REMEMBER

➡ The absolute value of an integer is its numerical value regardless of its sign.

MULTIPLE CHOICE QUESTIONS

1. 12×12–12+12÷12–12=?
   (a) 121
   (b) –121
   (c) 133
   (d) –131

2. [16–{5+ (2–7)}]–[12–{7–(3–4)}]?
   (a) 12
   (b) –12
   (c) 8
   (d) – 4

3. 25 + 16 ÷ 4 × 3 – 5 + 7 of (–3) = ?
   (a) 11
   (b) –11
   (c) 12
   (d) 13

4. In a class test containing 15 questions 4 marks are given for every correct answer and (–2) marks are given for every incorrect answer. Mohan attempts all questions but only 9 of his answers are correct. What is his total score?
   (a) 36
   (b) 48
   (c) 24
   (d) 28

5. The smallest integer is _____.
   (a) 0
   (b) –1
   (c) 1
   (d) Not defined

6. If p and q are two integers such that p is the successor of q, then the value of $q - p - 4$ is
   (a) –5
   (b) –4
   (c) –3
   (d) –2

7. The value of the expression 63 – 98 – (–58) + 115 + (–172) + 78 + (–62) + 131 is:
   (a) 341
   (b) 113
   (c) 279
   (d) –3

8. A shopkeeper earns a profit of ₹1 by selling one copy and incure a loss of 40 paise per pen while selling pens of his old stock. In a particular month he incurs a loss of ₹5. In this period he sold 45 copies. How many pens did he sell in this period?
   (a) 175
   (b) 150
   (c) 125
   (d) 100

9. If p and q are two integers such that $p > q$, then $(-p)$ _____ $(-q)$.
   (a) >
   (b) <
   (c) =
   (d) None of these

10. The temperature of a place is 8°C. Next day the temperature falls by 11°C. What was the temperature of the place on the second day?
    (a) 3°C
    (b) 19°C
    (c) –3°C
    (d) –19°C

11. A cement company earns a profit of ₹ 8 per bag of white cement sold and a loss of ₹ 5 per bag of grey cement sold. The company sells 3000 bags of white cement and 5000 bags of grey cement in a month. What is its profit or loss?
    (a) ₹ 1000 Loss
    (b) ₹ 1200 Loss
    (c) ₹ 1000 Profit
    (d) ₹ 1200 Profit

12. Sum of two negative numbers is always _____.
    (a) Positive
    (b) Negative
    (c) 0
    (d) 1

13. The temperature at 12 noon was 10° C. It decreased at the rate of 2°C per hour until midnight. At what time would the temprature be 8°C below zero?
    (a) 6 P.M.
    (b) 7 P.M.
    (c) 8 P.M.
    (d) 9 P.M.

14. The price of a stock decreases ₹35 per day for seven consecutive days. What will be the price of the stock after a week if its current price is ₹500?
    (a) ₹ 235
    (b) ₹ 265
    (c) ₹ 245
    (d) ₹ 255

15. A group of hikers started descending from a mountain peak at a rate of 500 metres per hour. At what height are the hikers standing on the mountain after 7 hours if the total height of the mountain is 6048 metres?
    (a) 2548 metres
    (b) 2458 metres
    (c) 3548 metres
    (d) 3500 metres

16. An elevator descends into a mine shaft at the rate of 4 m/min. If the descent starts from 14m above the ground level, how long will it take to reach 250 m underground?

(a) 64 min (b) 65 min
(c) 66 min (d) 67 min
17. (888 – 777 + 555) = 111 × _____.
(a) 5 (b) 6
(c) 7 (d) 8
18. What is simplified value of
$[14 - \{12 - \{9 - (7 - \overline{6 - 2})\}\}]$?
(a) 4 (b) 6
(c) 8 (d) 12
19. Kiran got on an elevator and rode up 13 floors. Next, she rode down 5 floors. After that she went up 6 floors. Finally, she went down 8 floors. When she got off the elevator, she was on 7th floor. From which floor did she start her ride?
(a) 6th (b) 1st
(c) 5th (d) 2nd
20. Which of the following will always be an odd integer for all values of p?
(a) 2011p (b) p^3
(c) $p^2 + 2011$ (d) $2p^2 + 2011$
21. When the integers 9, –7, –2, –4, 1, –1 and 3 are arranged in ascending order, then which of the following integer will come in the middle?
(a) –1 (b) 1
(c) 3 (d) –2
22. Observe the number line and state which of the following statement is not true?

(a) B is greater than –4.
(b) A is smaller than 7.
(c) B is smaller than –5.
(d) A is greater than 2.
23. Which of the following letter represents the integer 0?

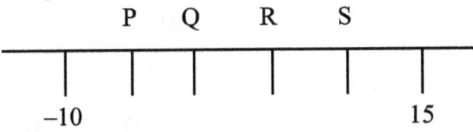

(a) P (b) Q
(c) R (d) S
24. If @, #, $ and & represent some integers on the number line, then the ascending order of the integers is:

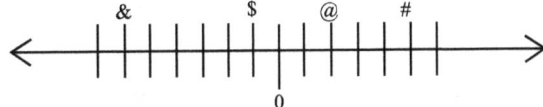

(a) &$@# (b) @$#&
(c) $#&@ (d) #@$&
25. Which of the following shows the maximum rise in temperature?
(a) 23° to 32° (b) –10° to +1°
(c) –18° to –11° (d) –5° to 5°
26. Which of the following is different from the others?
(a) 20 + (–25) (b) (–37) – (–32)
(c) (–5) × (–1) (d) (45) ÷ (–9)
27. The multiplication fact (–5) × (–10) = 50 is same as which of the following division fact?
(a) (–50) ÷ (–10) = (–5) (b) 50 ÷ (–5) = 10
(c) (–50) ÷ 5 = (–10) (d) 50 ÷ 10 = (–5)
28. –99 × 101 can be written as:
(a) (100 – 1) × (100 + 1)
(b) (100 – 1) × (100 – 1)
(c) (1 – 100) × (1 – 100)
(d) (1 – 100) × (1 + 100)
29. The additive inverse of (–65) ÷ (–13):
(a) Is greater than –3
(b) Is smaller than –3
(c) Lies between –3 and 3
(d) Lies between 1 and –3
30. If we multiply eleven negative integers and eight positive integers, the result will be _____.
(a) Positive (b) Negative
(c) 0 (d) None of these

Integers

HOTS

1. N is the number 1111...11 formed by writing 1004 ones in a row. What is the sum of the digits of the product 1004 x N?
   (a) 10,040
   (b) 11,004
   (c) 4,016
   (d) 5,020

2. Sunita lights a candle every fifteen minutes. Each candle burns for 45 minutes and then goes out. How many candles are alight 75 minutes after Sunita lit the first candle?
   (a) 4
   (b) 5
   (c) 6
   (d) 7

3. An ion is a charged particle whose charge is the sum of the charge on electrons (–1) and the charge on protons (+1). What is the charge on the electrons of an oxide ion having a charge of (–2) and whose proton charge is 8?
   (a) 6
   (b) 8
   (c) –10
   (d) –9

4. A diver descends 20 feet in the water from a boat at the surface of a lake. He then rose 12 feet and descends another 18 feet. At this point what is his depth in water?
   (a) 10 feet
   (b) 26 feet
   (c) 12 feet
   (d) 18 feet

5. In a test (+5) marks are given for every correct answer and (–2) marks are given for every incorrect answer. Sapna answered all the questions and scored 30 marks and got 10 correct answers. Karan also answered all the questions and scored (–12) marks though he got 4 correct answers. How many incorrect answers had they attempted altogether?
   (a) 10
   (b) 16
   (c) 18
   (d) 26

SUBJECTIVE QUESTIONS

1. Fill in the blanks using < or >.
   (a) –3 ...... –4
   (b) 6 ...... –20
   (c) –8 ...... –2
   (d) 5 ...... –7
   Answer:
   (a) –3 > –4
   (b) 6 > –20
   (c) –8 < –2
   (d) 5 > –7

2. Solve the following:
   (i) (–8) × (–5) + (–6)
   (ii) [(–6) × (–3)] + (–4)
   (iii) (–10) × [(–13) + (–10)]
   (iv) (–5) × [(–6) + 5]
   Answer:
   (i) (–8) × (–5) + (–6)
   = (–) × (–) × [8 × 5] + (-6)
   = 40 – 6
   = 34
   (ii) [(–6) × (–3)] + (–4)
   = (–) × (–) × [6 × 3] + (–4)
   = 18 – 4
   = 14
   (iii) (–10) × [(–13) + (–10)]
   = (–10) × (–23)
   = (–) × (–) × [10 × 23]
   = 230
   (iv) (–5) × [(–6) + 5]
   = (–5) × (–1)
   = (–) × (–) × 5 × 1
   = 5

3. Starting from (-7) × 4, find (–7) × (–3)
   Answer:
   (–7) × 4 = –28
   (–7) × 3 = –21 = [–28 + 7]
   (–7) × 2 = –14 = [–21 + 7]
   (–7) × 1 = –7 = [–14 + 7]
   (–7) × 0 = 0 = [–7 + 7]
   (–7) × (–1) = 7 = [0 + 7]
   (–7) × (–2) = 14 = [7 + 7]
   (–7) × (–3) = 21 = [14 + 7]

4. Using number line, find:
   (i) 3 × (–5)
   (ii) 8 × (–2)

Answer:
(i) 3 × (–5)

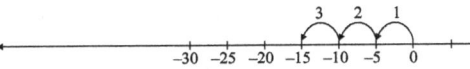

From the number line, we have
(–5) + (–5) + (–5) = 3 × (–5) = –15

(ii) 8 × (–2)

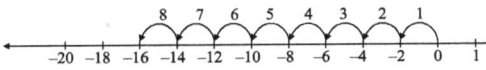

From the number line, we have
(–2) + (–2) + (–2) + (–2) + (–2) + (–2) + (–2) + (–2) = 8 × (–2) = –16

5. Write five pair of integers (*m, n*) such that *m* ÷ *n* = –3. One of such pair is (–6, 2).
   Answer:
   (i) (–3, 1) = (–3) ÷ 1 = –3
   (ii) (9, –3) = 9 ÷ (–3) = –3
   (iii) (6, –2) = 6 ÷ (–2) = –3
   (iv) (–24, 8) = (–24) ÷ 8 = –3
   (v) (18, –6) = 18 ÷ (–6) = –3

Fractions and Decimals   2

Learning Objectives : In this chapter, students will learn about:
- ✓ Fractions and its operations
- ✓ Decimals and its operations

CHAPTER SUMMARY

Fractions
Fractions are numbers of the form $\frac{p}{q}$ where p and q are natural numbers.

Types of Fractions
Proper Fractions: $\frac{1}{2}, \frac{3}{7}, \frac{5}{9}, \ldots$ These fractions have denominator greater than the numerator.

Improper Fractions: $\frac{3}{2}, \frac{15}{4}, \frac{9}{7}, \ldots$ These fractions have denominator smaller than the numerator.

Mixed Fractions: $1\frac{1}{2}, 2\frac{3}{4}, 3\frac{4}{7}, \ldots$ These fractions are a combination of a whole number and a fractional number.

Like Fractions: $\frac{7}{9}, \frac{2}{9}, \frac{15}{9}, \ldots$ These fractions have same denominators.

Unlike Fractions: $\frac{1}{2}, \frac{13}{7}, \frac{5}{9}, \ldots$ These fractions have different denominators.

Unit Fractions: $\frac{1}{2}, \frac{1}{7}, \frac{1}{6}, \ldots$ These fractions have 1 in their numerator.

Equivalent Fractions: $\frac{1}{2}, \frac{2}{4}, \frac{3}{6}, \ldots$ These are different looking fractions which represent the same fraction.

Operations on Fractions
- To add/subtract fractions, we first convert the fractions into like fractions by taking LCM of their denominators and then perform the addition/subtraction.

  Examples :
  (i) $\frac{2}{5} + \frac{3}{4} = \frac{8}{20} + \frac{15}{20} = \frac{23}{20} = 1\frac{3}{20}$

  (ii) $\frac{3}{4} - \frac{2}{5} = \frac{15}{20} - \frac{8}{20} = \frac{7}{20}$

- To multiply a fraction by a whole number, we multiply the whole number with the numerator of the fraction keeping the denominator same.

  Examples : $2 \times \frac{3}{5} = \frac{2 \times 3}{5} = \frac{6}{5}$

- To multiply two fractions, we multiply the numerators and the denominators separately.

  Examples : $\frac{3}{5} \times \frac{2}{7} = \frac{3 \times 2}{5 \times 7} = \frac{6}{35}$

- To find the reciprocal of a fraction, we interchange the numerator and the denominator.

  Examples : Reciprocal of $\frac{3}{5}$ is $\frac{5}{3}$

- To divide a whole number by a fraction, we take the reciprocal of the fraction and multiply with the whole number.

  Examples : $3 \div \frac{3}{2} = 3 \times \frac{2}{3} = 2$

- To divide a fraction by a whole number, we take the reciprocal of the whole number and multiply with the fraction.

  Examples : $\dfrac{3}{2} \div 3 = \dfrac{3}{2} \times \dfrac{1}{3} = \dfrac{1}{2}$

- To divide two fractions, we take the reciprocal of the second fraction and multiply with the first fraction.

  Examples : $\dfrac{3}{4} \div \dfrac{3}{2} = \dfrac{3}{4} \times \dfrac{2}{3} = \dfrac{1}{2}$

Note:
  (i) The product of two proper fractions is always less than each of the fractions.
  (ii) The product of two improper fractions is always more than each of the fractions.
  (iii) The operator 'of' stands for multiplication.

TRIVIA

The equals sign was invented in 1557 by Welsh mathematician Robert Recorde. The word 'equal' is from the Latin word aequalis as meaning uniform, identical, or equal.

Decimals

Decimals are the numbers which are represented in decimal forms. For example, 5.7, 12.523, 7.429 etc. Decimal numbers are made up of whole number part, decimal point and a decimal part

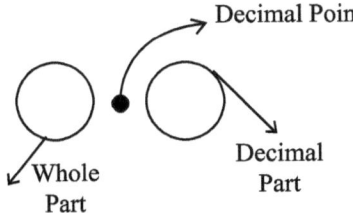

- The number of digits in the decimal part of a decimal number shows its decimal places.
- Adding zeros after the last digit of the decimal part does not change the value of the decimal number.

Like decimals: 4.23, 5.26, 7.74,... These decimals have same number of decimal places.

Unlike decimals: 3.617, 2.95, 7.0684,... These decimals have different number of decimal places.

Operations on Decimals

- To compare two decimals, we first convert the decimals into like decimals then compare them.

  Example: Compare 2.4 and 2.25
  2.4 = 2.40
  40 > 25 so 2.4 > 2.25

- To convert a decimal into fraction, we first write the number without decimal point in the numerator and write 1 followed by as many zeros as the decimal places in the denominator and then reduce it into simplest form.

  Example: $3.5 = \dfrac{35}{10} = \dfrac{7}{2} = 3\dfrac{1}{2}$

- To convert a fraction into decimal, we divide the numerator by the denominator till we reach zero as a remainder.

  Example: $\dfrac{3}{4} = 0.75$

$$\begin{array}{r} 0.75 \\ 4\overline{)3.00} \\ \underline{20} \\ 20 \\ \underline{-20} \\ 0 \end{array}$$

To add/subtract decimal numbers, we write the decimal numbers in a column keeping all decimal points aligned and then perform the addition/subtraction.

Examples: (i) 3.2 + 1.45 = 4.65

(ii) 3.2 − 1.45 = 1.75

- To multiply a decimal number by a power of 10, we move the decimal point as many places to the right as the number of zeros in the power of 10.

  Example: 4.693 × 100 = 469.3

Fractions and Decimals   17

```
    3 . 2 0        3 . 2 0
  + 1 . 4 5      - 1 . 4 5
  ─────────      ─────────
    4   6 5        1 . 7 5
```

- To multiply two decimal numbers, we first multiply the numbers without decimal point then place the
- decimal point after as many places from right as they are in both the decimal numbers put together.

  Example: 1.5×2.6

- $15 \times 26 = 390$ so $1.5 \times 2.6 = 3.90$

- To divide a decimal number by a power of 10, we move the decimal point as many places to the left as the
- number of zeros in the power of 10.

  Example: $56.2 \div 100 = 0.562$

- To divide two decimal numbers, we convert the divisor into whole number by multiplying it with a suitable power of 10. Then we multiply the same power of 10 with the dividend and then perform the division.

  Example: $4.8 \div 0.04 = \dfrac{4.8 \times 100}{0.04 \times 100} = \dfrac{480}{4} = 120$

MUST REMEMBER

➧ The product of two proper fractions is always less than each of the fractions.
➧ The product of two improper fractions is always more than each of the fractions.

MULTIPLE CHOICE QUESTIONS

1. Pictorial representation of $3 \times \frac{2}{3}$ is

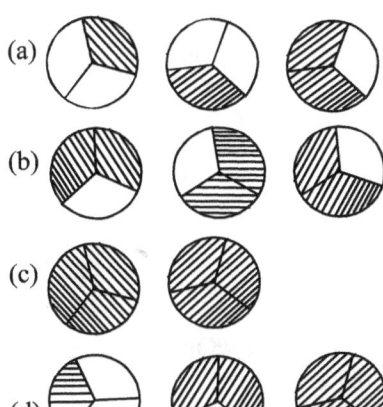

2. One packet of biscuit requires $2\frac{1}{2}$ cups of flour and $1\frac{2}{3}$ cups of sugar. Estimated total quantity of both ingredients used in 10 such packets of biscuits will be
   (a) less than 30 cups
   (b) between 30 cups and 40 cups
   (c) between 40 cups and 50 cups
   (d) above 50 cups

3. $\frac{4}{5}$ of 5 kg apples were used on Monday. The next day $\frac{1}{3}$ of what was left was used, Weight (in kg) of apples left now is
   (a) $\frac{2}{7}$ (b) $\frac{1}{14}$
   (c) $\frac{2}{3}$ (d) $\frac{4}{21}$

4. The picture

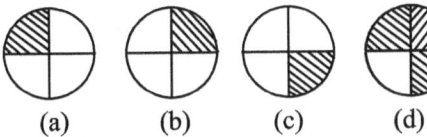

which picture represents 3/4 th part of the circle?

(a) $\frac{1}{4} \div 3$ (b) $3 \times \frac{1}{4}$
(c) $\frac{3}{4} \times 3$ (d) $3 \div \frac{1}{4}$

5. Reciprocal of –1 is _____
   (a) 1   (b) –1
   (c) 0   (d) None of these

6. Which letter comes $\frac{2}{5}$ of the way between A and J?
   (a) D   (b) E
   (c) F   (d) G

7. If $\frac{2}{3}$ of a number is 10, then what is 1.75 times of that number?
   (a) 26.24   (b) 24.26
   (c) 25.26   (d) 26.25

8. In a class of 40 students, $\frac{1}{5}$ of the total number of students like to eat rice only, $\frac{2}{5}$ of the total number of students like to eat chapati only and the remaining students like to eat both. What fraction of the total number of students like to eat both?
   (a) $\frac{1}{5}$ (b) $\frac{4}{5}$
   (c) $\frac{2}{5}$ (d) $\frac{3}{5}$

9. Reetu read $\frac{1}{5}$ th pages of a book. If she reads further 40 pages, she would have read $\frac{7}{10}$ th pages of the book. How many pages are left to be read?
   (a) 23   (b) 24
   (c) 25   (d) 26

Fractions and Decimals

10. The quotient of $7\frac{1}{6} \div 3\frac{2}{3}$ is:
    (a) Equal to 1.5 (b) Less than 1.5
    (c) Greater than 1.5 (d) None of these

11. Simplify: $\dfrac{2\frac{1}{2}+\frac{1}{5}}{2\frac{1}{2}\div\frac{1}{5}}$
    (a) $\dfrac{18}{125}$ (b) $\dfrac{12}{125}$
    (c) $\dfrac{36}{125}$ (d) $\dfrac{27}{125}$

12. The normal body temperature is 98.6° F. When Savitri was ill, her temperature rose to 103.1° F. How many degrees above normal was that?
    (a) 4.5°F (b) 2.5°F
    (c) 1.5°F (d) 3.5°F

13. What number divided by 520 gives the same quotient as 85 divided by 0.625?
    (a) 72000 (b) 77200
    (c) 70720 (d) 72700

14. How much cloth will be used in making 6 shirts, if each shirt requires $2\frac{1}{4}$ m of cloth, allowing $\frac{1}{8}$ m for waste in cutting and finishing each shirt?
    (a) $12\frac{1}{4}$ m (b) $12\frac{3}{4}$ m
    (c) $14\frac{3}{4}$ m (d) $14\frac{1}{4}$ m

15. A picture hall has seats for 820 people. At a recent film show, one usher guessed it was $\frac{3}{4}$ full, another that it was $\frac{2}{3}$ full. The ticket office reported 648 sales. Which usher (first or second) made the better guess?
    (a) First usher (b) Second usher
    (c) Both ushers (d) None of them

16. How many pieces of plywood each 0.35 cm thick are required to make a pile 1.89 m high?
    (a) 520 (b) 530
    (c) 540 (d) 560

17. A car covers a distance of 31.8 km in 2.4 litres of petrol. How much distance will it cover in 5 litres of petrol ?
    (a) 64.25 km (b) 66.25 km
    (c) 66.75 km (d) None of these

18. Each side of a polygon is 3.9 cm and its perimeter is 31.2 cm. How many sides does the polygon have?
    (a) 6 (b) 7
    (c) 8 (d) 9

19. $0.4 \div 0.4 \div 0.4 = ?$
    (a) 0.25 (b) 0.025
    (c) 2.5 (d) None of these

20. Mukesh bought 17.5 litres of mustard oil for ₹ 1550.50. What is the cost per litre?
    (a) ₹ 86.7 (b) ₹ 87.6
    (c) ₹ 88.6 (d) ₹ 89.6

21. A bus can cover 31.25 km in half an hour. How much distance can it cover in 16 hours ?
    (a) 750 km (b) 850 km
    (c) 950 km (d) 1000 km

22. $(0.25)^2 - (0.19)^2 = ?$
    (a) 0.0264 (b) 0.264
    (c) 2.64 (d) 0.204

23. What is the product of $11.1 \times 1.1 \times 0.11$?
    (a) 13.401 (b) 1.3031
    (c) 13.431 (d) 1.3431

24. Mohan purchased a notebook for ₹ 27.75, a pencil for ₹ 4.25 and a pen for ₹ 26.45. He gives a 100 rupee note to the shopkeeper. What amount did he get back ?
    (a) ₹ 41.55 (b) ₹ 42.55
    (c) ₹ 43.55 (d) None of these

25. Find the simplified value of
    $79.1 - 27.73 + 18.07 - 46.37$
    (a) 23.07 (b) 24.07
    (c) 23.87 (d) 23.67

26. Naresh bought 4 kg 270 g potato, 2 kg 170 g onion and some tomatoes. If the total weight of these vegetables is 11 kg 230 g, what is the weight of tomatoes?

(a) 2.790 kg (b) 4.790 kg
(c) 3.790 kg (d) None of these

27. What is the correct ascending order?
    (a) 7.09 < 7.9 < 7.19 < 7.90
    (b) 6.03 < 6.13 < 6.19 < 6.201
    (c) 18.3 < 18.09 < 18.325
    (d) None of these

28. In a school ₹ 18400 is distributed equally among student of class VII. If each student gets ₹ 287.5 how many students are there in class VII?
    (a) 62 (b) 63
    (c) 64 (d) 66

29. The total weight of some bags of cement is 3024.80 kg. If each bag weighs 39.8 kg how many bags are there?
    (a) 72 (b) 74
    (c) 76 (d) 78

30. 69 buckets of equal capacity can be filled with 586.5 litres of water. What is the capacity of each bucket?
    (a) 8.5 litres (b) 8.25 litres
    (c) 8.75 litres (d) None of these

HOTS

1. Look at the alphabets given.

   P R A S A D

   What fraction of alphabets are made of semicircles and straight lines?
   (a) 1 2 (b) 2 5
   (c) 5 6 (b) 4 5

2. Which of the following is an improper fraction?
   (a)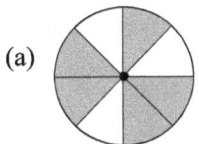
   (b)
   (c)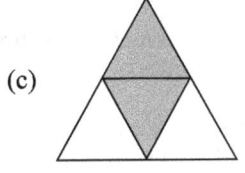
   (d)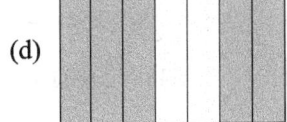

3. What does the shaded part of the following strip represent?

   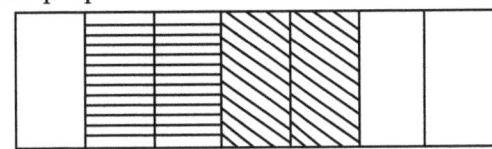

   (a) 2⁄7 − 1⁄7 + 2⁄7 = 3⁄7
   (b) 2⁄7 + 1⁄7 − 2⁄7 = 1⁄7
   (c) 2⁄7 + 1⁄7 = 3⁄7
   (d) 1⁄7 + 2⁄7 + 2⁄7 = 5⁄7

4. What is the decimal fraction shown by the shaded part of the figure given?

   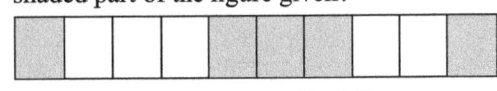

   (a) 2.5 (b) 0.5
   (c) 0.6 (d) 0.4

5. Find 78.5 ÷ 0.5?
   (a) 153 (b) 159
   (c) 158 (d) 157

SUBJECTIVE QUESTIONS

1. If 23 of a number is 6, find the number.
   Answer:
   Let x be the required number.
   $\therefore \dfrac{2}{3}$ of $x = 6 \Rightarrow \dfrac{2}{3} \times x = 6$
   $\Rightarrow x = 6 \div \dfrac{2}{3} = 6 \times \dfrac{3}{2} = 3 \times 3 = 9$
   Hence, the required number is 9.

2. Find the product of 67 and 223.
   Answer:
   $\dfrac{6}{7} \times 2\dfrac{2}{3} = \dfrac{6}{7} \times \dfrac{8}{3} = \dfrac{2 \times 8}{2 \times 1}$
   $= \dfrac{16}{7} = 2\dfrac{2}{7}$

   $7 \overline{)16} (2$
   $\underline{-14}$
   2

3. Solve the following:
   (a) $3 - 23$ \qquad (b) $4 + 25$
   Answer:
   (a) $3 - \dfrac{2}{3} = \dfrac{3}{1} - \dfrac{2}{3} = \dfrac{3 \times 3 - 2 \times 1}{3}$
   $= \dfrac{9 - 2}{3} = \dfrac{7}{3} = 2\dfrac{1}{3}$

   $3 \overline{)7} (2$
   $\underline{-6}$
   1

   (b) $4 + \dfrac{2}{5} = \dfrac{4}{1} + \dfrac{2}{5} = \dfrac{4 \times 5 + 2 \times 1}{5}$
   $= \dfrac{20 + 2}{5} = \dfrac{22}{5} = 4\dfrac{2}{5}$

   $7 \overline{)22} (4$
   $\underline{-20}$
   2

4. Arrange the following in ascending order:
   (i) $\dfrac{2}{7}, \dfrac{3}{5}, \dfrac{5}{6}$ \qquad (ii) $\dfrac{1}{5}, \dfrac{3}{7}, \dfrac{7}{10}, \dfrac{1}{6}$
   Answer:
   (i) We have $\dfrac{2}{7}, \dfrac{3}{5}$ and $\dfrac{5}{6}$
   LCM of 7, 5 and 6 = 210
   $\therefore \dfrac{2}{7} \times \dfrac{30}{30} = \dfrac{60}{210}$
   $\dfrac{3}{5} \times \dfrac{42}{42} = \dfrac{126}{210}$
   $\dfrac{5}{6} \times \dfrac{35}{35} = \dfrac{175}{210}$
   Since, the denominators are same.
   $\therefore 175 > 126 > 60$
   Hence, the required order is
   $\dfrac{5}{6} > \dfrac{3}{5} > \dfrac{2}{7}$

2	7, 5, 6
3	7, 5, 3
5	7, 5, 1
7	7, 1, 1
	1, 1, 1

   LCM = $2 \times 3 \times 5 \times 7$ = 210

   (ii) We have $\dfrac{1}{5}, \dfrac{3}{7}, \dfrac{7}{10}$ and $\dfrac{1}{6}$
   LCM of 5, 7, 10 and 6 = 210
   $\dfrac{1}{5} \times \dfrac{42}{42} = \dfrac{42}{210}$
   $\dfrac{3}{7} \times \dfrac{30}{30} = \dfrac{90}{210}$
   $\dfrac{7}{10} \times \dfrac{21}{21} = \dfrac{147}{210}$
   $\dfrac{1}{6} \times \dfrac{35}{35} = \dfrac{35}{210}$

2	5, 7, 10, 6
3	5, 7, 5, 3
5	5, 7, 5, 1
7	1, 7, 1, 1
	1, 1, 1, 1

   LCM = $2 \times 3 \times 5 \times 7$ = 210

   Since, the denominators are same.
   $\therefore 147 > 90 > 42 > 35$
   Hence, the required order is
   $\dfrac{7}{10} > \dfrac{3}{7} > \dfrac{1}{5} > \dfrac{1}{6}$

5. A picture hall has seats for 820 persons. At a recent film show, one usher guessed it was $\dfrac{3}{4}$ full, another that it was $\dfrac{2}{3}$ full. The ticket office reported 648 sales. Which usher (first or second) made the better guess?
   Answer:
   Total number of seats = 820
   Number of ticket sold = 648
   For first usher = $\dfrac{3}{4} \times 648 = 3 \times 162 = 486$
   For second usher = $\dfrac{2}{3} \times 648 = 2 \times 216 = 432$
   Since $432 < 486$
   Hence, the first usher guessed better.

Rational Numbers   3

Learning Objectives : In this chapter, students will learn about:
- ✓ Rational numbers and their properties
- ✓ Operation on rational numbers

CHAPTER SUMMARY

Rational Numbers
Rational numbers are of the form $\frac{p}{q}$, where p and q are integers and $q \neq 0$. For example, $\frac{-3}{9}, \frac{1}{5}$, etc.

Positive Rational Numbers: $-\frac{3}{8}, \frac{5}{11}, \ldots$ These rational numbers have positive numerator and denominator.

Negative Rational Numbers: $\frac{-2}{9}, \frac{6}{-15}, \ldots$ These rational numbers have either negative numerator or negative denominator.

Standard form: A rational number $\frac{a}{b}$ is said to be in standard form if b is positive and HCF of a and b is 1.

For example, $\frac{-2}{7}, \frac{6}{11}$, etc.

Note:
(i) Zero is a rational number as we can write 0 as $\frac{0}{1}$.
(ii) Every whole number is a rational number, but every rational number need not be a whole number.
(iii) Every fraction is a rational number, but every rational number need not be a fraction.
(iv) Every integer is a rational number, but every rational number need not be an integer.

Rational Numbers on Number Line
To represent rational numbers on a number line, we divide the number line into equal parts as the denominator of the rational number and then mark the numbers.

For example, let us represent $\frac{4}{7}$ on a number line

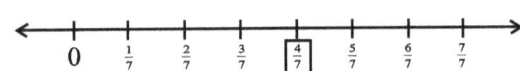

Properties of Rational Numbers
- If $\frac{a}{b}$ is a rational number and m is a non-zero integer, then $\frac{a}{b} = \frac{a \times m}{b \times m}$.

  Example: $\frac{2}{3} = \frac{2 \times 2}{3 \times 2} = \frac{4}{6}$

- If $\frac{a}{b}$ is a rational number and m is a common divisor, then $\frac{a}{b} = \frac{a \div m}{b \div m}$.

  Example: $\frac{10}{15} = \frac{10 \div 5}{15 \div 5} = \frac{2}{3}$

- Two rational numbers $\frac{a}{b}$ and $\frac{c}{d}$ are equal or equivalent if $a \times d = b \times c$.

  Example:
  (i) $\frac{3}{4}$ and $\frac{6}{8}$ are equivalent as $3 \times 8 = 4 \times 6 = 24$
  (ii) $\frac{2}{7}$ and $\frac{8}{21}$ are not equivalent as $2 \times 21 = 42$ and $7 \times 8 = 56$

- To compare two rational numbers, we compare the products $a \times d$ and $b \times c$.

Example: $\frac{5}{6}$ and $\frac{3}{4}$

$5 \times 4 = 20$ and $6 \times 3 = 18$

As $20 > 18$ so $\frac{5}{6} > \frac{3}{4}$.

- If a is any rational number, then exactly one of the following is true:
  (i) $a > 0$ (ii) $a < 0$
  (iii) $a = 0$

- If a and b are any two rational numbers, then exactly one of the following is true:
  (i) $a > b$ (ii) $a < b$
  (iii) $a = b$

- If a, b and c are any three rational numbers such that $a > b$ and $b > c$, then $a > c$.

- The absolute value of a rational number is its numerical value regardless of its sign.

Examples: (i) $\left|\frac{-3}{7}\right| = \frac{3}{7}$ (ii) $\left|\frac{2}{9}\right| = \frac{2}{9}$

TRIVIA

When an irrational number appears in a decimal expansion, it will come up without repetition.

Operations on Rational Numbers

- The operations on rational numbers are carried in the same manner as fractions with due consideration to their signs.

- If $\frac{a}{b}$ is a rational number, then its reciprocal is $\frac{b}{a}$

  Example: Reciprocal of $\frac{-3}{5}$ is $\frac{-5}{3}$.

Note:
(i) Reciprocal of 0 does not exist.
(ii) Reciprocal of 1 is 1 and that of -1 is -1.

➤ The absolute value of a rational number is its numerical value regardless of its sign.
➤ The operations on rational numbers are carried in the same manner as fractions with due consideration to their signs.

MULTIPLE CHOICE QUESTIONS

1. In the standard form of a rational number, the common factor of numerator and denominator is always
   (a) 0
   (b) 1
   (c) –2
   (d) 2

2. A student simplified a rational number $\frac{-24}{32}$ as $\frac{-3}{4}$. What error did the student make?
   (a) Divided numerator by –8
   (b) Divided denominator by –8
   (c) Divided numerator by 8
   (d) Divided denominator by 8

3. A body floats $\frac{2}{9}$ of its volume above the surface. What is the ratio of the volume of body submerged to its exposed volume?
   (a) 7:2
   (b) 2:7
   (c) 7:9
   (d) 9:7

4. 'a' and 'b' are two different numbers taken from the numbers 1–50. What is the largest value that $\frac{a-b}{a+b}$ can have?
   (a) $\frac{50}{51}$
   (b) $\frac{49}{51}$
   (c) $\frac{48}{51}$
   (d) $\frac{47}{51}$

5. If 12 shirts of equal size can be prepared from 27 m of cloth, what is the length of cloth required for each shirt?
   (a) $\frac{3}{4}$ m
   (b) $\frac{5}{4}$ m
   (c) $\frac{9}{4}$ m
   (d) $\frac{7}{4}$ m

6. From a rope 68 m long, pieces of equal size are cut. If length of one piece is $4\frac{1}{4}$ m, find the number of such pieces.
   (a) 13
   (b) 14
   (c) 15
   (d) 16

7. What should be divided by $\frac{-1}{2}$ to obtain the greatest negative integer?
   (a) $\frac{-1}{2}$
   (b) $\frac{1}{2}$
   (c) 1
   (d) –1

8. The product of two rational numbers is –10. If one of the numbers is 8, what is the other?
   (a) $\frac{4}{5}$
   (b) $\frac{5}{4}$
   (c) $-\frac{4}{5}$
   (d) $-\frac{5}{4}$

9. The sum of two rational numbers is –7. If one of the numbers is $-\frac{15}{6}$, what is the other?
   (a) $\frac{9}{2}$
   (b) $-\frac{9}{2}$
   (c) $\frac{7}{2}$
   (d) $-\frac{7}{2}$

10. Find the additive inverse of $\left(\frac{4}{5}+\frac{3}{7}\right)$.
    (a) $\frac{43}{35}$
    (b) $-\frac{43}{35}$
    (c) $-\frac{35}{43}$
    (d) $\frac{35}{43}$

11. What is the value of $\left(2-\frac{1}{2}-\frac{3}{4}\right)$?
    (a) $\frac{1}{4}$
    (b) $\frac{3}{4}$
    (c) $\frac{1}{2}$
    (d) $-\frac{3}{4}$

12. What is the simplest form of $\frac{84}{288}$?
    (a) $\frac{7}{12}$
    (b) $\frac{7}{48}$
    (c) $\frac{7}{24}$
    (d) None of these

Rational Numbers

13. Which of the following is correct?
    (a) $-\dfrac{2}{3} > \dfrac{-4}{3} > \dfrac{-7}{3} > \dfrac{-11}{3}$
    (b) $\dfrac{2}{3} > \dfrac{4}{3} > \dfrac{7}{3}$
    (c) $\dfrac{1}{2} < \dfrac{1}{3} < \dfrac{1}{4} < \dfrac{1}{5}$
    (d) None of these

14. By what rational number is $\dfrac{3}{13}$ multiplied to get -12?
    (a) -55 (b) -54
    (c) -53 (d) -52

15. Which of the following is incorrect?
    (a) $\dfrac{1}{2} > \dfrac{1}{3} > \dfrac{1}{4}$
    (b) $\dfrac{2}{5} < \dfrac{4}{5} < 1$
    (c) $\dfrac{2}{3} > \dfrac{3}{4} > \dfrac{7}{8}$
    (d) $\dfrac{1}{6} < \dfrac{2}{5} < \dfrac{3}{4}$

16. Which rational number is in between 2 and 3?
    (a) $\dfrac{8}{3}$ (b) $\dfrac{16}{3}$
    (c) $\dfrac{15}{4}$ (d) $\dfrac{11}{3}$

17. The cost of $4\dfrac{1}{2}$ metres of cloth is ₹ $98\dfrac{3}{4}$. What is the cost of cloth per metre?
    (a) $\dfrac{295}{18}$ (b) $\dfrac{395}{18}$
    (c) $\dfrac{495}{18}$ (d) None of these

18. What is the simplified value of $\left(\dfrac{3}{55} \times \dfrac{-33}{18}\right) - \left(\dfrac{39}{125} \times \dfrac{-15}{78}\right)$?
    (a) $\dfrac{1}{25}$ (b) $\dfrac{1}{50}$
    (c) $-\dfrac{1}{50}$ (d) $-\dfrac{1}{25}$

19. What is the reciprocal of $\left[\dfrac{2}{3} \div \dfrac{1}{3} - \dfrac{1}{2} \times \dfrac{1}{2}\right]$?
    (a) $\dfrac{4}{7}$ (b) $\dfrac{5}{7}$
    (c) $\dfrac{3}{7}$ (d) $\dfrac{-4}{7}$

20. The reciprocal of a rational number is $\dfrac{-7}{9}$. What is that rational number?
    (a) $\dfrac{-9}{7}$ (b) $\dfrac{9}{7}$
    (c) $\dfrac{7}{9}$ (d) 1

21. The sum of reciprocals of two rational numbers is $\dfrac{7}{4}$. If one of the numbers is $\dfrac{2}{3}$, what is the other?
    (a) 2 (b) -4
    (c) 4 (d) None of these

22. What is the value of x if $\dfrac{121}{13} = \dfrac{x}{104}$?
    (a) 948 (b) 968
    (c) 978 (d) 988

23. What result will be obtained when the sum of $\dfrac{65}{12}$ and $\dfrac{8}{3}$ is divided by their difference?
    (a) $\dfrac{33}{97}$ (b) $\dfrac{97}{33}$
    (c) $\dfrac{31}{97}$ (d) $\dfrac{97}{31}$

24. What is the multiplicative inverse of $\left(\dfrac{2}{3} + \dfrac{3}{4}\right)$?
    (a) $\dfrac{12}{17}$ (b) $-\dfrac{12}{17}$
    (c) 1 (d) 0

25. The cost of 15 articles is ₹ $87\dfrac{1}{2}$. What is the cost of one article?
    (a) ₹ $\dfrac{25}{6}$ (b) ₹ $\dfrac{35}{6}$
    (c) ₹ $\dfrac{37}{6}$ (d) None of these

26. A bus is moving at an average speed of $56\frac{2}{3}$ km/hour. How much distance will it cover in $3\frac{2}{5}$ hour?
    (a) $\frac{578}{3}$ km
    (b) $\frac{568}{3}$ km
    (c) $\frac{548}{3}$ km
    (d) None of these

27. What should be added to $\left(\frac{-23}{4}+\frac{-13}{8}\right)$ to get 1?
    (a) $\frac{57}{8}$
    (b) $\frac{59}{8}$
    (c) $\frac{67}{8}$
    (d) None of these

28. How many pieces each of length $3\frac{3}{4}$ m can be cut from a rope of length 60 m?
    (a) 14
    (b) 15
    (c) 16
    (d) 17

29. By what rational number should $\frac{-8}{65}$ be multiplied to obtain $\frac{5}{39}$?
    (a) $-\frac{5}{24}$
    (b) $\frac{25}{24}$
    (c) $\frac{5}{24}$
    (d) $\frac{-25}{24}$

30. Which rational number should be subtracted from 1 to get $-\frac{3}{7}$?
    (a) $\frac{7}{10}$
    (b) $\frac{10}{7}$
    (c) $\frac{-7}{10}$
    (d) $\frac{-10}{7}$

HOTS

1. Which one of the following statement is false?
    (a) The product of 10 negative integers and 15 positive integers is always positive
    (b) The product of 15 positive integers and 10 negative integers is always negative
    (c) The product of rational number and its reciprocal is always 1
    (d) If a is reciprocal of p then p will be reciprocal of a

2. Steve has a negative rational number which is reciprocal of itself. If he multiplies the rational number with
$$x=\left[\frac{1}{7}\times 4\frac{3}{5}+4\frac{3}{5}+7\frac{3}{5}+4\frac{9}{17}\div 8\frac{7}{17}\right]$$
then which one of the following is the correct statement?
    (a) When x multiplied by that number product will be reciprocal of x
    (b) When x multiplied by that number product will be additive inverse of x
    (c) x will be $\frac{3}{4}$ times
    (d) x will be doubled

3. Which of the following rational numbers are equal?
    (a) $\left(\frac{-9}{12}\right)$ and $\left(\frac{8}{-12}\right)$
    (b) $\left(\frac{-12}{20}\right)$ and $\left(\frac{20}{-25}\right)$
    (c) $\left(\frac{-7}{21}\right)$ and $\left(\frac{3}{-9}\right)$
    (d) $\left(\frac{-8}{-14}\right)$ and $\left(\frac{13}{21}\right)$

Rational Numbers

4. Arrange the following rational numbers in ascending order:

$\left(\dfrac{3}{5}\right), \left(\dfrac{-17}{-30}\right), \left(\dfrac{8}{-15}\right), \left(\dfrac{-7}{10}\right)$

(a) $\left(-\dfrac{7}{10}\right) < \left(\dfrac{8}{-15}\right) < \left(\dfrac{-17}{30}\right) < \left(\dfrac{3}{5}\right)$

(b) $\left(\dfrac{-17}{30}\right) < \left(\dfrac{-7}{10}\right) < \left(\dfrac{8}{-15}\right) < \left(\dfrac{3}{5}\right)$

(c) $\left(\dfrac{8}{-15}\right) < \left(\dfrac{-7}{10}\right) < \left(\dfrac{-17}{30}\right) < \left(\dfrac{3}{5}\right)$

(d) $\left(\dfrac{-7}{10}\right) < \left(\dfrac{-17}{30}\right) < \left(\dfrac{8}{-15}\right) < \left(\dfrac{3}{5}\right)$

5. Arrange the following rational numbers in descending order:

$\left(\dfrac{7}{8}\right), \left(\dfrac{64}{16}\right), \left(\dfrac{39}{-12}\right), \left(\dfrac{5}{-4}\right), \left(\dfrac{140}{28}\right)$

(a) $\left(\dfrac{-3}{10}\right) > \left(\dfrac{7}{-15}\right) > \left(\dfrac{-11}{20}\right) > \left(\dfrac{17}{-30}\right)$

(b) $\left(\dfrac{7}{-15}\right) > \left(\dfrac{-3}{10}\right) > \left(\dfrac{-11}{20}\right) > \left(\dfrac{17}{-30}\right)$

(c) $\left(\dfrac{-11}{20}\right) > \left(\dfrac{7}{-15}\right) > \left(\dfrac{-3}{10}\right) > \left(\dfrac{17}{-30}\right)$

(d) $\left(\dfrac{-3}{10}\right) > \left(\dfrac{7}{-15}\right) > \left(\dfrac{17}{-30}\right) > \left(\dfrac{-11}{20}\right)$

SUBJECTIVE QUESTIONS

1. List five rational numbers between:
    (i) -1 and 0
    (ii) -2 and -1
    (iii) $\dfrac{-4}{5}$ and $\dfrac{-2}{3}$
    (iv) $\dfrac{1}{2}$ and $\dfrac{2}{3}$

    Answer:
    (i) -1 and 0
    $\dfrac{-1}{10}, \dfrac{-1}{20}, \dfrac{-1}{30}, \dfrac{-1}{40}, \dfrac{-1}{50}$

    (ii) -2 and -1
    $-2 = \dfrac{-12}{6}$ and $-1 = \dfrac{-6}{6}$
    Five rational numbers are
    $\dfrac{-11}{6}, \dfrac{-10}{6}, \dfrac{-9}{6}, \dfrac{-8}{6}, \dfrac{-7}{6}$

    (iii) $\dfrac{-4}{5}$ and $\dfrac{-2}{3}$
    $\dfrac{-4}{5} = \dfrac{-4 \times 9}{5 \times 9} = \dfrac{-36}{45}$ and
    $\dfrac{-2}{3} = \dfrac{-2 \times 15}{3 \times 15} = \dfrac{-30}{45}$
    Five rational numbers are
    $\dfrac{-35}{45}, \dfrac{-34}{45}, \dfrac{-33}{45}, \dfrac{-32}{45}, \dfrac{-31}{45}$

    (iv) $\dfrac{1}{2}$ and $\dfrac{2}{3}$
    $\dfrac{1}{2} = \dfrac{1 \times 18}{2 \times 18} = \dfrac{18}{36}$ and $\dfrac{2}{3} = \dfrac{2 \times 12}{3 \times 12} = \dfrac{24}{36}$
    Five rational numbers are
    $\dfrac{19}{36}, \dfrac{20}{36}, \dfrac{21}{36}, \dfrac{22}{36}, \dfrac{23}{36}$

2. The points P, Q, R, S, T, U, A and B on the number line are such that, TR = RS = SU and AP = PQ = QB. Name the rational numbers represented by P, Q, R and S.

    Answer:
    Distance between U and T = 1 unit
    It is divided into 3 equal parts.
    TR = RS = SU = $\dfrac{1}{3}$
    $R = -1 - \dfrac{1}{3} = -\dfrac{3}{3} - \dfrac{1}{3} = \dfrac{-4}{3}$
    $S = -1 - \dfrac{2}{3} = -\dfrac{3}{3} - \dfrac{2}{3} = -\dfrac{5}{3}$

Similarly,
AB = 1 unit
It is divided into 3 equal parts.

$P = 2 + \dfrac{1}{3} = \dfrac{6}{3} + \dfrac{1}{3} = \dfrac{7}{3}$

$Q = 2 + \dfrac{2}{3} = \dfrac{6}{3} + \dfrac{2}{3} = \dfrac{8}{3}$

Exponents and Powers 4

Learning Objectives : In this chapter, students will learn about:
- ✓ Irrational Numbers
- ✓ Laws of exponents

CHAPTER SUMMARY

Irrational Numbers
Irrational numbers are those which cannot be written in the form $\frac{p}{q}$, where p and q are integers and $q \neq 0$
For example, $\sqrt{2}, \pi$, etc.

Surds
Surds are basically an expression involving a root. Root can be a square root, cube root, fourth root, etc.
For example: $\sqrt{2}, \sqrt[3]{4}$, etc.

Important Rules
If 'a' and 'b' are two positive real numbers, then
- $\sqrt{ab} = \sqrt{a} \times \sqrt{b}$
- $\sqrt{\frac{a}{b}} = \frac{\sqrt{a}}{\sqrt{b}}$
- $(\sqrt{a} + \sqrt{b})(\sqrt{a} - \sqrt{b}) = a - b$
- $(a + \sqrt{b})(a - \sqrt{b}) = a^2 - b$
- $(\sqrt{a} + \sqrt{b})(\sqrt{c} + \sqrt{d}) = \sqrt{ac} + \sqrt{ad} + \sqrt{bc} + \sqrt{bd}$
- $(\sqrt{a} + \sqrt{b})^2 = a + 2\sqrt{ab} + b$
- $(\sqrt{a})^2 = a$
- $\sqrt{a} + \sqrt{a} = 2\sqrt{a}$
- $\sqrt{a} - \sqrt{a} = 0$

Rationalising Surds
If a is a real number, then

- The rationalising factor of $\sqrt{a}$ is $\sqrt{a}$
- The rationalising factor of $\sqrt[3]{a}$ is $a^{\frac{2}{3}}$
- To rationalise $\frac{1}{\sqrt{a}}$, we multiply the numerator and denominator by $\sqrt{a}$
- To rationalise $\frac{1}{a+\sqrt{b}}$, we multiply the numerator and denominator by $a - \sqrt{b}$
- To rationalise $\frac{1}{a-\sqrt{b}}$ we multiply the numerator and denominator by $a + \sqrt{b}$
- To rationalise $\frac{1}{\sqrt{a}+\sqrt{b}}$, we multiply the numerator and denominator by $\sqrt{a} - \sqrt{b}$
- To rationalise $\frac{1}{\sqrt{a}-\sqrt{b}}$, we multiply the numerator and denominator by $\sqrt{a} + \sqrt{b}$

Example:

$$\frac{1}{2-\sqrt{3}} = \frac{1}{2-\sqrt{3}} \times \frac{2+\sqrt{3}}{2+\sqrt{3}} = \frac{2+\sqrt{3}}{2^2 - (\sqrt{3})^2} = \frac{2+\sqrt{3}}{4-3} = 2+\sqrt{3}$$

n^{th} Root of a Rational Number
If $a > 0$ is a real number and 'n' is a positive integer, then nth root of 'a' is given as $\sqrt[n]{a} = b$, if $b^n = a$ and $b > 0$.

Exponents or Indices
When a number is multiplied by itself n number of times, then it is written as $a \times a \times a.....$

(n times) $= a^n$, where a is the base, n is the exponent and a^n is the nth power of a.

TRIVIA

The polar diameter of the Earth is quite close to (within 0.1%) half a billion inches.

Important Results

- $(-x_1) \times (-x_2) \times (-x_3) \times \ldots \times (-x_n) = -(x_1 \times x_2 \times x_3 \times \ldots \times x_n)$ when n is odd.
- $(-x_1) \times (-x_2) \times (-x_2) \times \ldots \times (-x_n) = (-x_n) = (x_1 \times x_2 \times x_3 \times \ldots \times x_n)$ when n is even
- $(-x) \times (-x) \times (-x) \times \ldots \times n$ times $= -x^n$ when n is odd.
- $(-x) \times (-x) \times (-x) \times \ldots \times n$ times $= x^n$ when n is even.
- $(-1) \times (-1) \times (-1) \ldots n$ times $= -1$ when n is odd.
- $(-1) \times (-1) \times (-1) \ldots n$ times $= 1$ when n is even.

Laws of Exponents

If m and n are rational numbers and a is a positive real number, then
- $a^m \times a^n = a^{m+n}$
- $a^m \div a^n = a^{m-n}$
- $(a^m)^n = a^{mn}$
- $a^m \times b^m = (ab)^m$
- $\left(\dfrac{a}{b}\right)^m = \dfrac{a^m}{b^m}$
- $a^0 = 1$
- $a^{-n} = \dfrac{1}{a^n}$

Standard Form of Numbers

A number is said to be in standard form if it is expressed as $p \times 10^n$, where p is a real number such that $1 \leq p < 10$ and n is an integer.

Examples: (i) $7560000000 = 7.56 \times 10^9$
(ii) $0.00000039 = 3.9 \times 10^{-7}$

MUST REMEMBER

➡ Surds are basically an expression involving a root.

Exponents and Powers

MULTIPLE CHOICE QUESTIONS

1. If $x = 3 + 2\sqrt{2}$, then the value of $\sqrt{x} - \dfrac{1}{\sqrt{x}}$ is:
   - (a) 1
   - (b) 2
   - (c) $2\sqrt{2}$
   - (d) $3\sqrt{3}$

2. $\left(\dfrac{x^b}{x^c}\right)^{(b+c-a)} \cdot \left(\dfrac{x^c}{x^a}\right)^{(c+a-b)} \cdot \left(\dfrac{x^a}{x^b}\right)^{(a+b-c)} = ?$
   - (a) x^{abc}
   - (b) 1
   - (c) $x^{ab+bc+ca}$
   - (d) x^{a+b+c}

3. If m and n are whole numbers such that $m^n = 121$, the value of $(m-1)^{n+1}$ is:
   - (a) 1
   - (b) 10
   - (c) 121
   - (d) 1000

4. $(256)^{0.16} \times (256)^{0.09} = ?$
   - (a) 4
   - (b) 16
   - (c) 64
   - (d) 256.25

5. The value of $[(10)^{150} \div (10)^{146}]$ is
   - (a) 1000
   - (b) 10000
   - (c) 100000
   - (d) 10^6

6. If $(25)^{7.5} \times (5)^{2.5} \div (125)^{1.5} = 5^x$ then $x = ?$
   - (a) 8.5
   - (b) 13
   - (c) 16
   - (d) 17.5

7. $(0.04)^{-1.5} = ?$
   - (a) 25
   - (b) 125
   - (c) 250
   - (d) 625

8. If $3^{(x-y)} = 27$ and $3^{(x+y)} = 243$, then x is equal to:
   - (a) 0
   - (b) 2
   - (c) 4
   - (d) 6

9. If $5^a = 3125$, then the value of $5^{(a-3)}$ is:
   - (a) 25
   - (b) 125
   - (c) 625
   - (d) 1625

10. Given that $10^{0.48} = x$, $10^{0.70} = y$ and $x^z = y^2$, then the value of z is close to:
    - (a) 1.45
    - (b) 1.88
    - (c) 2.9
    - (d) 3.7

11. $(17)^{3.5} \times (17)^? = 17^8$
    - (a) 2.29
    - (b) 2.75
    - (c) 4.25
    - (d) 4.5

12. Find the value of $\sqrt{300}$.
    - (a) 15.36
    - (b) 30
    - (c) 9
    - (d) 17.32

13. Evaluate: $\sqrt{75} + \sqrt{147} = ?$
    - (a) 20.7846
    - (b) 22.3698
    - (c) 18.336
    - (d) 21.7586

14. Find the value of:
    $\sqrt{80} + 3\sqrt{245} - \sqrt{125} = ?$
    - (a) 38.6395
    - (b) 44.7214
    - (c) 50.2136
    - (d) 3.2365

15. Find $\sqrt{242} \div \sqrt{72}$.
    - (a) 1.2
    - (b) 2
    - (c) $\dfrac{4}{5}$
    - (d) $1\dfrac{5}{6}$

16. $(18a^8b^6) \div (3a^2b^2)$ simplifies to
    - (a) $6a^4b^3$
    - (b) $6a^{10}b^8$
    - (c) $6a^6b^4$
    - (d) $15a^6b^3$

17. Replace question mark with the suitable answer:
    $$56 - 45 - \sqrt{?} = \sqrt{36}$$
    - (a) 25
    - (b) 35
    - (c) 15
    - (d) 5

18. Replace question mark with the suitable answer:
    $$(?)^2 = \dfrac{4}{25}$$
    - (a) 1
    - (b) 1.5
    - (c) 2/5
    - (d) 3

19. Find $\sqrt{210\dfrac{1}{4}} = ?$
    - (a) $13\dfrac{1}{2}$
    - (b) $15\dfrac{1}{2}$
    - (c) $14\dfrac{1}{2}$
    - (d) $17\dfrac{1}{2}$

20. What is the value of $(0.003)^3$?
    - (a) 0.09
    - (b) 0.000000027
    - (c) 0.00027
    - (d) 0.27

21. The value of $\dfrac{10^{22}+10^{20}}{10^{20}}$ is
    (a) 10
    (b) 10^{42}
    (c) 101
    (d) 10^{22}

22. The standard form of the number 12345 is
    (a) 1234.5×10^1
    (b) 123.45×10^2
    (c) 12.345×10^3
    (d) 1.2345×10^4

23. If $2^{1998} - 2^{1997} - 2^{1996} + 2^{1995} = k \cdot 2^{1995}$, then the value of k is
    (a) 1
    (b) 2
    (c) 3
    (d) 4

24. Which of the following is equal to 1?
    (a) $2^0 + 3^0 + 4^0$
    (b) $2^0 \times 3^0 \times 4^0$
    (c) $(3^0 - 2^0) \times 4^0$
    (d) $(3^0 - 2^0) \times (3^0 + 2^0)$

25. Which of the following is not equal to $\left(\dfrac{-5}{4}\right)^4$?
    (a) $\dfrac{(-5)^4}{4^4}$
    (b) $\dfrac{5^4}{(-4)^4}$
    (c) $-\dfrac{5^4}{4^4}$
    (d) $\left(-\dfrac{5}{4}\right) \times \left(-\dfrac{5}{4}\right) \times \left(-\dfrac{5}{4}\right) \times \left(-\dfrac{5}{4}\right)$

26. Which of the following is not equal to 1?
    (a) $\dfrac{2^3 \times 3^2}{4 \times 18}$
    (b) $[(-2)^3 \times (-2)^4] \div (-2)^7$
    (c) $\dfrac{3^0 \times 5^3}{5 \times 25}$
    (d) $\dfrac{2^4}{(7^0 + 3^0)^3}$

27. In standard form, the number 829030000 is written as $K \times 10^8$, where k is equal to
    (a) 82903
    (b) 829.03
    (c) 82.903
    (d) 8.2903

28. Which of thre following has the largest value?
    (a) 0.0001
    (b) $\dfrac{1}{1000}$
    (c) $\dfrac{1}{10^6}$
    (d) $\dfrac{1}{10^6} \div 0.1$

29. Which of the following is not true?
    (a) $3^2 > 2^3$
    (b) $4^3 = 2^6$
    (c) $3^3 = 9$
    (d) $2^5 > 5^2$

30. Which power of 8 is equal 2^6?
    (a) 3
    (b) 2
    (c) 1
    (d) 4

HOTS

1. If you express 450 as a product of powers of their prime factors, it will be:
   (a) $3 \times 2^2 \times 5^2$
   (b) $2 \times 4^2 \times 5^2$
   (c) $2 \times 3^2 \times 5^2$
   (d) $1 \times 3^2 \times 5^2$

2. If you express 24000 as a product of powers of their prime factors, it will be:
   (a) $6^6 \times 3 \times 2^3$
   (b) $4^6 \times 3 \times 5^3$
   (c) $1 \times 3 \times 5^3$
   (d) $2^6 \times 3 \times 5^3$

3. Correct value of $\left(\dfrac{-1}{2}\right)^2 \times 2^3 \times \left(\dfrac{3}{4}\right)^2$:
   (a) $\dfrac{9}{8}$
   (b) $\dfrac{4}{7}$
   (c) $\dfrac{8}{9}$
   (d) $\dfrac{1}{16}$

4. Correct value of $\left(\dfrac{-1}{2}\right)^2 \times 2^3 \times \left(\dfrac{3}{4}\right)^2$:
   (a) $\dfrac{24}{12225}$
   (b) $\dfrac{14}{16225}$
   (c) $\dfrac{64}{18225}$
   (d) $\dfrac{34}{18225}$

5. If $a = 2$ and $b = 3$, the value of $\left(\left(\dfrac{a}{b}\right) + \left(\dfrac{b}{a}\right)\right)^a$
   (a) $\dfrac{129}{36}$
   (b) $\dfrac{169}{36}$
   (c) $\dfrac{139}{36}$
   (d) $\dfrac{169}{26}$

Exponents and Powers

SUBJECTIVE QUESTIONS

1. Express 343 as a power of 7.
   Answer:
   We have $343 = 7 \times 7 \times 7 = 7^3$
   Thus, $343 = 7^3$

7	343
7	49
7	7
	1

2. Which is greater 3^2 or 2^3?
   Answer:
   We have $3^2 = 3 \times 3 = 9$
   $2^3 = 2 \times 2 \times 2 = 8$
   Since $9 > 8$
   Thus, $3^2 > 2^3$

3. Express the following number as a powers of prime factors
   (i) 144 (ii) 225
   Answer:
   (i) We have
   $144 = 2 \times 2 \times 2 \times 2 \times 3 \times 3 = 2^4 \times 3^2$
   Thus, $144 = 2^4 \times 3^2$

2	144
2	72
2	36
2	18
2	9
2	3
	1

   (ii) We have
   $225 = 3 \times 3 \times 5 \times 5 = 3^2 \times 5^2$
   Thus, $225 = 3^2 \times 5^2$

3	225
3	75
5	25
5	5
	1

4. Find the value of:
   (i) $(-1)^{1000}$ (ii) $(1)^{250}$
   (iii) $(-1)^{121}$ (iv) $(10000)^0$
   Answer:
   (i) $(-1)1000 = 1$ [$\because$ (–1)even number = 1]
   (ii) $(1)250 = 1$ [$\because$ (1)even number = 1]
   (iii) $(-1)121 = -1$ [$\because$ (–1)odd number = –1]
   (iv) $(10000)0 = 1$ [$\because a0 = 1$]

5. Express the following in exponential form:
   (i) $5 \times 5 \times 5 \times 5 \times 5$
   (ii) $4 \times 4 \times 4 \times 5 \times 5 \times 5$
   (iii) $(-1) \times (-1) \times (-1) \times (-1) \times (-1)$
   (iv) $a \times a \times a \times b \times c \times c \times c \times d \times d$
   Answer:
   (i) $5 \times 5 \times 5 \times 5 \times 5 = (5)^5$
   (ii) $4 \times 4 \times 4 \times 5 \times 5 \times 5 = 4^3 \times 5^3$
   (iii) $(-1) \times (-1) \times (-1) \times (-1) \times (-1) = (-1)^5$
   (iv) $a \times a \times a \times b \times c \times c \times c \times d \times d = a^3 b^1 c^3 d^2$

Ratio and Percentage

5

Learning Objectives : In this chapter, students will learn about:
- ✓ Concept of ratio and percentage

CHAPTER SUMMARY

Ratio

Ratio is used to compare similar quantities using division. The ratio of a to b is written as *a* : *b* where *a* is the antecedent and *b* is consequent.

Properties of Ratio
- The order of terms in a ratio is very important. The ratio 3 : 4 is not same as the ratio 4 : 3.
- If we multiply or divide the numerator and denominator of a ratio by the same number, the ratio remains the same.
- Ratio exists between quantities of similar kind. For example, we cannot take ratio of a height of student and its marks.
- Ratio has no units.
- In order to find the ratio of the given quantities, the quantities must be in the same unit.
- To compare two ratios, we first convert them into like fractions and then compare them.
- A ratio *a* : *b* is in its lowest term if HCF of *a* and *b* is 1.
- If a quantity increases or decreases in the ratio *a* : *b*, then

   New Quantity = $\frac{b}{a}$ × Original Quantity

Note: When two numbers are in the ratio *a* : *b*, we write them as *ax* and *bx*. For example, two numbers are in the ratio 3 : 4 so the numbers are 3*x* and 4*x*.

Proportion

If two ratios *a* : *b* and *c* : *d* are equal, we say that the terms a, b, c and d are in proportion and we express it as *a* : *b* :: *c* : *d*, where *a* and *d* are extremes while *b* and *c* are means.

- Product of extremes = Product of means
- *a*, *b* and *c* are said to be in continued proportion if *a* : *b* :: *b* : *c*, i.e.

   $\frac{a}{b} = \frac{b}{c} \Rightarrow b^2 = ac \Rightarrow b = \sqrt{ac}$

- In proportion, the first two quantities should be of same kind and the last two quantities should be same kind.

TRIVIA
The ratio of males to females in the world is 102:100, so there are slightly more men on the planet than women.

Unitary Method

In this method, the value of the require quantity is calculated by finding the value of the unit quantity.

Example: The cost of 5 bars of a soap is ₹92.50. What is the cost of three dozen bars of soap?

Solution: Cost of 5 bars of soap = ₹92.50

Cost of 1 bar of soap = $\frac{92.50}{5}$ = ₹18.5

Cost of three dozen bars of soap = ₹18.5 × 36
= ₹666
he cost of three dozen bars of soap is ₹666.

Percent

By a certain percent, we mean that many hundredths. Thus, x percent means x hundredths, written as $x\%$. For example, 25%, 3.9%, etc.

Conversions

- To convert a decimal or a fraction into percentage, we multiply it by 100.

  Example: (i) $2.5 \times 100 = 250\%$
  (ii) $\frac{1}{2} \times 100 = 50\%$

  To convert a percentage into a fraction or a decimal, we devide it by 100.

  Example: $75\% = \frac{75}{100} = \frac{3}{4} = 0.75$

Percentage Increase /Decrease

Percentage increase
$$= \frac{\text{New Number} - \text{Original Number}}{\text{Original Number}} \times 100$$

Percentage decrease
$$= \frac{\text{Original Number} - \text{New Number}}{\text{Original Number}} \times 100$$

If the price of the commodity increases by R%, then the reduction in consumption so as not to increase the expenditure is: $\left[\frac{R}{(100+R)} \times 100\right]\%$

If the price of the commodity decreases by R%, then the increase in consumption so as not to decrease the expenditure is: $\left[\frac{R}{(100-R)} \times 100\right]\%$

If A is R% more than B, then B is less than A by $\left[\frac{R}{(100+R)} \times 100\right]\%$

If A is R% less than B, then B is more than A by $\left[\frac{R}{(100-R)} \times 100\right]\%$

Population

Let the population of a town be P and suppose it increase at the rate of R% per annum, then:

- Population after n years $= P\left(1 + \frac{R}{100}\right)^n$

- Population n years ago $= \dfrac{P}{\left(1 + \dfrac{R}{100}\right)^n}$

Depreciation

Let the present value of a machine be P. suppose it depriciates at the rate of R% per annum, then:

- Value of the machine after n years
$$= P\left(1 - \frac{R}{100}\right)^n$$

- Value of the machine n years ago $= \dfrac{P}{\left(1 - \dfrac{R}{100}\right)^n}$

MUST REMEMBER

➡ In order to find the ratio of the given quantities, the quantities must be in the same unit.

MULTIPLE CHOICE QUESTIONS

1. A batsman scored 110 runs which included 3 boundaries and 8 sixes. What percent of his total score did he make by running between the wickets?
   (a) 45%
   (b) $45\frac{5}{11}\%$
   (c) 54%
   (d) 55%

2. Two students appeared in an examination. One of them secured 9 marks more than the other and his marks were 56% of the sum of their marks. The marks obtained by them are:
   (a) 39, 30
   (b) 41, 32
   (c) 42, 33
   (d) 43, 34

3. A fruit seller had some apples. He sells 40% apples and still has 420 apples. Originally, he had:
   (a) 588 apples
   (b) 600 apples
   (c) 672 apples
   (d) 700 apples

4. What percentage of numbers from 1 to 70 has 1 or 9 in the unit's digit?
   (a) 1
   (b) 14
   (c) 20
   (d) 21

5. If A = $x\%$ of y and B = $y\%$ of x, then which of the following is true?
   (a) A is smaller than B
   (b) A is greater than B
   (c) Relationship between A and B cannot be determined
   (d) None of these

6. If 20% of $a = b$, then $b\%$ of 20 is the same as:
   (a) 4% of a
   (b) 5% of a
   (c) 20% of a
   (d) None of these

7. In a certain school, 20% of students are below 8 years of age. The number of students above 8 years of age is 2/3 of the number of students of 8 years of age which is 48. What is the total number of students in the school?
   (a) 72
   (b) 80
   (c) 120
   (d) 100

8. Two numbers A and B are such that the sum of 5% of A and 4% of B is two-third of the sum of 6% of A and 8% of B. Find the ratio of A : B.
   (a) 2 : 3
   (b) 1 : 1
   (c) 3 : 4
   (d) 4 : 3

9. A student multiplied a number by 3/5 instead of 5/3. What is the percentage error in the calculation?
   (a) 34%
   (b) 44%
   (c) 54%
   (d) 64%

10. In an election between two candidates, one got 55% of the total valid votes, 20% of the votes were invalid. If the total number of votes was 7500, the number of valid votes that the other candidate got, was:
    (a) 2700
    (b) 2900
    (c) 3000
    (d) 3100

11. Three candidates contested an election and received 1136, 7636 and 11628 votes respectively. What percentage of the total votes did the winning candidate get?
    (a) 57%
    (b) 60%
    (c) 65%
    (d) 90%

12. Two tailors X and Y are paid a total of ₹ 550 per week by their employer. If X is paid 120 percent of the sum paid to Y, how much is Y paid per week?
    (a) ₹ 200
    (b) ₹ 250
    (c) ₹ 300
    (d) None of these

13. Gauri went to the stationers and bought things worth ₹ 25, out of which 30 paise went on sales tax on taxable purchases. If the tax rate was 6%, then what was the cost of the tax-free items?
    (a) ₹ 15
    (b) ₹ 15.70
    (c) ₹ 19.70
    (d) ₹ 20

14. Rajeev buys goods worth ₹ 6650. He gets a rebate of 6% on it. After getting the rebate, he pays sales tax @ 10%. Find the amount he will have to pay for the goods.
    (a) ₹ 6876.10
    (b) ₹ 6999.20
    (c) ₹ 6654
    (d) ₹ 7000

15. The population of a town increased from 1,75,000 to 2,62,500 in a decade. The average percent increase of population per year is:
    (a) 4.37%
    (b) 5%
    (c) 6%
    (d) 8.75%

Ratio and Percentage

16. The population of a town has increased from 60,000 to 65,000. Find the increase percent.
    (a) $8\frac{1}{3}\%$ (b) $7\frac{1}{2}\%$
    (c) $6\frac{2}{3}\%$ (d) $9\frac{2}{3}\%$

17. Ram's salary is increased from ₹ 630 to ₹ 700. Find the increase percent.
    (a) $8\frac{1}{2}\%$ (b) $11\frac{1}{9}\%$
    (c) $13\frac{2}{9}\%$ (d) $9\frac{1}{9}\%$

18. In an election of two candidates, the candidate who gets 41% is rejected by a majority of 2412 votes. Find the total number of votes polled.
    (a) 12600 (b) 11300
    (c) 13400 (d) 15600

19. A man loses 12.5% of his money and after spending 70% of the remainder he is left with ₹ 210. How much did he have at first?
    (a) ₹ 800 (b) ₹ 950
    (c) ₹ 1200 (d) ₹ 1050

20. 3.5% of income is taken as tax and 12.5% of the remaining is saved. This leaves ₹ 4,053 to spend. What is the income?
    (a) ₹ 6000 (b) ₹ 7200
    (c) ₹ 5600 (d) ₹ 4800

21. If 2 litres of water is evaporated on boiling from 8 litres of sugar solution containing 5% sugar, find the percentage of sugar in the remaining solution.
    (a) $6\frac{2}{3}\%$ (b) $8\frac{1}{3}\%$
    (c) $7\frac{1}{2}\%$ (d) $9\frac{2}{3}\%$

22. Due to fall in manpower, the production in a factory decreases by 25%. By what percent should working hours be increased to restore the original production?
    (a) $36\frac{2}{3}\%$ (b) $34\frac{1}{3}\%$
    (c) $33\frac{1}{3}\%$ (d) $26\frac{2}{5}\%$

23. 12% of a certain sum of money is ₹ 43.5 Find the sum.
    (a) ₹ 340.50 (b) ₹ 362.50
    (c) ₹ 421.75 (d) ₹ 263.30

24. Two numbers are respectively 20% and 50% more than the third. What percent is the first of the second?
    (a) 60% (b) 82%
    (c) 75% (d) 80%

25. Two numbers are respectively 20% and 25% of a third number. What percent is the first of the second?
    (a) 60% (b) 45%
    (c) 80% (d) 35%

HOTS

1. An error 2% in excess is made while measuring the side of a square. The percentage of error in the calculated area of the square is:
   (a) 2% (b) 2.02%
   (c) 4% (d) 4.04%

2. A towel, when bleached, was found to have lost 20% of its length and 10% of its breadth. The percentage of decrease in area is:
   (a) 10% (b) 10.08%
   (c) 20% (d) 28%

3. Three pipes A, B and C can fill an empty tank fully in 30 minutes, 20 minutes, and 10 minutes respectively. When the tank is empty, all the three pipes are opened. A, B and C discharge chemical solutions P, Q and R respectively. What is the proportion of the solution R in the liquid in the tank after 3 minutes?
   (a) 5/11 (b) 6/11
   (c) 7/11 (d) 8/11

4. Mr. Sharma left one-third of his property to his daughter, one-fourth to his son and the remainder to his wife. If his wife's share is ₹18000 what was the worth of Mr. Sharma's total property?
   (a) ₹ 41200   (b) ₹ 42200
   (c) ₹ 43200   (d) ₹ 44200

5. The ages of Simran and Ranjna are in the ratio 5:3. After 6 years their ages will be in the ratio 7:5. What is the present age of Ranjna?
   (a) 9 years   (b) 12 years
   (c) 14 years   (d) 15 years

SUBJECTIVE QUESTIONS

1. Find the ratio of:
   (a) 5 km to 400 m
   (b) 2 hours to 160 minutes
   Answer:
   (a) 5 km = 5 × 1000 = 5000 m
      Ratio of 5 km to 400 m
      = 5000 m : 400 m
      = 25 : 2
      Required ratio = 25 : 2
   (b) 2 hours = 2 × 60 = 120 minutes
      Ratio of 2 hours to 160 minutes
      = 120 : 160
      = 3 : 4
      Required ratio = 3 : 4

2. State whether the following ratios are proportional or not:
   (i) 20 : 45 and 4 : 9
   (ii) 9 : 27 and 33 : 11
   Answer:
   (i) 20 : 45 and 4 : 9
      Product of extremes = 20 × 9 = 180
      Product of means = 45 × 4 = 180
      Here, the product of extremes = Product of means
      Hence, the given ratios are in proportion.
   (ii) 9 : 27 and 33 : 11
      Product of extremes = 9 × 11 = 99
      Product of means = 27 × 33 = 891
      Here, the product of extremes ≠ Product of means
      Hence, the given ratios are not in proportion.

3. Find the mean proportional between 9 and 16.
   Answer:
   Let x be the mean proportional between 9 and 16.
   $9 : x :: x : 16$
   $\Rightarrow x \times x = 9 \times 16$
   $\Rightarrow x^2 = 144$
   $\Rightarrow x = \sqrt{144} = 12$
   Hence, the required mean proportional = 12

Ratio and Percentage

Profit and Loss 6

Learning Objectives : In this chapter, students will learn about:
- ✓ Concept of profit and loss
- ✓ Calculating discount

CHAPTER SUMMARY

Cost Price (C.P.): The price at which an article is purchased.

Selling Price (S.P.): The price at which an article is sold.

Profit (P): If S.P. is greater than C.P., the seller gains a profit.

Loss (L): If S.P. is smaller than C.P., the seller incurs a loss.

Discount: It is the reduction in price offered by the seller to sell his goods to dispose off the stock.

Marked Price (M.P.): The printed price of the article.

Note:
(i) Profit or loss is always reckoned on C.P.
(ii) Discount is always calculated on M.P of the article.

Important Formulae
- Profit = S.P. − C.P.
- Loss = C.P − S.P.
- Profit % = $\frac{P}{C.P} \times 100$
- Loss% = $\frac{L}{C.P.} \times 100$
- Selling Price = $\frac{100 + P\%}{100} \times C.P.$
- Selling Price = $\frac{100 - L\%}{100} \times C.P.$
- Cost Price = $\frac{100}{100 + P\%} \times S.P.$
- Cost Price = $\frac{100}{100 - L\%} \times S.P.$
- Discount = M.P. − S.P.
- Discount% = $\frac{Discount}{M.P.} \times 100$
- Selling price = M.P. $\times \left\{\frac{100 - Discount\%}{100}\right\}$
- M.P. = $\frac{100 \times S.P.}{100 - Discount\%}$
- When a person sells two similar items, one at a profit of x% and the other at a loss of x%, then the seller always incurs a loss which is given by:

  Loss % = $\left(\frac{x\%}{10}\right)^2$

- If a trader professes to sell his goods at cost price, but uses false weights, then

  Profit % = $\left[\frac{Error}{true\ value - Error} \times 100\right]\%$

- Two successive discounts x% and y% on an article is equivalent to a single discount of $\left(x + y - \frac{xy}{100}\right)\%$

TRIVIA
A number if multiply by 11 is just you bring down the last digits add the digit to the number on it's left and bring down the first number.

- Profit or loss is always reckoned on C.P.
- Discount is always calculated on M.P of the article.

MULTIPLE CHOICE QUESTIONS

1. Alfred buys an old scooter for ₹ 4700 and spends ₹ 800 on its repairs. If he sells the scooter for ₹ 5800, his gain percent is:
   (a) $4\frac{4}{7}\%$ (b) $5\frac{5}{11}\%$
   (c) 10% (d) 12%

2. The cost price of 20 articles is the same as the selling price of x articles. If the profit is 25%, then the value of x is:
   (a) 15 (b) 16
   (c) 18 (d) 25

3. If selling price is doubled, the profit triples. Find the profit percent.
   (a) 66% (b) 100%
   (c) 105% (d) 110%

4. In a certain store, the profit is 320% of the cost. If the cost increases by 25% but the selling price remains constant, approximately what percentage of the selling price is the profit?
   (a) 30% (b) 70%
   (c) 100% (d) 250%

5. A vendor bought toffees at 6 for a rupee. How many for a rupee must he sell to gain 20%?
   (a) 3 (b) 4
   (c) 5 (d) 6

6. The percentage profit earned by selling an article for ₹ 1920 is equal to the percentage loss incurred by selling the same article for ₹ 1280. At what price should the article be sold to make 25% profit?
   (a) ₹ 2000
   (b) ₹ 2200
   (c) ₹ 2400
   (d) Data inadequate

7. A shopkeeper expects a gain of 22.5% on his cost price. If in a week, his sale was of ₹ 392, what was his profit?
   (a) ₹ 18.20 (b) ₹ 70
   (c) ₹ 72 (d) ₹ 88.25

8. A man buys a cycle for ₹ 1400 and sells it at a loss of 15%. What is the selling price of the cycle?
   (a) ₹ 1090 (b) ₹ 1160
   (c) ₹ 1190 (d) ₹ 1202

9. Sam purchased 20 dozens of toys at the rate of ₹ 375 per dozen. He sold each one of them at the rate of ₹ 33. What was his percentage profit?
   (a) 3.5 (b) 4.5
   (c) 5.6 (d) 6.5

10. Some articles were bought at 6 articles for ₹ 5 and sold at 5 articles for ₹ 6. Gain percent is:
    (a) 30% (b) 33%
    (c) 35% (d) 44%

11. On selling 17 balls at ₹ 720, there is a loss equal to the cost price of 5 balls. The cost price of a ball is:
    (a) ₹ 45 (b) ₹ 50
    (c) ₹ 55 (d) ₹ 60

12. When a plot is sold for ₹ 18,700, the owner loses 15%. At what price must that plot be sold in order to gain 15%?
    (a) ₹ 21,000 (b) ₹ 22,500
    (c) ₹ 25,300 (d) ₹ 25,800

13. 100 oranges were bought at the rate of ₹ 350 and sold at the rate of ₹ 48 per dozen. The percentage of profit or loss is:
    (a) $14\frac{2}{7}\%$ Gain (b) 15% Loss
    (c) $14\frac{2}{7}\%$ Loss (d) 15% Gain

14. A shopkeeper sells one transistor for ₹ 840 at a gain of 20% and another for ₹ 960 at a loss of 4%. His total gain or loss percent is:
    (a) $5\frac{15}{17}\%$ Loss (b) $5\frac{15}{17}\%$ Gain
    (c) $6\frac{2}{3}\%$ Gain (d) $6\frac{2}{3}\%$ Loss

15. A trader mixes 26 kg of rice at ₹ 20 per kg with 30 kg of rice of other variety at ₹ 36 per kg and sells the mixture at ₹ 30 per kg. His profit percent is:
    (a) No profit, no loss   (b) 5%
    (c) 8%   (d) 10%

16. A trader uses 800 gm weight instead of 1 kg. Find his profit %.
    (a) 20%   (b) 25%
    (c) 35%   (d) 200%

17. A trader uses 1 kg weight for 800 gm and increases the price by 20%. Find his profit/loss %.
    (a) 4% profit   (b) 4% loss
    (c) 6 profit   (d) 8% loss

18. A milk vendor mixes water to milk such that he gains 25%. Find the percentage of water in the mixture.
    (a) 30%   (b) 25%
    (c) 20%   (d) 45%

19. A person buys an item at ₹ 120 and sells to another at a profit of 25%. If the second person sells the item to another at ₹ 180, what is the profit % of the second person?
    (a) 15%   (b) 18%
    (c) 25%   (d) 20%

20. A trader allows a discount of 25% on his articles but wants to gain 50%. How many times of the C.P. should be marked on the items?
    (a) 4 times   (b) 5 times
    (c) 2 times   (d) 8 times

21. By selling an item at a price a trader gains 40%. What is the profit / loss % if the item is sold at half the price?
    (a) 30% profit   (b) 60% profit
    (c) 30% loss   (d) 45% loss

22. A trader gets a profit of 25% on an article. If he buys the article at 10% lesser price and sells it for ₹ 2 less, he still gets 25% profit. Find the actual C.P. of the article.
    (a) ₹ 26   (b) ₹ 18
    (c) ₹ 36   (d) ₹ 16

23. A trader gets a discount of 20% from the dealer and marks it at 20% more price than the actual MP to the customer. Find his overall gain %.
    (a) 50%   (b) 60%
    (c) 30%   (d) 75%

24. If the cost price of 20 articles is equal to the selling price of 25 articles, what is the % profit or loss made by the merchant?
    (a) 25% loss   (b) 25% profit
    (c) 20% loss   (d) 20% profit

25. Sam buys 10 apples for ₹ 1. At what price should he sell a dozen apples if he wishes to make a profit of 25%?
    (a) ₹ 0.125   (b) ₹ 1.25
    (c) ₹ 0.25   (d) ₹ 1.5

26. By selling an article at 80% of its marked price, a merchant makes a loss of 12%. What will be the percent profit made by the merchant if he sells the article at 95% of its marked price?
    (a) 5% profit   (b) 1% loss
    (c) 10% profit   (d) 4.5% profit

27. What is the maximum percentage discount that a merchant can offer on her Marked Price so that she ends up selling at no profit or loss, if she had initially marked her goods up by 50%?
    (a) 50%   (b) 20%
    (c) 25%   (d) 33.33%

28. A merchant who marked his goods up by 50% subsequently offered a discount of 20%. What is the percentage profit that the merchant makes after offering the discount?
    (a) 30%   (b) 125%
    (c) 20%   (d) 25%

29. If oranges are bought at the rate of 30 for a rupee, how many oranges must be sold for a rupee in order to gain 25%?
    (a) 36   (b) 24
    (c) 28   (d) 32

30. Satish marks his goods 25% above cost price but allows 12.5% discount for cash payment. If he sells the article for ₹ 875, find his cost price.
    (a) ₹ 800   (b) ₹ 890
    (c) ₹ 120   (d) ₹ 960

Profit and Loss

HOTS

1. A factory makes a profit of ₹1446 on every batch of juice produced and loses ₹106 on every batch because of the juice which gets spilled during production. The factory sold 90 batches of juice in a day. Find the total profit or loss made by the factory.
   (a) Profit of ₹1,20,600
   (b) Loss of ₹1,20,600
   (c) Profit of ₹1,60,200
   (d) Loss of ₹1,60,200

2. A shopkeeper sells some articles at the profit of 25% on the original price. What is the exact amount of profit? To find the answer, which of the following information given in statements I and II is/are necessary?
   I. Sale price of the article
   II. Number of articles sold
   (a) Only I is necessary
   (b) Only II is necessary
   (c) Either I or II is necessary
   (d) Both I and II are necessary

3. A shopkeeper sells some toys at ₹ 250 each. What percent profit does he make? To find the answer, which of the following information given in statements I and II is/are necessary?
   I. Number of toys sold
   II. Cost price of each toy
   (a) Only I is necessary
   (b) Only II is necessary
   (c) Both I and II are necessary
   (d) Either I or II is necessary

4. A man mixes two types of rice (X and Y) and sells the mixture at the rate of ₹ 17 per kg. Find his profit percentage.
   I. The rate of X is ₹ 20 per kg
   II. The rate of Y is ₹ 13 per kg
   (a) I alone sufficient while II alone not sufficient to answer
   (b) II alone sufficient while I alone not sufficient to answer
   (c) Either I or II alone sufficient to answer
   (d) Both I and II are not sufficient to answer

5. By selling a product with 20% profit, how much profit was earned?
   I. The difference between cost and selling price is ₹ 40.
   II. The selling price is 120 percent of the cost price.
   (a) I alone sufficient while II alone not sufficient to answer
   (b) II alone sufficient while I alone not sufficient to answer
   (c) Either I or II alone sufficient to answer
   (d) Both I and II are not sufficient to answer

6. By selling an article what is the profit percent gained?
   I. 5% discount is given on list price.
   II. If discount is not given, 20% profit is gained.
   III. The cost price of the articles is ₹ 5000.
   (a) Only I and II
   (b) Only II and III
   (c) Only I and III
   (d) All I, II and III

7. What was the percentage of discount given?
   I. 23.5% profit was earned by selling an almirah for ₹ 12,350.
   II. If there were no discount, the earned profit would have been 30%.
   III. The cost price of the almirah was ₹ 10,000.
   (a) Only I and II
   (b) Only II and III
   (c) Only I and III
   (d) None of these

8. What is the percent profit earned by the shopkeeper on selling the articles in his shop?
   I. Labelled price of the articles sold was 130% of the cost price.

II. Cost price of each article was ₹ 550.
III. A discount of 10% on labelled price was offered.
(a) Only I
(b) Only II
(c) I and III
(d) All the three are required

9. A milk vendor mixes water to 20 litres of milk such that the ratio of milk and water is 4:3. He buys the milk at ₹ 10 per litre and sells the mixture at ₹ 12 per litre. Find the profit % of the vendor.
(a) 110%
(b) 130%
(c) 125%
(d) 90%

10. A trader buys some apples at a price of 10 apples for ₹ 8 and sells them at a price of 8 apples for ₹ 10. Find his profit or loss %.
(a) 56.25 % Gain
(b) 56.25 % Loss
(c) 62.5 % Gain
(d) 45.60 % Loss

SUBJECTIVE QUESTIONS

1. Given the following values, find the unknown values:
   (i) C.P. = ₹ 1200, S.P. = ₹ 1350 Profit/Loss?
   (ii) C.P. = Rs 980, S.P. = ₹ 940 Profit/Loss = ?
   (iii) C.P. = Rs 720, S.P. =?, Profit = ₹ 55.50
   (iv) C.P. =? S.P. = ₹ 1254, Loss = ₹ 32
   Answer:
   (i) Given CP = ₹ 1200, SP = ₹ 1350
   Clearly CP < SP. So, profit.
   Profit = SP – CP
   = ₹ (1350 – 1200)
   = ₹ 150
   (ii) Given CP = ₹ 980, SP = ₹ 940
   Clearly CP > SP. So, loss.
   Loss = CP – SP
   = ₹ (980 – 940)
   = ₹ 40
   (iii) CP = ₹ 720, SP =?, profit = ₹ 55.50
   Profit = SP – CP
   55.50 = SP – 720
   SP = (55.50 + 720)
   = ₹ 775.50
   (iv) CP =?, SP = ₹ 1254, loss = ₹ 32
   Loss = CP – SP
   32 = CP – 1254
   CP = (1254 + 32)
   = ₹ 1286

2. Fill in the blanks in each of the following:
   (i) C.P. = ₹ 1265, S.P. = ₹ 1253, Loss = ₹ ....
   (ii) C.P. = ₹......., S.P. = ₹ 450, Profit = ₹ 150
   (iii) C.P. = ₹ 3355, S.P. = ₹ 7355,…….. = ₹......
   (iv) C.P. = ₹…., S.P. = ₹ 2390, Loss = ₹ 5.50
   Answer:
   (i) Loss = ₹ 12
   Given CP = ₹ 1265, SP = ₹ 1253
   Loss = CP – SP
   = ₹ (1265 – 1253)
   = ₹ 12
   (ii) C.P. = ₹ 300
   Given CP = ?, SP = ₹ 450, profit = ₹ 150
   Profit = SP – CP
   150 = 450 – CP
   CP = ₹ (450 – 150)
   = ₹ 300
   (iii) Profit = ₹ 4000
   Given CP = ₹ 3355, SP = ₹ 7355,
   Here SP > CP, so profit.
   Profit = SP – CP
   Profit = ₹ (7355 – 3355)
   = ₹ 4000
   (iv) C. P. = Rs 2395.50
   Given CP = ?, SP = ₹ 2390, loss = ₹ 5.50
   Loss = CP – SP

Profit and Loss

$5.50 = CP - 2390$
$= ₹ (5.50 + 2390)$
$= ₹ 2395.50$

3. Calculate the profit or loss and profit or loss percent in each of the following cases:
   (i) C.P. = ₹ 4560, S.P. = ₹ 5000
   (ii) C.P. = ₹ 2600, S.P. = ₹ 2470

   Answer:
   (i) Given CP = ₹ 4560, SP = ₹ 5000
   Here, clearly SP > CP. So, profit.
   Profit = SP – CP
   = ₹ (5000 – 4560)
   = ₹ 440

   Profit % = {(Profit/CP) × 100} %
   = {(440/4560) × 100} %
   = {0.0965 × 100} %
   Profit % = 9.65%

   (ii) Given CP = ₹ 2600, SP = ₹ 2470.
   Here, clearly CP > SP. So, loss.
   Loss = CP – SP
   = ₹ (2600 – 2470)
   = ₹ 130
   Loss % = {(Loss/CP) × 100} %
   = {(130/2600) × 100} %
   = {0.05 × 100} %
   Loss % = 5%

Simple and Compound Interest

Learning Objectives : In this chapter, students will learn about:
- ✓ Simple interest
- ✓ Compound Interest

CHAPTER SUMMARY

Simple Interest (S.I.)

Simple interest is calculated uniformly on the original principal throughout the loan period. When we need a large sum of money for buying house, car, etc. we borrow money either from bank or from some agency. The money borrowed is called loan and we become the borrower. When we borrow money in the form of loan we have to return that in a specified period of time by giving them extra fees. This extra fee levied on the loan is called as the Simple Interest (S.I).

Principal Money borrowed.

Rate: It is the percentage of the principal charged as interest each year. The rate is expressed as a decimal fraction, so percentages must be divided by 100.

Example: $5\% = \dfrac{5}{100} = 0.05$

Amount: The total money which the borrower pays back to the lender at the end of the specified period is called the amount.

Time: Time in years of the loan.

Important Formulae

Let Principal = P, Rate = R% per annum (p.a.) and Time = T years. Then

$$\text{S.I.} = \dfrac{P \times R \times T}{100}$$

- If the time is given in month, then

$$\text{S.I.} = \dfrac{P \times R \times T}{100 \times 12}$$

- If the time is given in days, then

$$\text{S.I.} = \dfrac{P \times R \times T}{100 \times 365}$$

$$P = \left(\dfrac{100 \times S.I.}{R \times T}\right); R = \left(\dfrac{100 \times S.I}{P \times T}\right) \text{ and }$$

$$T = \left(\dfrac{100 \times S.I.}{P \times R}\right)$$

Compound Interest

The interest calculated on a sum of money which includes principal and interest calculated for previous year is called Compound Interest. The SI (Simple Interest) and CI (Compound Interest) for first year are same and for second and subsequent years both differ by an amount which is arrived by calculating interest on amount for previous years.

In other words, Compound Interest can be defined as the investment rate that grows exponentially, not linearly as in the case of Simple Interest.

The following table illustrates the conceptual working of simple interest and compound interest.

Rate of interest per annum is 10%.

Year	Simple Interest		Compound Interest	
	Principal	SI	Principal	CI
1st	1000	100	1000	100
2nd	1000	100	1000 + 100 = 1100	110
3rd	1000	100	1100 + 110 = 1210	121

On the basis of above calculation, it is clear that:
(i) Simple interest for each year is constant.
(ii) Compound interest calculated for each year is the interest on amount calculated for previous year.

Important Formulae

Let Principal = P, Rate = $R\%$ per annum, Time = n years.

- When interest is compounded annually:
  $$\text{Amount} = P\left[1+\frac{R}{100}\right]^n$$

- When interest is compounded half-yearly:
  $$\text{Amount} = P\left[1+\frac{R/2}{100}\right]^{2n}$$

- When interest is compounded quarterly:
  $$\text{Amount} = P\left[1+\frac{R/4}{100}\right]^{4n}$$

- When interest is compounded annually but time is in fraction, say $3\frac{2}{5}$ years,
  $$\text{Amount} = P\left(1+\frac{R}{100}\right)^3 \times \left(1+\frac{\frac{2}{5}R}{100}\right)$$

- When rates are different for different years, say $R_1\%$, $R_2\%$, $R_3\%$ for 1st, 2nd and 3rd year respectively.
  Then,
  $$\text{Amount} = P(1+\frac{R_1}{100}) \times (1+\frac{R_2}{100}) \times (1+\frac{R_3}{100})$$

- Present worth of ₹ x due n years hence is given by:
  $$\text{Present Worth} = \frac{x}{(1+\frac{R}{100})}$$

More important Formulae

To find compound interest for two years, when simple interest is given:

Compound Interest = Total simple interest + (Simple interest for one year × Rate of interest)

If the difference between the compound interest and simple interest on a certain sum of money for 2 years at R% per annum rate is Rs. 'D', then

$$\text{Difference (D)} = \left(\frac{R}{100}\right)^2 P$$

If the difference between the compound interest and simple interest on a certain sum of money for 2 years at R% per annum rate is Rs. 'D',

$$\text{The Sum (P)} = \left(\frac{100}{R}\right)^2 D$$

If the difference between the compound interest and simple interest on a certain sum of money for 3 years at R% per annum rate is Rs. 'D', then

$$\text{Difference (D)} = \frac{(300+R)}{100^3}$$

If the difference between the compound interest and simple interest on a certain sum of money for 3 years at R% per annum rate is Rs, 'D', then

$$\text{The sum (P)} = \frac{D \times 100^3}{R^2(300+R)}$$

TRIVIA

You can remember the value of Pi (3.1415926) by counting each word's letters in 'May I have a large container of coffee?'.

True Discount

Suppose a man has to pay ₹156 after 4 years and the rate of interest is 14% per annum. Clearly, ₹100 at 14% will amount to ₹ 156 in 4 years. So, the payment of ₹ 100 now will clear off the debt of ₹ 156 due 4 years hence we say that:

Sum due = ₹156 due 4 years hence:

Present Worth (P.W) = ₹ 100;

True Discount (T.D.) = ₹ (156 – 100)

= ₹ 56 = (Sum due) – (P.W.)

We define: T.D. = Interest on P.W.; Amount = (P.W.) + (T.D.)

Interest is reckoned on P.W. whereas true discount is reckoned on the amount.

Important Formulae

Let rate = $R\%$ per annum and Time = T years.
Then,

- P.W. = $\dfrac{100 \times Amount}{100 + (R \times T)} = \dfrac{100 \times T.D.}{R \times T}$

- T.D. = $\dfrac{(P.W.) \times (R \times T)}{100} = \dfrac{Amount \times R \times T}{R \times T}$

- Sum = $\dfrac{(S.I.) \times (T.D.)}{(S.I.) - (T.D.)}$

- (S.I.) – (T.D.) = S.I. on T.D.

- When the sum is put at compound interest, then P.W. = $\dfrac{Amount}{\left(1 + \dfrac{R}{100}\right)^T}$

MUST REMEMBER

→ Compound Interest can be defined as the investment rate that grows exponentially, not linearly as in the case of Simple Interest.

MULTIPLE CHOICE QUESTIONS

1. A man wants to sell his scooter. There are two offers, one at ₹ 12,000 cash and the other a credit of ₹ 12,880 to be paid after 8 months, money being at 18% per annum. Which is the better offer?
   (a) ₹ 12,000 in cash
   (b) ₹ 12,880 at credit
   (c) Both are equally good
   (d) None of the above

2. The present worth of ₹ 1404 due in two equal half-yearly instalments at 8% per annum simple interest is:
   (a) ₹ 1325   (b) ₹ 1300
   (c) ₹ 1350   (d) ₹ 1500

3. If the true discount on a sum due 2 years hence at 14% per annum is ₹ 168, then the sum due is:
   (a) ₹ 768   (b) ₹ 968
   (c) ₹ 1960   (d) ₹ 2400

4. A sum of money amounts to ₹ 9800 after 5 years and ₹ 12005 after 8 years at the same rate of simple interest. The rate of interest per annum is:
   (a) 5%   (b) 8%
   (c) 12%   (d) 15%

5. Reena took a loan of ₹ 1200 with simple interest for as many years as the rate of interest. If she paid ₹ 432 as interest at the end of the loan period, what was the rate of interest?
   (a) 3.6
   (b) 6
   (c) 18
   (d) Cannot be determined

6. Steve invested $ 10,000 in a savings bank account that earned 2% simple interest. Find the interest earned if the amount was kept in the bank for 4 years.
   (a) $ 500   (b) $ 650
   (c) $ 775   (d) $ 800

7. Ryan borrowed $ 15,000 from a bank to buy a car at 10% simple interest. If he paid $ 9,000 as interest while clearing the loan, find the time for which the loan was given.
   (a) 5.5 years   (b) 6 years
   (c) 8.5 years   (d) 9 years

8. In what time does a sum of money become four times at the simple interest rate of 5% per annum?
   (a) 40 years   (b) 45 years
   (c) 60 years   (d) 80 years

9. The simple interest on ₹ 1650 will be less than the interest on ₹ 1800 at 4% simple interest by ₹ 30. Find the time.
   (a) 3 years   (b) 5 years
   (c) 7 years   (d) 9 years

10. Bobby invested a certain sum of money at 8% p.a. simple interest for 'n' years. At the end of 'n' years, Bobby got back 4 times his original investment. What is the value of n?
    (a) 50 years
    (b) 25 years
    (c) 12 years 6 months
    (d) 37 years 6 months

11. In what time will ₹1000 become ₹1331 at 10% per annum compounded annually?
    (a) 2 years   (b) 3 years
    (c) 4 years   (d) 7 years

12. If the simple interest on a sum of money at 5% per annum for 3 years is ₹ 1200, find the compound interest on the same sum for the same period at the same rate.
    (a) 1251   (b) 1261
    (c) 1271   (d) 1281

13. What will be the compound interest on a sum of ₹25,000 after 3 years at the rate of 12 % per annum?
    (a) ₹ 9000.30   (b) ₹ 9720
    (c) ₹ 10123.20   (d) ₹ 10483.20

14. The compound interest on ₹ 30,000 at 7% per annum is ₹ 4347. The period (in years) is
    (a) 2   (b) 5
    (c) 3   (d) 4

15. The difference between compound interest and simple interest on an amount of ₹ 15,000 for 2 years is ₹ 96. What is the rate of interest per annum?

(a) 8
(b) 10
(c) 9
(d) Cannot be determined

16. The compound interest on a certain sum for 2 years at 10% per annum is ₹ 525. The simple interest on the same sum for double the time at half the rate percent per annum is:
(a) ₹ 400 (b) ₹ 500
(c) ₹ 600 (d) ₹ 800

17. At what rate of compound interest per annum will a sum of ₹ 1200 become ₹ 1348.32 in 2 years?
(a) 6% (b) 6.5%
(c) 7% (d) 7.5%

18. The least number of complete years in which a sum of money invested at 20% compound interest will be more than double is:
(a) 3 (b) 4
(c) 5 (d) 6

19. The effective annual rate of interest corresponding to a nominal rate of 6% per annum payable half-yearly is:
(a) 6.06% (b) 6.07%
(c) 6.08% (d) 6.09%

20. There is 60% increase in an amount in 6 years at simple interest. What will be the compound interest of ₹ 12,000 after 3 years at the same rate?
(a) ₹ 2160 (b) ₹ 3120
(c) ₹ 3972 (d) ₹ 6240

21. A person borrows ₹ 5000 for 2 years at 4% p.a. simple interest. He immediately lends it to another person at 6.25% p.a. for 2 years. Find his gain in the transaction per year.
(a) ₹ 112.50 (b) ₹ 125
(c) ₹ 150 (d) ₹ 167.50

22. A certain amount earns simple interest of ₹ 1750 after 7 years. Had the interest been 2% more, how much more interest would it have earned?
(a) ₹ 35
(b) ₹ 245
(c) ₹ 350
(d) Cannot be determined

23. What will be the ratio of simple interest earned by certain amount at the same rate of interest for 6 years and that for 9 years?
(a) 1 : 3 (b) 1 : 4
(c) 2 : 3 (d) Data inadequate

24. A sum of ₹ 12,500 amounts to ₹ 15,500 in 4 years at the rate of simple interest. What is the rate of interest?
(a) 3% (b) 4%
(c) 5% (d) 6%

25. A lent ₹ 5000 to B for 2 years and ₹ 3000 to C for 4 years on simple interest at the same rate of interest and received ₹ 2200 in all from both of them as interest. The rate of interest per annum is:
(a) 5% (b) 7%
(c) 7.5% (d) 10%

26. Find compound interest on ₹ 7500 at 4% per annum for 2 years, compounded annually.
(a) ₹512 (b) ₹552
(c) ₹612 (d) ₹622

27. Find the compound interest on ₹16, 000 at 20% per annum for 9 months, compounded quarterly.
(a) ₹ 2552 (b) ₹ 2512
(c) ₹ 2592 (d) ₹ 2572

28. Simple interest on a certain sum of money for 3 years at 8% per annum is half the compound interest on ₹ 4000 for 2 years at 10% per annum. The sum placed on simple interest is:
(a) ₹ 1550 (b) ₹ 1650
(c) ₹ 1750 (d) ₹ 2000

29. The present worth of ₹169 due in 2 years at 4% per annum compound interest is:
(a) ₹150.50 (b) ₹154.75
(c) ₹156.25 (d) ₹158

30. On a sum of money, the simple interest for 2 years is ₹ 660, while the compound interest is ₹696.30, the rate of interest being the same in both the cases. The rate of interest is:
(a) 10% (b) 11%
(c) 12% (d) 10.5%

HOTS

1. A trader owes a merchant ₹ 10,028 due 1 year hence. The trader wants to settle the account after 3 months. If the rate of interest is 12% per annum, how much cash should he pay?
   (a) ₹ 9025.20 (b) ₹ 9200
   (c) ₹ 9600 (d) ₹ 9560

2. An automobile financier claims to be lending money at simple interest, but he includes the interest every six months for calculating the principal. If he is charging an interest of 10%, the effective rate of interest becomes:
   (a) 10% (b) 10.25%
   (c) 10.5% (d) None of these

3. Mr. Thomas invested an amount of ₹ 13,900 in two different schemes A and B at the simple interest rate of 14% p.a. and 11% p.a. respectively. If the total amount of simple interest earned in 2 years is ₹ 3508, what was the amount invested in Scheme B?
   (a) ₹ 6400 (b) ₹ 6500
   (c) ₹ 7200 (d) ₹ 7500

4. Anita invested a certain sum of money in a bank that paid simple interest. The amount grew to ₹ 240 at the end of 2 years. She waited for another 3 years and got a final amount of ₹ 300. What was the principal amount that she invested at the beginning?
   (a) ₹ 200 (b) ₹ 150
   (c) ₹ 210 (d) ₹ 175

5. Pratap invested a certain sum of money in a simple interest bond whose value grew to ₹ 300 at the end of 3 years and to ₹ 400 at the end of another 5 years. What was the rate of interest in which he invested his sum?
   (a) 12.5% (b) 6.67%
   (c) 6.25% (d) 8.33%

SUBJECTIVE QUESTIONS

1. Find the simple interest, when:
   (i) Principal = ₹ 2000, Rate of Interest = 5% per annum and Time = 5 years.
   (ii) Principal = ₹ 500, Rate of Interest = 12.5% per annum and Time = 4 years.
   (iii) Principal = ₹ 4500, Rate of Interest = 4% per annum and Time = 6 months.
   (iv) Principal = ₹ 12000, Rate of Interest = 18% per annum and Time = 4 months.
   (v) Principal = ₹ 1000, Rate of Interest = 10% per annum and Time = 73 days.

   Solution:
   (i) Given Principal = ₹ 2000, Rate of Interest = 5% per annum and Time = 5 years.
   We know that simple interest
   $$= \frac{(P \times T \times R)}{100}$$
   On substituting these values in the above equation, we get
   $$SI = \frac{(2000 \times 5 \times 5)}{100}$$
   $$= ₹ 500$$

   (ii) Given Principal = ₹ 500, Rate of Interest = 12.5% per annum and Time = 4 years.
   We know that simple interest
   $$= \frac{(P \times T \times R)}{100}$$
   On substituting these values in the above equation, we get
   $$SI = \frac{(500 \times 4 \times 12.5)}{100}$$
   $$= ₹ 250$$

(iii) Given Principal = ₹ 4500, Rate of Interest = 4% per annum and

Time = 6 months = $\frac{1}{2}$ years

We know that simple interest
$= \frac{(P \times T \times R)}{100}$

On substituting these values in the above equation, we get

$SI = \frac{\left(4500 \times \frac{1}{2} \times 4\right)}{100}$

$SI = \frac{(4500 \times 1 \times 4)}{100 \times 2}$

$= ₹ 90$

(iv) Given Principal = ₹ 12000, Rate of Interest = 18% per annum and

Time = 4 months = $\left(\frac{4}{12}\right) = \left(\frac{1}{3}\right)$ years

We know that simple interest
$= \frac{(P \times T \times R)}{100}$

On substituting these values in the above equation, we get

$SI = \frac{\left(12000 \times \left(\frac{1}{3}\right) \times 18\right)}{100}$

$SI = \frac{(12000 \times 1 \times 18)}{100 \times 3}$

$= ₹ 720$

(v) Given Principal = ₹ 1000, Rate of Interest = 10% per annum and

Time = 73 days = $\left(\frac{73}{365}\right)$ days

We know that simple interest =
$= \frac{(P \times T \times R)}{100}$

On substituting these values in the above equation, we get

$SI = \frac{\left(1000 \times \left(\frac{73}{365}\right) \times 10\right)}{100}$

$SI = \frac{(1000 \times 73 \times 10)}{100 \times 365}$

$= ₹ 20$

Simple and Compound Interest

Algebraic Expressions 8

Learning Objectives : In this chapter, students will learn about:
- ✓ Concept of algebraic expressions

CHAPTER SUMMARY

Constant
A symbol having a fixed numerical value is called a constant. For example, 2, –4, etc.

Variable
A symbol having various numerical values is called variable.

Example: $C = 2\pi r$ Here C and r are variables and 2 and π are constants.

Algebraic Expressions
A combination of constants and variables connected by some or all of the four basic operations +, –, × & ÷ is called an algebraic expression. For example, $7x^2 - 3xy + y^2z - 5$.

Types of Algebraic Expressions
(1) **Monomial:** An algebraic expression with only one term is called monomial.
   Example: $3x^2, -5xy, 4y^2$ etc.
(2) **Binomial:** An algebraic expression having two terms is called binomial.
   Example: $a + b, 3a^2 - 5b^2$ etc.
(3) **Trinomial:** An algebraic expression having three terms is called trinomial.
   Example: $ax^2 + bx + c, 5x^2 - 3x + 2$ etc.
(4) **Polynomial:** An algebraic expression having two or more terms is called polynomial.
   Example: $6x^2 - 5x + 1, x^3 - x^2 - x + 3$ etc.

Literal
The variable factor is called as literal. For example: x, y, a, b etc.

Numeral
The constant factor is called as numeral. For example 2, –3 etc.

Like Terms
In an algebraic expression, the terms having the same literal factor are called like terms.
Example: In $3x^2 - 2x + 2x^2 - 3xy$, $3x^2$ and $2x^2$ are like terms.

Unlike Terms
In an algebraic expression, the terms having different literal factors are called unlike terms.
Example: In $x^3 - 3x^2 + 5x + 3$ all terms are unlike terms.

Operations on Algebraic Expressions
In addition, combine all the like terms and add the coefficients of all the like terms.

In subtractions, change the sign of the subtrahend and then proceed as addition.

The product of two factors with like sign is positive and the product of two factors with unlike sign is negative.

Algebraic Identities
$(a + b)^2 = a^2 + 2ab + b^2$
$a^2 + b^2 = (a + b)^2 - 2ab$
$(a - b)^2 = a^2 - 2ab + b^2$
$a^2 + b^2 = (a - b)^2 + 2ab$
$(a + b + c)^2 = a^2 + b^2 + c^2 + 2(ab + bc + ca)$
$(a + b)^3 = a^3 + b^3 + 3ab(a + b)$

$a^3 + b^3 = (a + b)^3 - 3ab(a + b)$

$(a - b)^3 = a^3 - b^3 - 3ab(a - b)$

$a^3 - b^3 = (a - b)^3 + 3ab(a - b)$

$a^2 - b^2 = (a + b)(a - b)$

$a^3 - b^3 = (a - b)(a^2 + ab + b)^2$

$a^3 + b^3 = (a + b)(a^2 - ab + b^2)$

TRIVIA

The mathematical name for # (number sign) is octothorpe.

FACTOR THEOREM

If $(x + a)$ is a factor of polynominal P(x), then remainder = 0

$\Rightarrow \quad P(-a) = 0$

Solving Numerical Expressions

A numerical expression consists of four operations (+, −, ×, ÷) and four brackets ((), {}, [], −). Sometimes in complex expressions, some operations are performed prior to the others. We use **BODMAS** rule to solve these expressions. B – brackets, O – operator 'of', D – division, M – multiplication, A – addition, S – subtraction. The order of solving brackets is:

Brackets	Name
—	Vinclum
( )	Parentheses or common brackets
{ }	Braces or curly brackets
[ ]	Square or Box brackets

Example: Simplify $36 - [18 - \{14 - (15 - 4 \div 2 \times 2)\}]$

Solution:

Given expression:

$= 36 - [18 - \{14 - (15 - 4 \div 2 \times 2)\}]$

$= 36 - [18 - \{14 - (15 - 2 \times 2)\}]$

$= 36 - [18 - \{14 - (15 - 4)\}]$

$= 36 - [18 - \{14 - 11\}]$

$= 36 - [18 - 3]$

$= 36 - 15$

$= 21$

MUST REMEMBER

→ A symbol having a fixed numerical value is called a constant.
→ An algebraic expression with only one term is called monomial.
→ An algebraic expression having two terms is called binomial.
→ An algebraic expression having three terms is called trinomial.
→ An algebraic expression having two or more terms is called polynomial.

MULTIPLE CHOICE QUESTIONS

1. Which expression is obtained when $2x^2 - 5x + 7$ is subtracted from $5x^2 - 2x + 6$?
   (a) $3x^2 - 3x + 1$
   (b) $3x^2 + 3x - 1$
   (c) $3x^2 - 3x - 1$
   (d) None of these

2. What is the sum of $5x - 2x^2 + 3$, $3x^2 - 2x + 7$ and $4x^2 - 5x - 6$?
   (a) $5x^2 - 2x + 4$
   (b) $5x^2 + 2x - 4$
   (c) $5x^2 - 2x - 4$
   (d) None of these

3. What is the result when $x^2 - xy + y^2$ is subtracted from $2xy - 3y^2 + 2x^2$?
   (a) $x^2 - 2xy + 4y^2$
   (b) $2x^2 + 3xy - 4y^2$
   (c) $x^2 + 2xy + 4y^2$
   (d) $x^2 + 3xy - 4y^2$

4. Find the expression if the sum of $6a + 5a^2 + 7$ and $-7a - 8 + 7a^2$ is subtracted from -5.
   (a) $-12a^2 + a - 4$
   (b) $12a^2 + a - 4$
   (c) $12a^2 - a + 4$
   (d) None of these

5. What is obtained after simplification of the expression $[7 - 2x + 3y - \{2x - y\}] - (4x + 7y - 5)$?
   (a) $8x - 3y + 12$
   (b) $-8x - 3y + 12$
   (c) $8x + 3y - 12$
   (d) None of these

6. What is the product of $-3m^2np$, $\frac{1}{3}nm^3p^2$ and $\frac{2}{3}m^2n^2p^2$?
   (a) $-\frac{1}{3}m^5n^4p^4$
   (b) $-\frac{2}{3}m^7n^4p^4$
   (c) $-\frac{2}{3}m^7n^4p^5$
   (d) $-\frac{2}{3}m^6n^3p^6$

7. What is the product of $-xyz^2$, $-2yx^2z$ and $\frac{1}{2}x^3yz$?
   (a) $x^6y^3z^4$
   (b) $x^6y^2z^3$
   (c) $x^6y^3z^3$
   (d) $x^6y^2z^2$

8. $5 - (3x + 2y) - 3(x - y) + 7x + y = ?$
   (a) $x + 2y + 5$
   (b) $x - 2y + 5$
   (c) $2x + 2y + 5$
   (d) None of these

9. Find the product of the sum of $3x^2 + 5y^2$ and $x^2 - 4y^2$ and the difference of $(x^2 - y^2)$ and $2x^2 + 3y^2$.
   (a) $4x^4 - 16x^2y^2 + 4y^4$
   (b) $4x^4 + 17x^2y^2 + 4y^4$
   (c) $4x^4 - 15x^2y^2 + 4y^4$
   (d) None of these

10. Find the value of $(2.3a^5b^2) \times (1.2a^2b^2)$ when $a = 1$ and $b = 0.5$.
    (a) 0.10725
    (b) 0.1275
    (c) 0.1525
    (d) 0.1725

11. Find the value of $(2.6\ m^2n) \times (5mn^2)$ when $m = \frac{1}{2}$ and $n = \frac{1}{3}$.
    (a) $\frac{13}{162}$
    (b) $\frac{13}{216}$
    (c) $\frac{3}{216}$
    (d) $\frac{130}{216}$

12. Find the product of ab^2c, $-a^2bc^2$, $-abc^3$ and $-a^2bc$.
    (a) $-a^6b^5c^7$
    (b) $a^6b^6c^7$
    (c) $-a^6b^6c^5$
    (d) $-a^5b^5c^5$

13. What is obtained when $(3x - \frac{4}{5}xy^2)$ is multiplied by $\frac{1}{3}xy$?
    (a) $x^2y^2 - \frac{4}{15}x^2y^3$
    (b) $x^2y - \frac{4}{15}x^2y^3$
    (c) $xy^2 - \frac{4}{15}xy^2$
    (d) None of these

14. Find the numerical value of the product $3s(s^2 - st)$ when $s = 2$ and $t = 5$.
    (a) -32
    (b) -36
    (c) -38
    (d) None of these

15. What is the simplified value of $a(b - c) + b(c - a) + c(a - b)$?
    (a) 0
    (b) 1
    (c) -1
    (d) None of these

16. Simplify $a(b - 2c) + 2b(c - 2a) + c(3a - 2b)$.
    (a) $2ab - ac$
    (b) $ab - ac$
    (c) $ac - 3ab$
    (d) $ab - 3ab$

17. What is the product of $-3x^2y^2z^2$ and $-5xy^2z$
    (a) $15 x^2y^2z^2$
    (b) $15 x^3y^2z^2$
    (c) $15 x^3y^3z^3$
    (d) $15 x^3y^4z^3$

18. Find the simplest expression of
    $a(b - c) - b(c - 2a) - c(2a - b)$
    (a) $3ab - ac$
    (b) $3a(b - c)$
    (c) $2(ab - ac)$
    (d) $2ab - 3ac$

19. What is product of $(x^4 - \dfrac{1}{x^4})$ and $(x + \dfrac{1}{x})$?
    (a) $x^5 + x^3 - \dfrac{1}{x^3} - \dfrac{1}{x^5}$
    (b) $x^5 + x^4 - \dfrac{1}{x^4} - \dfrac{1}{x^5}$
    (c) $x^5 + x^3 - \dfrac{1}{x^4} - \dfrac{1}{x^5}$
    (d) None of these

20. What is the product of $(x^3 + y^3)$ and $(x^2 - y^2)$?
    (a) $x^5 + x^3y^2 - x^2y^3 - y^5$
    (b) $x^5 - x^3y^2 + x^2y^3 - y^5$
    (c) $x^5 - x^2y^2 + x^3y^3 - y^5$
    (d) None of these

21. Find the difference of $x^2 - xy + y^2 + yz$ and $2x^2 - 3xy - y^2 - yz$.
    (a) $x^2 - 2xy - 2y^2 - 2yz$
    (b) $x^2 + 2xy + 2y^2 - 2yz$
    (c) $x^2 - 2xy - y^2 + 2yz$
    (d) None of these

22. What is the result when the sum of $(-5x^2 + 7xy + 2y^2)$ and $(x^2 - 3xy - y^2)$ is subtracted from -7?
    (a) $4x^2 - 4xy + y^2 + 7$
    (b) $4x^2 - 4xy - y^2 - 7$
    (c) $4x^2 - xy + y^2 + 7$
    (d) $4x^2 + 4xy - 4y^2 - 7$

23. What is the product of $(0.8m - 0.7n)$ and $(1.5n - 1.7m)$?
    (a) $2.39 mn - 1.05 n^2 - 1.36 m^2$
    (b) $1.19 mn - 1.15 n^2 + 1.36 m^2$
    (c) $1.39 mn - 1.05 n^2 + 1.36 m^2$
    (d) None of these

24. Find the sum of $0.3x^2 - 3xy + 0.8y^2$ and $4x^2 - 2y^2 + 0.7xy$?
    (a) $4.3x^2 - 1.3xy + 1.2 y^2$
    (b) $4.3x^2 - 2.3xy + 1.2 y^2$
    (c) $4.3x^2 - 2.3xy - 1.2 y^2$
    (d) None of these

25. Find the product of $(7x^2 - x + 11)$ and $(x^2 - 3)$.
    (a) $7x^4 - x^3 - 10x^2 + 3x - 33$
    (b) $7x^4 + x^3 - 21x^2 + 3x - 33$
    (c) $7x^4 - x^3 + 11x^2 - 3x - 33$
    (d) None of these

26. What is the product of $1.5 a(10a^2b - 100ab^2)$
    (a) $15a^3b - 150a^2b^2$
    (b) $15a^2b - 1500a^2b^2$
    (c) $150a^3b - 150a^2b^2$
    (d) None of these

27. Find the simplified expression of
    $7x^2 - [x^2 - 3x - \{x + y\}] - (5x - 3y + 3)$.
    (a) $6x^2 - 2x + 4y + 3$
    (b) $6x^2 - x + 4y - 3$
    (c) $6x^2 - 2x - 4y - 3$
    (d) None of these

28. Find the result of
    $x(x + 4) + 3x(2x^2 - 3) + 4x^2 + 5$?
    (a) $6x^3 + 5x^2 - 13x + 5$
    (b) $6x^3 + 4x^2 - 5x + 5$
    (c) $6x^3 + 5x^2 - 5x + 5$
    (d) None of these

29. $4mn(m - n) - 6m^2(n - n^2) - 3n^2(2m^2 - m) = ?$
    (a) $2m^2n - n^2m$
    (b) $-mn(2m - n)$
    (c) $m^2n - 2n^2m$
    (d) $-mn(2m + n)$

30. $a^2b(a - b^2) - ab^2(3ab - a^2) - a^3b(1 - 2b) = ?$
    (a) $3a^3b^2 - 4a^2b^3$
    (b) $3a^3b^2 - 3a^2b^3$
    (c) $a^3b^2 - 4a^2b^3$
    (d) $3a^3b^2 + 4a^2b^3$

Algebraic Expressions

HOTS

1. What should be added to $xy - 3yz + 4zx$ to get $4xy - 3zx + 4yz + 7$?
   (a) $3xy - 7zx + 7yz + 7$
   (b) $3xy - 4zx + 7yz + 7$
   (c) $3xy - 2zx + 5yz + 7$
   (d) $3xy - 7zx + 1yz + 7$

2. What should be subtracted from $x^2 - xy + y^2 - x + y + 3$ to obtain $-x^2 + 3y^2 - 4xy + 1$?
   (a) $2x^2 + 3xy - 2y^2 - x + y + 2$
   (b) $2x^2 + xy - 2y^2 - x + y + 2$
   (c) $2x^2 + 5xy - 2y^2 - x + y$
   (d) $x^2 + 3xy - 2y^2 - x + y + 2$

3. How much is $x^2 - 2xy + 3y^2$ less than $2x^2 - 3y^2 + xy$?
   (a) $x^2 - 6y^2 + 3xy$
   (b) $x^2 - 9y^2 + 3xy$
   (c) $4x^2 - y^2 + 3xy$
   (d) $6x^2 - 6y^2 + xy$

4. How much does $a^2 - 3ab + 2b^2$ exceed $2a^2 - 7ab + 9b^2$?
   (a) $5a^2 + ab - 7b^2$
   (b) $a^2 + 4ab - 7b^2$
   (c) $2a^2 + 4ab - 7b^2$
   (d) $7a^2 - 4ab - 7b^2$

5. If $P = a^2 - b^2 + 2ab$, $Q = a^2 + 4b^2 - 6ab$, $R = b^2 + b$, $S = a^2 - 4ab$ and $T = -2a^2 + b^2 - ab + a$. Find $P + Q + R + S - T$.
   (a) $5a^2 + b^2 - 6ab - a + b$
   (b) $a^2 + 3b^2 - 7ab - 7a + b$
   (c) $5a^2 + 3b^2 - 7ab - a + b$
   (d) $5a^2 + 3b^2 - 7ab - a - b$

SUBJECTIVE QUESTIONS

1. Identify the monomials, binomials, trinomials and quadrinomials from the following expressions:
   (i) a^2
   (ii) $a^2 - b^2$
   (iii) $x^3 + y^3 + z^3$
   (iv) $x^3 + y^3 + z^3 + 3xyz$

   Answer:
   (i) Given a^2
       a^2 is a monomial expression because it contains only one term
   (ii) Given $a^2 - b^2$
       $a^2 - b^2$ is a binomial expression because it contains two terms
   (iii) Given $x^3 + y^3 + z^3$
       $x^3 + y^3 + z^3$ is a trinomial because it contains three terms
   (iv) Given $x^3 + y^3 + z^3 + 3xyz$
       $x^3 + y^3 + z^3 + 3xyz$ is a quadrinomial expression because it contains four terms

2. Write all the terms of each of the following algebraic expressions:
   (i) $3x$
   (ii) $2x - 3$
   (iii) $2x^2 - 7$
   (iv) $2x^2 + y^2 - 3xy + 4$

   Answer:
   (i) Given $3x$
       $3x$ is the only term of the given algebraic expression.
   (ii) Given $2x - 3$
       $2x$ and -3 are the terms of the given algebraic expression.
   (iii) Given $2x^2 - 7$
       $2x^2$ and -7 are the terms of the given algebraic expression.
   (iv) Given $2x^2 + y^2 - 3xy + 4$
       $2x^2$, y^2, $-3xy$ and 4 are the terms of the given algebraic expression.

3. Identify the terms and also mention the numerical coefficients of those terms:
   (i) $4xy, -5x^2y, -3yx, 2xy^2$
   (ii) $7a^2bc, -3ca^2b, -(5/2) abc^2, 3/2abc^2, (-4/3)cba^2$

   Answer:
   (i) Like terms $4xy$, $-3yx$ and Numerical coefficients $4, -3$
   (ii) Like terms $(7a^2bc, -3ca^2b)$ and $(-4/3cba^2)$ and their Numerical coefficients $7, -3, (-4/3)$

Like terms are $(-5/2abc^2)$ and $(3/2\ abc^2)$ and numerical coefficients are $(-5/2)$ and $(3/2)$

4. Identify the like terms in the following algebraic expressions:
   (i) $a^2 + b^2 - 2a^2 + c^2 + 4a$
   (ii) $3x + 4xy - 2yz + 52zy$
   (iii) $abc + ab^2c + 2acb^2 + 3c^2ab + b^2ac - 2a^2bc + 3cab^2$

   Answer:
   (i) Given $a^2 + b^2 - 2a^2 + c^2 + 4a$
       The like terms in the given algebraic expressions are a^2 and $-2a^2$.
   (ii) Given $3x + 4xy - 2yz + 52zy$
       The like terms in the given algebraic expressions are $-2yz$ and $52zy$.
   (iii) Given $abc + ab^2c + 2acb^2 + 3c^2ab + b^2ac - 2a^2bc + 3cab^2$
       The like terms in the given algebraic expressions are ab^2c, $2acb^2$, b^2ac and $3cab^2$.

5. Write the coefficient of x in the following:
   (i) $-12x$ (ii) $-7xy$

   Answer:
   (i) Given $-12x$
       The numerical coefficient of x is -12.
   (ii) Given $-7xy$
       The numerical coefficient of x is $-7y$.

Linear Equations in One Variable — 9

 **Learning Objectives :** In this chapter, students will learn about:
- Linear equation of one variable and its solution

CHAPTER SUMMARY

Linear Equation
An equation consisting of only a linear polynomial is known as linear equation.
Example: $2x + 3 = 9$
$3P - 3 = 6$

Solution of a Linear Equation
The value of the variable which makes the equation a true statement is called the solution of a linear equation.

Example 1: Solve $5x - 6 = 4x - 2$.
Solution: Given $5x - 6 = 4x - 2$
$\Rightarrow 5x - 4x = -2 + 6$
$\Rightarrow x = 4$

Example 2: Solve $\dfrac{x}{4} + \dfrac{x}{6} = \dfrac{x}{2} + \dfrac{3}{4}$

Solution: Here $\dfrac{x}{4} + \dfrac{x}{6} = \dfrac{x}{2} + \dfrac{3}{4}$

$\Rightarrow \dfrac{x}{4} + \dfrac{x}{6} - \dfrac{x}{2} = \dfrac{3}{4}$

$\Rightarrow \dfrac{3x + 2x - 6x}{12} = \dfrac{3}{4}$

$\Rightarrow \dfrac{-x}{12} = \dfrac{3}{4}$

$\Rightarrow x = \dfrac{12 \times 3}{-4} = -9$

Example 3: If $\dfrac{2x-1}{3} = \dfrac{x-2}{3} + 1$, then $x = ?$

Solution: Given $\dfrac{2x-1}{3} - \dfrac{x-2}{3} + 1$

$\Rightarrow \dfrac{2x-1}{3} - \dfrac{x-2}{3} = 1$

$\Rightarrow \dfrac{2x-1-(x-2)}{3} = 1$

$\Rightarrow 2x - 1 - x + 2 = 3$

$\Rightarrow x + 1 = 3 \Rightarrow x = 3 - 1 = 2$

Example 4: If $\dfrac{2x-3}{5} + \dfrac{x+3}{4} = \dfrac{4x+1}{7}$, find x.

Solution: We have $\dfrac{2x-3}{5} + \dfrac{x+3}{4} = \dfrac{4x+1}{7}$

$\Rightarrow \dfrac{4(2x-3)+5(x+3)}{20} = \dfrac{4x+1}{7}$

$\Rightarrow \dfrac{8x-12+5x+15}{20} = \dfrac{4x+1}{7}$

$\Rightarrow \dfrac{13x+3}{20} = \dfrac{4x+1}{7}$

$\Rightarrow 91x + 21 = 80x + 20$

$\Rightarrow 91x - 80x = 20 - 21$

$\Rightarrow 11x = -1$

$x = \dfrac{-1}{11}$

Example 5: The denominator of a fraction is 4 more than its numerator. If 2 is added to both numerator and denominator, the fraction becomes $\dfrac{2}{3}$. Find the fraction.

Solutions: Let the numerator be x.

∴ Denominator = $x + 4$

Fraction = $\dfrac{x}{x+4}$

∴ $\dfrac{x+2}{x+4+2} = \dfrac{2}{3}$

⇒ $\dfrac{x+2}{x+6} = \dfrac{2}{3}$

⇒ $3x + 6 = 2x + 12$

⇒ $3x - 2x = 12 - 6$

⇒ $x = 6$

Hence, fraction = $\dfrac{6}{6+4} = \dfrac{6}{10} = \dfrac{3}{5}$

Example 6: When a number is added to its two–thirds, it gives 55. What is that number?

Solution: Let the number be x.

∴ $x + \dfrac{2x}{3} = 55$

⇒ $\dfrac{3x+2x}{3} = 55$

⇒ $\dfrac{5x}{3} = 55$

⇒ $5x = 55 \times 3$

⇒ $x = \dfrac{55 \times 3}{5} = 33$

Example 7: The length of a rectangle is twice its breadth. If the perimeter of rectangle is 150m, what is its length?

Solution: Let the breadth of rectangle = x

∴ Length = $2x$

Perimeter = 150

⇒ $2(2x + x) = 150$

⇒ $3x = \dfrac{150}{2}$

⇒ $3x = 75 \Rightarrow x = \dfrac{75}{3} = 25$

∴ Length = $2x = 2 \times 25 = 50$ m

Example 8: Two complementary angle differ by 12°. What are the angles ?

Solution: Let one angle be x.

and other angle = $x + 12$

∴ $x + x + 12 = 90°$

⇒ $2x = 90° - 12°$

⇒ $2x = 78°$

⇒ $x = \dfrac{78°}{2} = 39°$

Hence, the angles are 39° and 51°.

TRIVIA

Giuseppe Peano denoted the rationals into Q in 1895. It was taken from the Italian word of quoziente referring to quotient.

MUST REMEMBER

➡ An equation consisting of only a linear polynomial is known as linear equation.

Linear Equations in One Variable

MULTIPLE CHOICE QUESTIONS

1. Mr. Sharma left one-third of his property to his daughter, one-fourth to his son and the remainder to his wife. If his wife's share is ₹18000 what was the worth of Mr. Sharma's total property?
   (a) ₹ 41200
   (b) ₹ 42200
   (c) ₹ 43200
   (d) ₹ 44200

2. In an examination, a student requires 40% of the total marks to pass. If Manoj gets 185 marks and fails by 15 marks what is the total marks?
   (a) 400
   (b) 500
   (c) 550
   (d) 600

3. 50 kg of an alloy of nickel and iron contains 60% nickel. How much nickel must be melted into it to make the alloy contain 75% of nickel?
   (a) 20 kg
   (b) 30 kg
   (c) 35 kg
   (d) 40 kg

4. The sum of digits of a two digit number is 9. If 27 is added to the number its digits get interchanged. What is the number?
   (a) 36
   (b) 63
   (c) 46
   (d) 64

5. Solve for x, $x - \left(2x - \dfrac{3x-4}{7}\right) = \dfrac{4x-27}{3} - 3$.
   (a) 40
   (b) 60
   (c) 50
   (d) 45

6. A bookseller earned a profit of 5% by selling a book for ₹ 714. What is the cost price of the book?
   (a) ₹ 620
   (b) ₹ 640
   (c) ₹ 660
   (d) ₹ 680

7. The length of a rectangle is three times of its breadth. Its perimeter is 128m, what is its length?
   (a) 24 m
   (b) 36 m
   (c) 48 m
   (d) None of these

8. Ramesh travelled $\dfrac{3}{5}$ of his journey by rail, $\dfrac{1}{4}$ by a car, $\dfrac{1}{8}$ by a bus and the remaining 4 km on foot. What is the length of total journey?
   (a) 120 km
   (b) 140 km
   (c) 160 km
   (d) 180 km

9. A number consists of two-digits whose sum is 8. If 18 is added to the number its digits are reversed. What is that number?
   (a) 35
   (b) 36
   (c) 53
   (d) 63

10. A number is as much greater than 21 as it is less than 71. What is that number?
    (a) 36
    (b) 46
    (c) 48
    (d) 56

11. Two supplementary angles differ by 20°. What is the measure of smaller angle?
    (a) 30
    (b) 40
    (c) 80
    (d) 100

12. A number when multiplied by 5 is increased by 80. What is that number?
    (a) 15
    (b) 16
    (c) 18
    (d) 20

13. The sum of three consecutive odd numbers is 99. What is the difference of smallest and largest odd number?
    (a) 1
    (b) 2
    (c) 3
    (d) 4

14. The ages of Simran and Ranjna are in the ratio 5:3. After 6 years their ages will be in the ratio 7:5. What is the present age of Ranjna?
    (a) 9 years
    (b) 12 years
    (c) 14 years
    (d) 15 years

15. Thrice a number when increased by 6 gives 84. What is that number?
    (a) 26
    (b) 28
    (c) 32
    (d) 34

16. The sum of two consecutive even number is 96. What is the smaller number?
    (a) 42 (b) 44
    (c) 46 (d) 48

17. On adding nine to the twice of a whole number gives 61. What is $\frac{5}{13}$ of that whole number?
    (a) 5 (b) 10
    (c) 15 (d) 20

18. After 12 years Manish will be three times as old as he was 4 years ago. What is his present age?
    (a) 12 years (b) 14 years
    (c) 16 years (d) 18 years

19. Niraj is 19 years younger than his cousin after 5 years their age will be in the ratio 2:3. What is the present age of Niraj?
    (a) 31 years (b) 33 years
    (c) 35 years (d) 36 years

20. What is the value of p in the given equation $8(2p-5) - 6(3p-7) = 1$?
    (a) 1 (b) $\frac{1}{2}$
    (c) $\frac{1}{3}$ (d) $\frac{1}{4}$

21. What is the value of y in the given equation $0.6y + 0.8 = 0.56y + 2.32$?
    (a) 34 (b) 36
    (c) 38 (d) 39

22. Two complementary angles are differ by 14°. What is the measure of larger angle?
    (a) 52° (b) 54°
    (c) 38° (d) None of these

23. The sum of three consecutive odd numbers is 147. What is the smallest odd number?
    (a) 45 (b) 47
    (c) 43 (d) 49

24. In an isosceles triangle, the vertex angle is thrice of its base angle. What is the measure of vertex angle?
    (a) 90° (b) 75°
    (c) 108° (d) 112°

25. A number is $\frac{2}{5}$ times of another number. If their sum is 140, find the larger number.
    (a) 70 (b) 80
    (c) 90 (d) 100

HOTS

1. Solving $2(5x-3) - 3(2x-1) = 9$ will give value of x as:
   (a) 3 (b) 5
   (c) 87 (d) 9

2. Solving $\left(\frac{x}{2}\right) + \left(\frac{3}{2}\right) = \left(\frac{2x}{5}\right) - 1$ will give value of x as:
   (a) −25 (b) −24
   (c) −45 (d) −5

3. Solving $3x - 2(2x-5) = 2(x+3) - 8$ will give value of x as:
   (a) 4 (b) 5
   (c) 8 (d) 6

4. Solving $\left(\frac{6x-2}{9}\right) + \left(\frac{3x+5}{18}\right) = \left(\frac{1}{3}\right)$ will give value of x as:
   (a) $\frac{4}{3}$ (b) $\frac{2}{3}$
   (c) $\frac{1}{3}$ (d) $\frac{10}{3}$

5. Solving $m - \frac{(m-1)}{2} = 1 - \frac{(m-2)}{3}$ will give value of m as:
   (a) $\frac{9}{5}$ (b) $\frac{2}{5}$
   (c) $\frac{1}{5}$ (d) $\frac{7}{5}$

Linear Equations in One Variable

SUBJECTIVE QUESTIONS

1. Verify by substitution that:
   (i) $x = 4$ is the root of $3x - 5 = 7$
   (ii) $x = 3$ is the root of $5 + 3x = 14$
   (iii) $x = 2$ is the root of $3x - 2 = 8x - 12$
   (iv) $x = 4$ is the root of $(3x/2) = 6$
   (v) $y = 2$ is the root of $y - 3 = 2y - 5$
   (vi) $x = 8$ is the root of $(1/2)x + 7 = 11$

   Answer:
   (i) Given $x = 4$ is the root of $3x - 5 = 7$.
   Now, substituting x = 4 in place of 'x' in the given equation, we get
   $= 3(4) - 5 = 7$
   $= 12 - 5 = 7$
   $7 = 7$
   Since, LHS = RHS
   Hence, $x = 4$ is the root of $3x - 5 = 7$.

   (ii) Given $x = 3$ is the root of $5 + 3x = 14$.
   Now, substituting x = 3 in place of 'x' in the given equation, we get
   $= 5 + 3(3) = 14$
   $= 5 + 9 = 14$
   $14 = 14$
   Since, LHS = RHS
   Hence, x = 3 is the root of $5 + 3x = 14$.

   (iii) Given $x = 2$ is the root of $3x - 2 = 8x - 12$.
   Now, substituting x = 2 in place of 'x' in the given equation, we get
   $= 3(2) - 2 = 8(2) - 12$
   $= 6 - 2 = 16 - 12$
   $4 = 4$
   Since, LHS = RHS
   Hence, $x = 2$ is the root of $3x - 2 = 8x - 12$.

   (iv) Given $x = 4$ is the root of $3x/2 = 6$.
   Now, substituting $x = 4$ in place of 'x' in the given equation, we get
   $= (3 \times 4)/2 = 6$
   $= (12/2) = 6$
   $6 = 6$
   Since, LHS = RHS
   Hence, $x = 4$ is the root of $(3x/2) = 6$.

   (v) Given $y = 2$ is the root of $y - 3 = 2y - 5$.
   Now, substituting $y = 2$ in place of 'y' in the given equation, we get
   $= 2 - 3 = 2(2) - 5$
   $= -1 = 4 - 5$
   $-1 = -1$
   Since, LHS = RHS
   Hence, $y = 2$ is the root of $y - 3 = 2y - 5$.

   (vi) Given $x = 8$ is the root of $(1/2)x + 7 = 11$.
   Now, substituting $x = 8$ in place of 'x' in the given equation, we get
   $= (1/2)(8) + 7 = 11$
   $= 4 + 7 = 11$
   $= 11 = 11$
   Since, LHS = RHS
   Hence, $x = 8$ is the root of $12x + 7 = 11$.

2. Solve each of the following equations by trial – and – error method:
   (i) $x + 3 = 12$
   (ii) $x - 7 = 10$
   (iii) $4x = 28$
   (iv) $(x/2) + 7 = 11$

   Answer:
   (i) Given $x + 3 = 12$
   Here LHS = $x + 3$ and RHS = 12

x	LHS	RHS	Is LHS = RHS
1	1 + 3 = 4	12	No
2	2 + 3 = 5	12	No
3	3 + 3 = 6	12	No
4	4 + 3 = 7	12	No
5	5 + 3 = 8	12	No
6	6 + 3 = 9	12	No
7	7 + 3 = 10	12	No
8	8 + 3 = 11	12	No
9	9 + 3 = 12	12	Yes

   Therefore, if $x = 9$, LHS = RHS.
   Hence, $x = 9$ is the solution to this equation.

   (ii) Given $x - 7 = 10$
   Here LHS = $x - 7$ and RHS = 10

x	LHS	RHS	Is LHS = RHS
9	9 - 7 = 2	10	No
10	10 - 7 = 3	10	No
11	11 - 7 = 4	10	No
12	12 - 7 = 5	10	No
13	19 - 7 = 6	10	No

14	14 − 7 = 7	10	No
15	15 − 7 = 8	10	No
16	16 − 7 = 9	10	No
17	17 − 7 = 10	10	Yes

Therefore if $x = 17$, LHS = RHS
Hence, $x = 17$ is the solution to this equation.
(iii) Given $4x = 28$
Here LHS = $4x$ and RHS = 28

x	LHS	RHS	Is LHS = RHS
1	4 × 1 = 4	28	No
2	4 × 2 = 8	28	No
3	4 × 3 = 12	28	No
4	4 × 4 = 16	28	No
5	4 × 5 = 20	28	No
6	4 × 6 = 24	28	No
7	4 × 7 = 28	28	Yes

Therefore if $x = 7$, LHS = RHS
Hence, $x = 7$ is the solution to this equation.
(iv) Given $(x/2) + 7 = 11$
Here LHS = $(x/2) + 7$ and RHS = 11
Since RHS is a natural number, $(x/2)$ must also be a natural number, so we must substitute values of x that are multiples of 2.

x	LHS	RHS	Is LHS = RHS
2	(2/2) + 7 = 1 + 7 = 8	11	No
4	(4/2) + 7 = 2 + 7 = 9	11	No
6	(6/2) + 7 = 3 + 7 = 10	11	No
8	(8/2) + 7 = 4 + 7 = 11	11	Yes

Therefore if $x = 8$, LHS = RHS
Hence, $x = 8$ is the solution to this equation.

Lines and Angles

10

Learning Objectives : In this chapter, students will learn about:
- ✓ Parallel lines
- ✓ Different types of angles

CHAPTER SUMMARY

Line
A line segment which may be extended endlessly on both sides is called a line.

Intersecting Lines
Two lines which have a common point is called as intersecting lines.

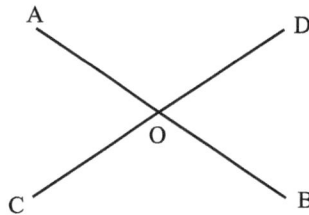

Concurrent Lines
Three or more lines in a plane are called concurrent lines if they pass though same common point.

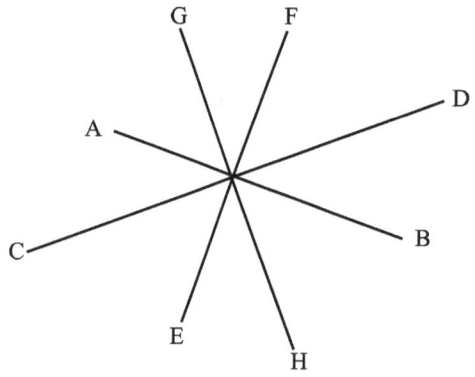

Point O is called point of concurrence.

Collinear Points
Three or more points in a plane are said to be collinear points if they lie on the same line.

Parallel Lines
Two lines in a plane are called parallel if their distance is always same and there is no common point between them.

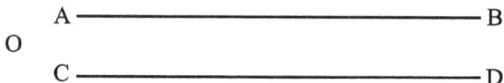

If two parallel lines cut by transversal then
(1) The corresponding angles are equal.
(2) Alternate angles are equal.
(3) Sum of interior angles of same side of transversal is 180°

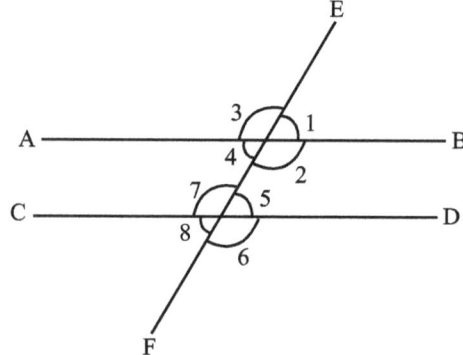

66 International Mathematics Olympiad – 7

Here, ∠1 and ∠5 are corresponding angles.
∠4 and ∠5, ∠2 and ∠7 are alternate angles.
∠2 and ∠5 and ∠4 and ∠7 are interior angles of same side of transversal.
∠2 + ∠5 = ∠4 + ∠7 = 180°

Vertically Opposite Angles

If two lines in a plane cross each other, thus angles obtained are called vertically opposite angles.

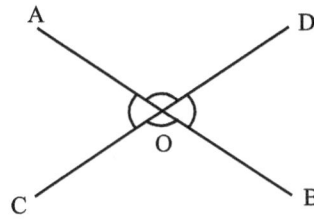

∠AOC = ∠BOD
∠AOD = ∠BOC

Straight Angle

An angle whose measure is 180°, is called a straight angle.

Complete Angle

An angle whose measure is 360°, is called a complete angle.

Example 1: Find x in the given figure

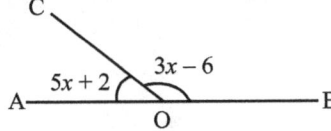

Solution: Here, $5x + 2 + 3x - 6 = 180°$

$\Rightarrow \quad 8x - 4 = 180°$

$\Rightarrow \quad 8x = 180° + 4$

$\Rightarrow \quad x = \dfrac{184°}{8} = 23°$

Example 2:

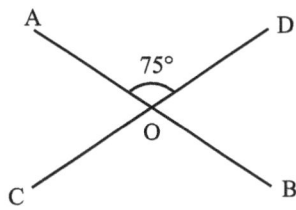

In figure ∠AOD = 73°, find ∠AOC and ∠BOC.

Solution: Here, ∠AOC + 73° = 180°

$\Rightarrow$ ∠AOC = 180° − 73° = 107°

and ∠AOD = ∠BOC = 73°

Example 3:

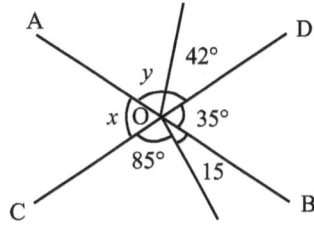

Find x and y in figure given above.

Solution: At point O, all lines meet.

$x = 35°$ (vertically opposite angles)

$y = 360° − (35° + 85° + 15° + 35° + 42°)$

$= 360° − 212° = 148°$

Example 4: In the given figure find x.

$l \parallel m$

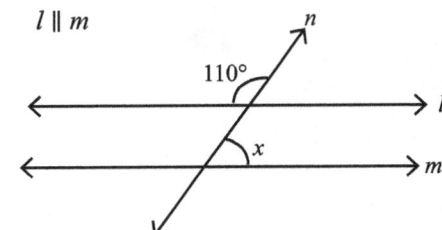

Solution:

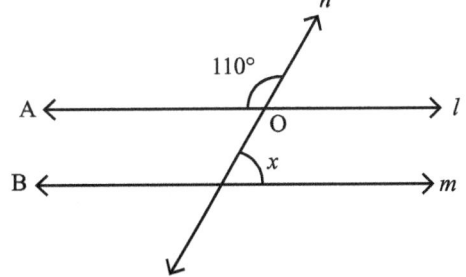

Lines and Angles

∠AOC = 180° − 110° = 70°

∴ x = 70° (alternate angles)

Example 5: Find x if AB ∥ CD.

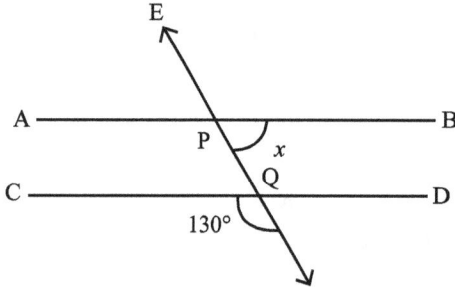

Solution: ∠PQD = 130° (vertically opposite angle)

∴ x + ∠PQD = 180°

⇒ x + 130° = 180°

⇒ x = 180° − 130° = 50°

Example 6: Find x and y in the figure given below, AB ∥ CD.

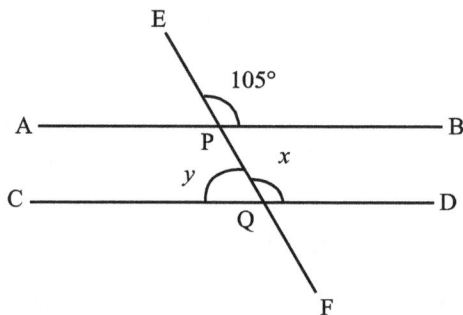

Solution: AB ∥ CD

∴ ∠EPB = x = 105°

⇒ x + y = 180°

⇒ 105° + y = 180°

⇒ y = 180° − 105° = 75°

TRIVIA

Zero is the number with the most names or synonyms. It is also known as nought, naught, ow, nil, zilch, zip, diddly-squat, love and scratch.

MUST REMEMBER

➡ A line segment which may be extended endlessly on both sides is called a line.

➡ Two lines in a plane are called parallel if their distance is always same and there is no common point between them.

MULTIPLE CHOICE QUESTIONS

1. What is the supplement of 64°?
   - (a) 106°
   - (b) 126°
   - (c) 116°
   - (d) 26°

2. What is the value of x in the given figure?

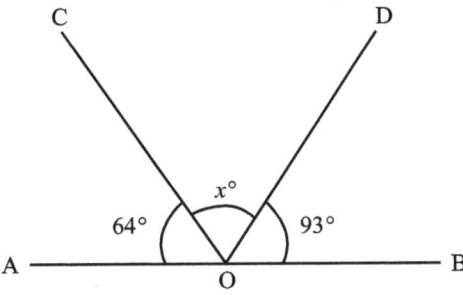

   - (a) 23°
   - (b) 33°
   - (c) 43°
   - (d) None of these

3. In the given figure two straight lines AB and PQ intersect at a point O. If $\angle AOP = 47°$ what is the measure of $\angle BOQ$?

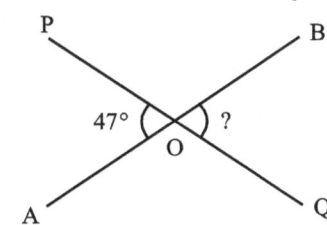

   - (a) 47°
   - (b) 133°
   - (c) 123°
   - (d) None of these

4. What is the complement of 67°?
   - (a) 33°
   - (b) 23°
   - (c) 43°
   - (d) None of these

5. In the following figure, if AB ∥ CD, $\angle BAP = 108°$ and $\angle PCD = 120°$, what is the measure of $\angle APC$?

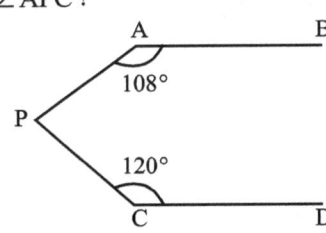

   - (a) 72°
   - (b) 92°
   - (c) 132°
   - (d) None of these

6. In the given figure MN ∥ PQ $\angle MNE = 120°$, $\angle EPQ = 100°$.
   What is the value of x?

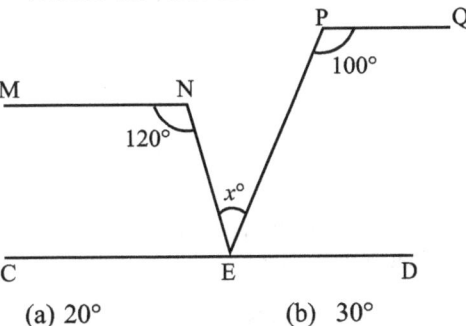

   - (a) 20°
   - (b) 30°
   - (c) 40°
   - (d) 60°

7. In the given figure AB ∥ CD and EF is transversal. If $\angle 1$ and $\angle 2$ are in the ratio 5:7 what is the measure of $\angle 8$?

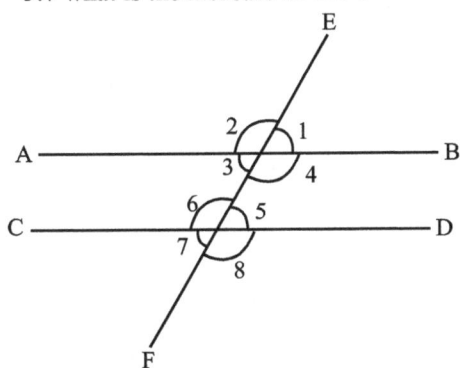

   - (a) 75°
   - (b) 105°
   - (c) 85°
   - (d) 115°

8. What is the value of x in the following figure?

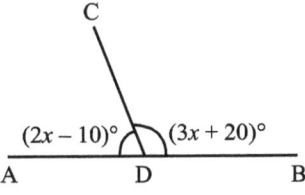

   - (a) 24°
   - (b) 34°
   - (c) 44°
   - (d) 54°

9. Which of the following angle is its complement?
   - (a) 30°
   - (b) 45°
   - (c) 60°
   - (d) 90°

10. In the given figure, ABC is a straight line. What is the value of y?

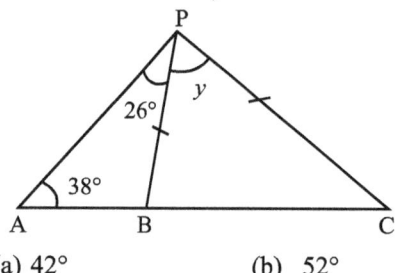

(a) 42° (b) 52°
(c) 62° (d) 32°

11. In the given figure, PQR is a straight line. What is the value of x?

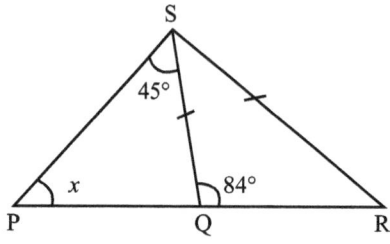

(a) 39° (b) 49°
(c) 59° (d) None of these

12. In the given figure, ABC is a straight line what is the value of z?

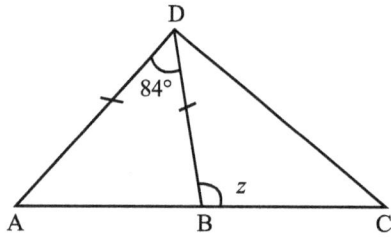

(a) 112° (b) 92°
(c) 132° (d) None of these

13. In the given figure, what is the length of BC if AB = AC?

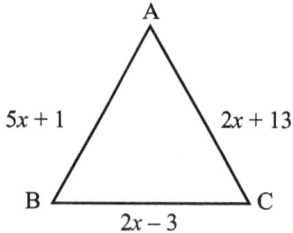

(a) 3 (b) 5
(c) 6 (d) 7

14. In the given figure △ACD is a right angled triangle. △ABC is an isosceles triangle with AB = AC. ACQ, EAD, are straight lines. What is the value of x?

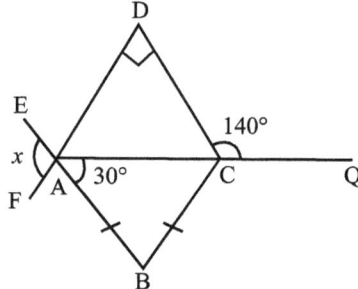

(a) 60° (b) 70°
(c) 80° (d) 90°

15. If the sides of a triangle are as given in the figure. The perimeter of triangle is 78 m. What is the measure of the highest side?

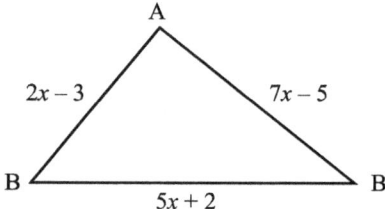

(a) 32 m (b) 37 m
(c) 35 m (d) 38 m

16. In the given figure △ABC is an equilateral triangle and △ACD is an isosceles triangle. What is the value of x?

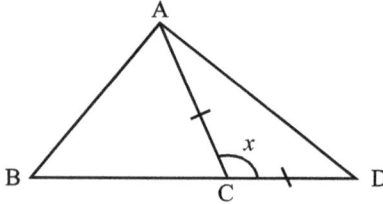

(a) 40° (b) 60°
(c) 120° (d) None of these

17. If $l \parallel m$, then what is the value of x?

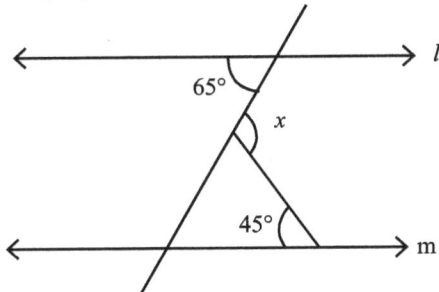

(a) 70° (b) 110°
(c) 65° (d) 25°

18. In the given figure, $\frac{y}{x} = 5$ and $\frac{z}{x} = 4$ then what is the value of x?

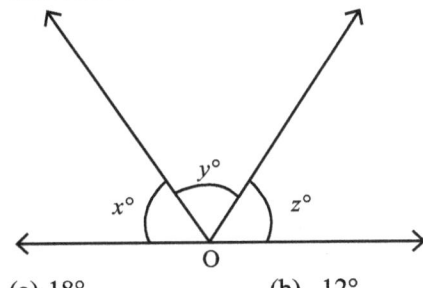

(a) 18° (b) 12°
(c) 28° (d) 15°

19. Find the value of x in figure given below.

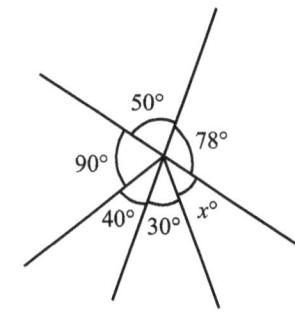

(a) 72° (b) 82°
(c) 92° (d) 42°

20. $\angle A = 56°$, CE $\parallel$ BA $\angle ECD = 73°$. What is the value of $\angle ACD$?

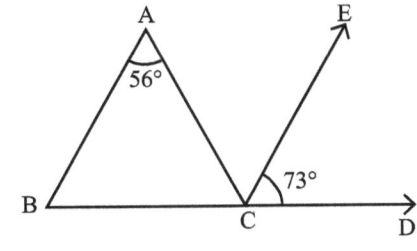

(a) 31° (b) 41°
(c) 51° (d) 61°

HOTS

1. In Figure below, OA and OB are opposite rays. If $x = 25°$, what is the value of y?

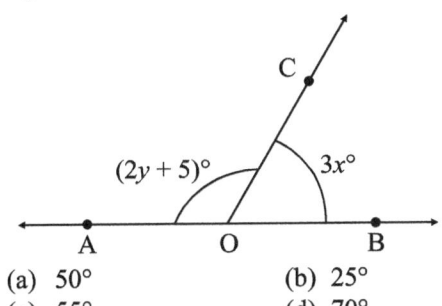

(a) 50° (b) 25°
(c) 55° (d) 70°

2. In Figure below, OA and OB are opposite rays. If $y = 35°$, what is the value of x?

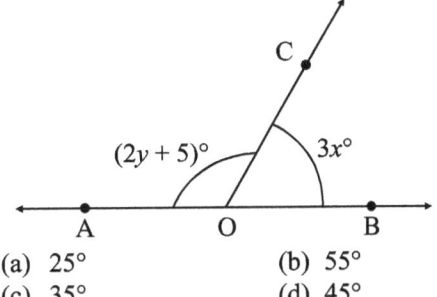

(a) 25° (b) 55°
(c) 35° (d) 45°

3. In Figure below, find ∠x. Further find ∠BOC.

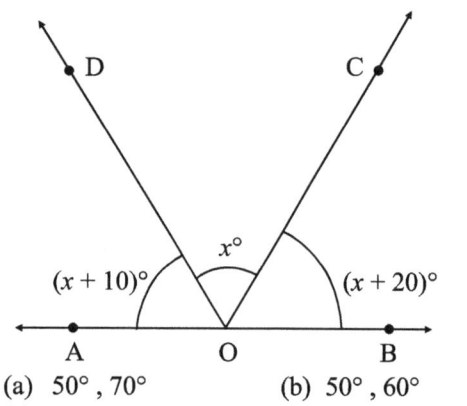

(a) 50°, 70°   (b) 50°, 60°
(c) 50°, 80°   (d) 50°, 40°

4. In Figure below, find ∠x. Further find ∠COD.

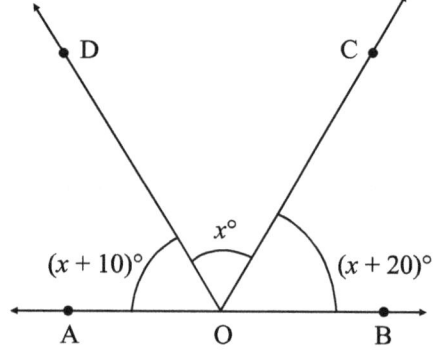

(a) 50°, 30°   (b) 50°, 50°
(c) 50°, 60°   (d) 50°, 70°

5. In Figure below, find ∠x. Further find ∠AOD.

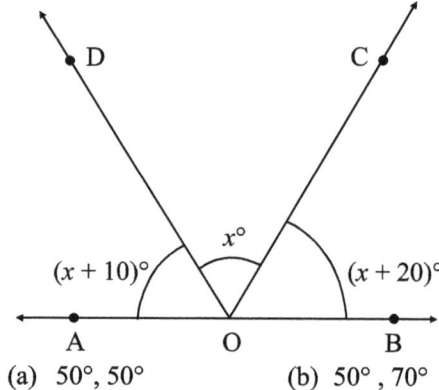

(a) 50°, 50°   (b) 50°, 70°
(c) 50°, 60°   (d) 50°, 80°

SUBJECTIVE QUESTIONS

1. Write down each pair of adjacent angles shown in figure below.

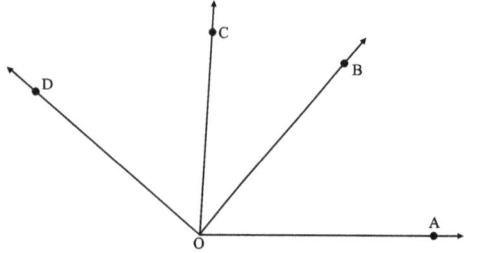

Answer:
The angles that have common vertex and a common arm are known as adjacent angles
Therefore the adjacent angles in given figure are:

∠DOC and ∠BOC
∠COB and ∠BOA

2. In Figure below, name all the pairs of adjacent angles.

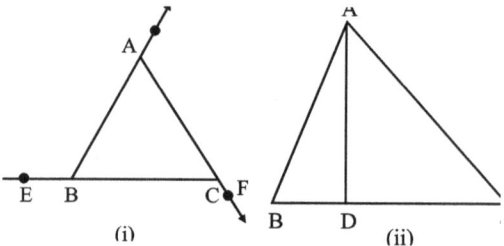

Answer:
The angles that have common vertex and a common arm are known as adjacent angles.

In fig (i), the adjacent angles are
∠EBA and ∠ABC
∠ACB and ∠BCF
∠BAC and ∠CAD
In fig (ii), the adjacent angles are
∠BAD and ∠DAC
∠BDA and ∠CDA

3. In figure below, write down
   (i) Each linear pair
   (ii) Each pair of vertically opposite angles.

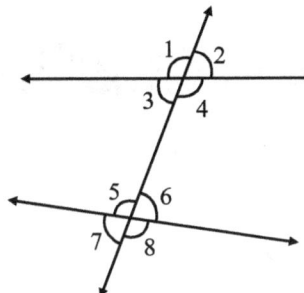

Answer:
(i) The two adjacent angles are said to form a linear pair of angles if their non – common arms are two opposite rays.
∠1 and ∠3
∠1 and ∠2
∠4 and ∠3
∠4 and ∠2
∠5 and ∠6
∠5 and ∠7
∠6 and ∠8
∠7 and ∠8
(ii) The two angles formed by two intersecting lines and have no common arms are called vertically opposite angles.
∠1 and ∠4
∠2 and ∠3
∠5 and ∠8
∠6 and ∠7

4. Find the complement of each of the following angles:
   (i) 35°   (ii) 72°
   (iii) 45°   (iv) 85°
   Answer:
   (i) The two angles are said to be complementary angles if the sum of those angles is 90o
   Complementary angle for given angle is 90° − 35° = 55°
   (ii) The two angles are said to be complementary angles if the sum of those angles is 90°
   Complementary angle for given angle is 90° − 72° = 18°
   (iii) The two angles are said to be complementary angles if the sum of those angles is 90°
   Complementary angle for given angle is 90° − 45° = 45°
   (iv) The two angles are said to be complementary angles if the sum of those angles is 90°
   Complementary angle for given angle is 90° − 85° = 5°

5. Find the supplement of each of the following angles:
   (i) 70°   (ii) 120°
   Answer:
   (i) The two angles are said to be supplementary angles if the sum of those angles is 180°. Therefore supplementary angle for the given angle is
   180° − 70° = 110°
   (ii) The two angles are said to be supplementary angles if the sum of those angles is 180°. Therefore supplementary angle for the given angle is
   180° − 120° = 60°

Triangles   11

Learning Objectives : In this chapter, students will learn about:
- Basic of Triangles
- Different types of Triangles

CHAPTER SUMMARY

Triangle
Triangle has three sides and three angles.

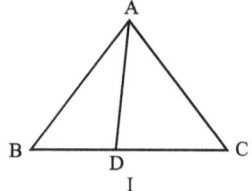

In the above figure, AB, BC, CA are sides of △ABC, ∠A, ∠B and ∠C are angles of a △ABC.

A, B, C are called vertex of a △ABC. The total measure of the three sides of a triangle is 180°.

Median
A median connects a vertex of a triangle to the mid – point of the opposite side.

Altitude
The height is the distance from any vertex.

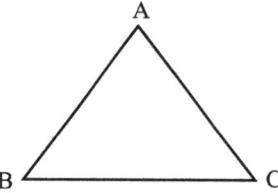

AD is the median.

In fig. II, AD is altitude of △ABC.

Exterior Angle
Exterior angle of a triangle is equal to the sum of its interior opposite angles.

∠ACD = ∠ABC + ∠BAC

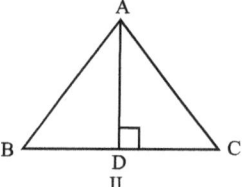

Equilateral Triangle
A triangle in which all the three sides are of equal length is called an equilateral triangle.

Isosceles Triangle
A triangle in which two sides are equal is called an isosceles triangle.

Example 1: Two angles of a triangle are 53° and 48°. What is the third angle?

Solution: Third angle = 180° – (53° + 48°)

= 180° – 101° = 79°

Example 2: In a right angled triangle one of the angle is 42°. What is the measure of third angle?

Solution: Third angle = 180° – (90° + 42°)

= 180° – 132° = 48°

Example 3: In the given figure, what is the value of x.

Solution: ∠BAC = 90°

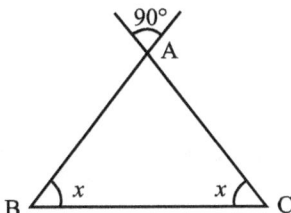

$x + x + 90° = 180°$
$\Rightarrow 2x = 180° - 90°$
$\Rightarrow 2x = 90°$
$\Rightarrow x = \dfrac{90°}{2} = 45°$

Example 4: What is the value of x?

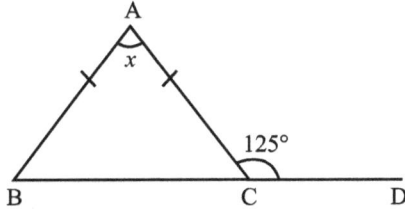

Solution: $\angle ACD = 125°$
$\angle ACB = 180° - 125° = 55°$
and $AB = AC$
$\angle ABC = \angle ACB = 55°$
$x + 55° + 55° = 180°$
$\Rightarrow x + 110° = 180°$
$\Rightarrow x = 180° - 110° = 70°$

■ The sum of lengths of any two sides of a triangle is greater than third side.

Example 5: The sides of a triangle are 3, 4, 7cm. Is triangle possible or not?

Solution: $3 + 4 = 7$
$4 + 7 > 3$
$3 + 7 > 4$

But, sum of any two sides of a triangle must be greater than third side.
$3 + 4 = 7$

So, triangle is not possible.

■ Sum of all sides of a triangle is called its perimeter.

Example 6: The sides of a triangle are 6, 7, 11cm. What is its perimeter?

Solution: Perimeter = $6 + 7 + 11 = 24$ cm

■ In right angled triangle, the side opposite to right angle is called hypotenuse.

The other two sides are called legs of the right angled triangle.

TRIVIA

The Reuleaux Triangle is a shape of constant width, the simplest and best known such curve other than a circle.

Pythagoras Theorem

In a right angled triangle, the sum of the squares of the legs is equal to the square of hypotenuse.

Example 7: In a right angled triangle, one side is 5cm, hypotenuse is 13cm. What is the length of third side?

Solution: In right angled triangle,
$$x^2 + 5^2 = 13^2$$
$\Rightarrow \quad x^2 + 25 = 163$
$\Rightarrow \quad x^2 = 169 - 25$
$\Rightarrow \quad x^2 = \sqrt{144}$
$\Rightarrow \quad x = 12$ cm

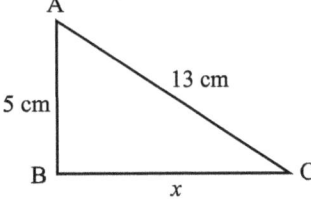

Triangles

MUST REMEMBER

- Exterior angle of a triangle is equal to the sum of its interior opposite angles.
- A triangle in which all the three sides are of equal length is called an equilateral triangle.
- In right angled triangle, the side opposite to right angle is called hypotenuse.

MULTIPLE CHOICE QUESTIONS

1. Two angles of a triangle are equal and the third angle measures 70°. Find the measure of each of the unknown angles.
   (a) 50° (b) 55°
   (c) 70° (d) 110°

2. In a $\triangle XYZ$, if $\angle X = 90°$ and $\angle Z = 48°$, find $\angle Y$.
   (a) 42° (b) 45°
   (c) 40° (d) 35°

3. Each of the two equal angles of an isosceles triangle is twice the third angle. Find the angles of the triangle.
   (a) 36°, 72°, 36° (b) 45°, 60°, 75°
   (c) 36°, 36°, 72° (d) 72°, 72°, 36°

4. What is the measure of each angle of an equilateral triangle?
   (a) 60° (b) 80°
   (c) 40° (d) 70°

5. Find the angles of a triangle which are in the ratio 4 : 3 : 2.
   (a) 15°, 20°, 25° (b) 20°, 20°, 40°
   (c) 80°, 60°, 40° (d) 40°, 80°, 60°

6. In the given figure, find the values of x and y.

   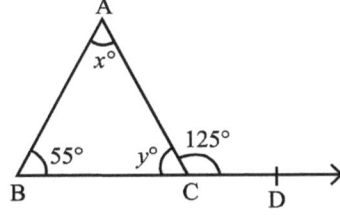

   (a) $x = 55°, y = 70°$ (b) $x = 55°, y = 55°$
   (c) $x = 50°, y = 70°$ (d) $x = 70°, y = 55°$

7. In the given figure, find the values of x and y.

   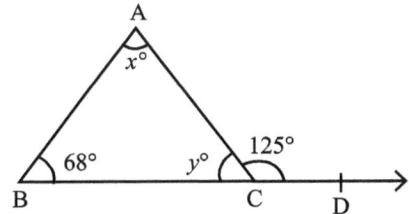

   (a) $y = 62°, x = 50°$
   (b) $x = 62°, y = 50°$
   (c) $x = 52°, y = 40°$
   (d) $x = 50°, y = 60°$

8. In the figure given alongside, $x : y = 2 : 3$ and $\angle ACD = 130°$ find the values of x, y and z.

   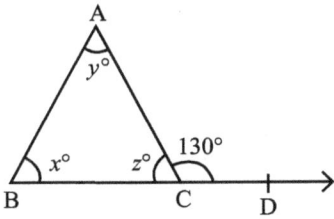

   (a) $x = 26°, y = 52°, z = 26°$
   (b) $x = 50°, y = 80°, z = 50°$
   (c) $x = 52°, y = 78°, z = 50°$
   (d) $x = 50°, y = 78°, z = 52°$

9. A man goes 24m due east and then 10m due north. How far is he away from his initial position?
   (a) 24 m (b) 28 m
   (c) 30 m (d) 26 m

10. The lengths of the sides of two triangles are given below. Which of them is right-angled?
    (i) $a = 8$ cm, $b = 5$ cm, and $c = 10$ cm
    (ii) $a = 7$ cm, $b = 24$ cm, and $c = 25$ cm
    (a) (i) and (ii) both
    (b) (ii) is but (i) not
    (c) (i) and (ii) both not
    (d) None of these

11. Two poles of height 9 cm and 14m stand upright on a plane ground. If the distance between their feet is 12 m. Find the distance between their tops.
    (a) 12 m (b) 13 m
    (c) 5 m   (d) 15 m

12. Two circles are congruent if they have
    (a) Same length   (b) Same breadth
    (c) Same radius   (d) None of these

Triangles

13. Two lines segments are congruent if they have
    (a) The same length   (b) Same breadth
    (c) Same radius   (d) None of these

14. In a $\triangle ABC$ it is given that $\angle B = 37°$ and $\angle C = 29°$. Then $\angle A = ?$
    (a) 57°   (b) 114°
    (c) 66°   (d) 86°

15. In a $\triangle ABC$, if $2\angle A = 3, \angle B = 6\angle C$ then $\angle B = ?$
    (a) 30°   (b) 90°
    (c) 60°   (d) 45°

16. In a $\triangle ABC$, $\angle A - \angle B = 33°$ and $\angle B - \angle C = 18°$, then $\angle B = ?$
    (a) 35°   (b) 55°
    (c) 45°   (d) 57°

17. The sum of all angles of a triangle is
    (a) 90°   (b) 150°
    (c) 100°   (d) 180°

18. In the given figure, what value of x will make AOB a straight line?

    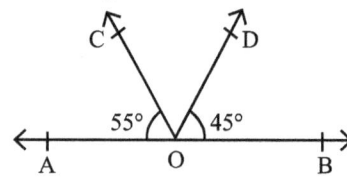

    (a) $x = 50$ (b) $x = 80$
    (c) $x = 100$ (d) $x = 60$

19. In the given figure, AOB is a straight line, $\angle AOC = (3x - 8)°$, $\angle COD = 50°$ and $\angle BOD = (x + 10)°$. The value of x is

    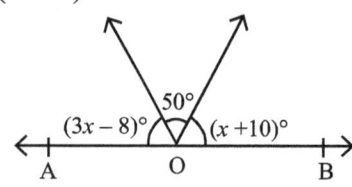

    (a) 42   (b) 52
    (c) 36   (d) 32

20. In $\triangle ABC$, $\angle B = 90°$, $AB = 5$cm and $AC = 13$cm then $BC = ?$

    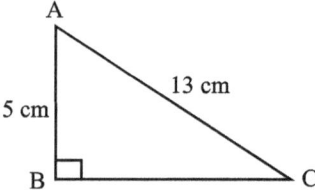

    (a) 18 cm   (b) 12 cm
    (c) 8 cm   (d) None of these

21. $\triangle ABC$ is an isosceles triangle with $\angle C = 90°$ and $AC = 5$ cm then $AB = ?$
    (a) $5\sqrt{2}$ cm   (b) 10 cm
    (c) 5 cm   (d) 2.5 cm

22. The angles of a triangle are $(3x)°$, $(2x - 7)°$ and $(4x - 11)°$. Then $x = ?$
    (a) 18   (b) 22
    (c) 20   (d) 30

23. The supplement of 45° is
    (a) 45°   (b) 75°
    (c) 135°   (d) 155°

24. An angle is one – fifth of its supplement. The measure of the angle is
    (a) 75°   (b) 150°
    (c) 15°   (d) 30°

25. In the given figure, AOB is a straight line, $\angle AOC = 68°$ and $\angle BOC = x°$, the value of x is.

    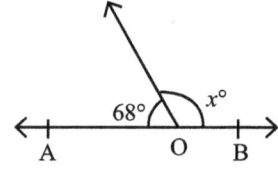

    (a) 112   (b) 132
    (c) 22   (d) 32

HOTS

1. In the following figure, if l ∥ m value of *a* will be:

   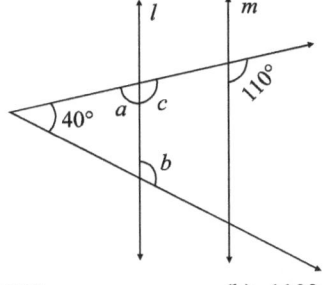

   (a) 180° (b) 110°
   (c) 70°   (d) 40°

2. In the following figure, if l ∥ m value of *b* will be:

   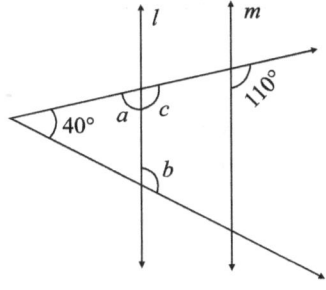

   (a) 180° (b) 110°
   (c) 70°   (d) 40°

3. Find the values of *a, b* and *c*.

   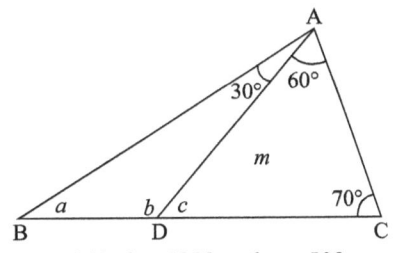

   (a) $a = 20°, b = 130°$ and $c = 50°$
   (b) $a = 50°, b = 130°$ and $c = 20°$
   (c) $a = 10°, b = 130°$ and $c = 20°$
   (d) $a = 20°, b = 30°$ and $c = 40°$

4. Find the values of *a, b* and *c*.

   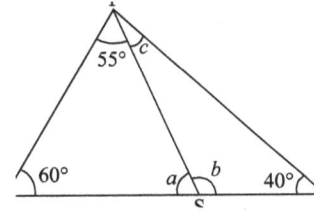

   (a) $a = 65°, b = 115°$ and $c = 25°$
   (b) $a = 25°, b = 75°$ and $c = 65°$
   (c) $a = 45°, b = 15°$ and $c = 55°$
   (d) $a = 65°, b = 15°$ and $c = 25°$

5. Two angles of a triangle are of measures 150° and 30°. The third angle will be:
   (a) 35° (b) 75°
   (c) 45° (d) 25°

SUBJECTIVE QUESTIONS

1. In ΔABC, write the following:
   (a) Angle opposite to side BC.
   (b) The side opposite to ∠ABC.
   (c) Vertex opposite to side AC.

   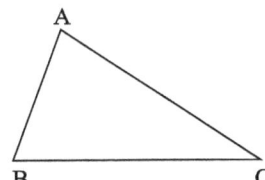

   Answer:
   (a) In ΔABC, Angle opposite to BC is ∠BAC
   (b) Side opposite to ∠ABC is AC
   (c) Vertex opposite to side AC is B

2. Classify the following triangle on the bases of sides

   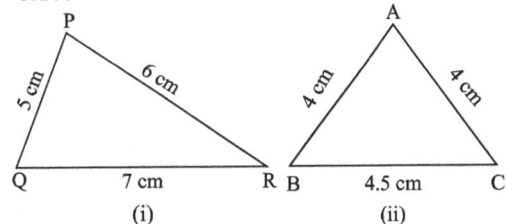

   (i) (ii)

Triangles

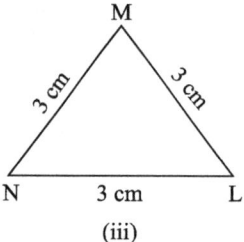

N   3 cm   L

(iii)

Answer:
(i) PQ = 5 cm, PR = 6 cm and QR = 7 cm
PQ ≠ PR ≠ QR
Thus, ΔPQR is a scalene triangle.
(ii) AB = 4 cm, AC = 4 cm
AB = AC
Thus, ΔABC is an isosceles triangle.
(iii) MN = 3 cm, ML = 3 cm and NL = 3 cm
MN = ML = NL
Thus, ΔMNL is an equilateral triangle.

3. In the given figure, name the median and the altitude. Here E is the midpoint of BC.
Answer:
In ΔABC, we have

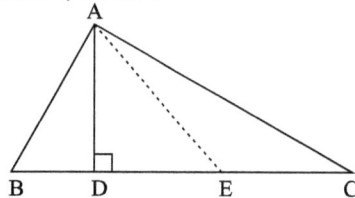

AD is the altitude.
AE is the median.

4. In the given diagrams, find the value of x in each case.

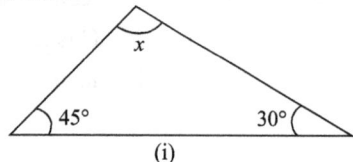

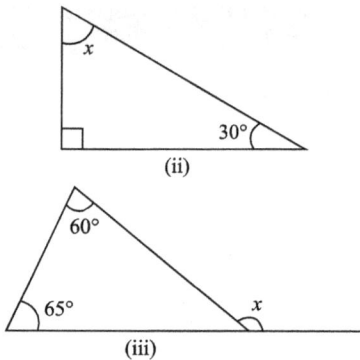

Answer:
(i) $x + 45° + 30° = 180°$ (Angle sum property of a triangle)
$\Rightarrow x + 75° = 180°$
$\Rightarrow x = 180° - 75°$
$x = 105°$
(ii) Here, the given triangle is right angled triangle.
$x + 30° = 90°$
$\Rightarrow x = 90° - 30° = 60°$
(iii) $x = 60° + 65°$ (Exterior angle of a triangle is equal to the sum of interior opposite angles)
$\Rightarrow x = 125°$

5. Which of the following cannot be the sides of a triangle?
(i) 4.5 cm, 3.5 cm, 6.4 cm
(ii) 2.5 cm, 3.5 cm, 6.0 cm
Answer:
(i) Given sides are, 4.5 cm, 3.5 cm, 6.4 cm
Sum of any two sides = 4.5 cm + 3.5 cm
= 8 cm
Since 8 cm > 6.4 cm (Triangle inequality)
The given sides form a triangle.
(ii) Given sides are 2.5 cm, 3.5 cm, 6.0 cm
Sum of any two sides = 2.5 cm + 3.5 cm
= 6.0 cm
Since 6.0 cm = 6.0 cm
The given sides do not form a triangle.

Data Handling 12

Learning Objectives : In this chapter, students will learn about:
- Basics of Data
- Frequency
- Mean and Median

CHAPTER SUMMARY

Data
A collection of numerical figures giving some particular type of information is called data.

Example: The weight of 5 students in a class are 65kg, 48kg, 52kg, 46kg, 40kg etc.

Frequency
The number of times a particular observation occurs is called its frequency.

Mean of Ungrouped Data

$$\text{Mean} = \frac{\text{Sum of the given observations}}{\text{Number of the given observations}}$$

Example 1: Find the mean of the numbers 45, 48, 62, 76, 57, 38.

Solution: Mean $= \dfrac{45+48+62+76+57+38}{6}$

$= \dfrac{326}{6} = 54.33$

Mean of Grouped (tabulated) Data

Let the frequencies of n observations $x_1, x_2, \ldots x_n$ be $f_1, f_2, f_3 \ldots f_n$ respectively, then

$$\text{Mean} = \frac{x_1 f_1 + x_2 f_2 + x_3 f_3 + \ldots\ldots x_n f_n}{f_1 + f_2 + f_3 + \ldots\ldots + f_n}$$

$$\text{Mean} = \frac{\sum x_i f_i}{\sum f_i}$$

where $\sum$ (Sigma) denotes summation.

Example 2: The given table shows the weight of 16 workers in a factory.

Weight (in kg)	56	60	62	65	68	72
No. of workers	3	4	2	2	3	2

Find the mean weight.

Solution:

Weight (in kg) (x_i)	No. of workers (f_i)	$x_i f_i$
56	3	168
60	4	240
62	2	124
65	2	130
68	3	204
72	2	144

$\sum f_i = 16 \quad \sum x_i f_i = 1010$

Mean weight $= \dfrac{\sum x_i f_i}{\sum f_i} = \dfrac{1010}{16} = 63.125$ kg

Example 3: Find the mean of first seven prime numbers.

Solution: The first seven prime numbers are 2, 3, 5, 7, 11, 13, 17.

Mean $= \dfrac{2+3+5+7+11+13+17}{7}$

$= \dfrac{58}{7} = 8.285$

Median of Ungrouped Data

When the given data is arranged in ascending or descending order, then the value of the middle most observation is called the median of the data.

Method for Finding Median

The ungrouped data is arranged in ascending or descending order.

When n is odd, then

Median = value of $\left(\dfrac{n+1}{2}\right)$th observation

When *n* is even, Then

Median $= \dfrac{\left[\dfrac{n}{2}th \text{ observation} + \left(\dfrac{n}{2}+1\right)th \text{ observation}\right]}{2}$

Example 4: The runs scored by 11 players of a cricket team are 36, 57, 43, 17, 87, 23, 29, 09, 67, 31, 64.

What is the median score?

Solution: The runs in the ascending order are 09, 17, 23, 29, 31, 36, 43, 57, 64, 67, 87

$n = 11$, which is odd.

Median score = $\left(\dfrac{11+1}{2}\right)$th observation

= 6th observation

= 36

Example 5: The heights of 12 workers in a factory are 162cm, 175cm, 160cm, 158cm, 164cm, 182cm, 166cm, 171cm, 170cm, 165cm, 159cm, 163cm. Find the median of the height of 12 workers in a factory.

Solution: The heights in ascending order are 158, 159, 160, 162, 163, 164, 165, 166, 170, 171, 175, 182

$n = 12$, which is even.

Median height $= \dfrac{\dfrac{12}{2}th + \left(\dfrac{12}{2}+1\right)th \text{ height}}{2}$

$= \dfrac{[6th + 7th] \text{ height}}{2}$

$= \dfrac{164+165}{2} = \dfrac{329}{2} = 164.5$ cm

TRIVIA

Using only addition, you can add 8's to get the number 1,000 by:
888 + 88 + 8 + 8 + 8 = 1,000.

Median of Grouped Data

First of all, the given data is arranged in ascending or descending order. Then we have to prepare a cumulative frequency table.

Let the total frequency be N.

If N is odd, then

Median = Size of $\left(\dfrac{N+1}{2}\right)$th term.

If *N* is even, then

Median = $\dfrac{\text{Size of } \dfrac{N}{2}th \text{ term} + \text{Size of } \left(\dfrac{N}{2}+1\right)th \text{ term}}{2}$

Example 6: Find the median of given frequency distribution.

Marks obtained (x_i)	42	27	53	45	38	43
No. of students (f_i)	8	10	7	3	6	9

Solution:

Marks obtained (x_i)	No. of students (f_i)	Cumulative frequency
27	10	10
38	6	6
42	8	24
43	9	33
45	3	36
53	7	43

$N = 43$

$N = 43$, which is odd.

Median of marks = Marks obtained by $\left(\dfrac{43+1}{2}\right)$nd student

= Marks obtained by 22nd student
= 42

Mode

It is the value of the variable having highest frequency.

Example 7: Find the mode of the given data.

15, 12, 17, 25, 38, 12, 15, 17, 15, 28, 15, 27, 15.

Solution: Mode = 15, as it occurs 5 times.

Empirical Formula for Calculating Mode

$$\text{Mode} = 3\text{ Median} - 2\text{ Mean}.$$

Example 8: Calculate the mode of the given data.

Marks	12	17	25	35	40	45	50	56
No. of students	3	5	8	6	2	4	10	2

Calculate mean and median also.

Solution: By observation of the above table.

Mode = 50

Marks (x_i)	No. of students (f_i)	Cumulative frequency	$x_i f_i$
12	3	3	36
17	5	8	85
25	8	16	200
35	6	22	210
40	2	24	80
45	4	28	180
50	10	38	500
56	2	40	112

$$N = 40$$
$$\Sigma x_i f_i = 1403$$

$$\text{Mean} = \frac{\Sigma x_i f_i}{\Sigma f_i} = \frac{1403}{40} = 35.075$$

$$\text{Median} = \frac{\left(\frac{40}{2}\right)th + \left(\frac{40}{2}+1\right)th \text{ term}}{2}$$

$$= \frac{35+35}{2} = \frac{70}{2} = 35$$

MUST REMEMBER

➡ A collection of numerical figures giving some particular type of information is called data.
➡ When the given data is arranged in ascending or descending order, then the value of the middle most observation is called the median of the data.

Data Handling

MULTIPLE CHOICE QUESTIONS

1. What is the mean of the following numbers 7.6, 6.8, 8.5, 9.4, 5.9, 6.4, 9.1, 4.7?
   (a) 7.1 (b) 7.2
   (c) 7.3 (d) 7.4

2. What is the mean of first nine even natural numbers?
   (a) 10 (b) 12
   (c) 11 (d) 13

3. What is the mean of first seven prime numbers?
   (a) 7.285 (b) 8.285
   (c) 7.685 (d) 8.625

4. What is the mean of first eight odd natural numbers?
   (a) 8 (b) 9
   (c) 10 (d) 11

5. The runs scored by 11 members of a cricket team are 35, 39, 53, 28, 65, 62, 0, 46, 31, 08, 24. What is the median score?
   (a) 28 (b) 31
   (c) 35 (d) 39

6. What is the median of first 15 odd numbers?
   (a) 15 (b) 17
   (c) 19 (d) 21

7. What is the median of first 50 whole numbers?
   (a) 25.5 (b) 24.5
   (c) 26.5 (d) None of these

8. What is the median of 21, 15, 8, 28, 19, 23, 40, 7, 16, 9, 22 ?
   (a) 16 (b) 19
   (c) 21 (d) 22

9. What is the mode of the following data 22, 28, 47, 43, 28, 27, 36, 43, 45, 42, 43, 46, ?
   (a) 22 (b) 28
   (c) 47 (d) None of these

10. If the mean of a given data is 51kg and its median is 50 kg, what is the mode of that data?
    (a) 52 kg (b) 51 kg
    (c) 53 kg (d) 54 kg

11. If the mode of the given data is 22.16, its median is 22. What is its mean?
    (a) 20.92 (b) 21.92
    (c) 22.92 (d) 23.92

12. What is the mean of first 12 multiples of 7?
    (a) 45 (b) 46
    (c) 45.5 (d) 46.5

13. What is the median of the given data?

Marks obtained (x_i)	17	20	25	22	15	30
Number of students (f_i)	5	9	6	4	3	10

    (a) 17 (b) 20
    (c) 22 (d) None of these

14. What is the mean of the given data?

Weight in kg	60	63	65	72	75	77
No. of labours	4	5	4	2	6	3

    (a) 67.33 (b) 64.33
    (c) 68.33 (d) None of these

15. What is the median of first 9 multiples of 12?
    (a) 36 (b) 48
    (c) 60 (d) 72

16. What is the mode of the given data 16, 20, 8, 17, 27, 34, 28, 32, 27, 15, 27, 54, 42.
    (a) 8 (b) 27
    (c) 54 (d) None of these

17. If the mean of the given data 16, 24, x, 34, 35, 25, 37, 42, 47, is 32. What is the value of x?
    (a) 26 (b) 27
    (c) 28 (d) 29

18. The heights of nine players of a team are 165cm, 168cm, 170cm, 174cm, 182cm, 160cm, 171cm, 173cm, 164cm. Find the median.
    (a) 168 cm (b) 170 cm
    (c) 171 cm (d) None of these

19. What is the mean of the following data?

Marks obtained	45	27	20	56	82	75	17
No. of students	5	3	8	7	2	4	12

(a) 34.22 (b) 36.22
(c) 37.22 (d) None of these

20. What is the median of the following data?

Marks obtained	72	47	62	57	42	52	67
No. of students	9	8	11	8	3	6	5

(a) 56.5 (b) 57.5
(c) 58.5 (d) 59.5

21. The ages in years of 15 teachers of a school are 41, 32, 51, 43, 24, 38, 49, 56, 42, 28, 37, 48, 45, 47, 50. What is the range of ages of teachers?
(a) 32 years (b) 30 years
(c) 28 years (d) None of these

22. A batsman scored the following number of runs in 8 innings. What is the arithmetic mean? 59, 36, 57, 35, 60, 55, 46, 50.
(a) 49.25 (b) 49.35
(c) 49.65 (d) 49.75

23. Following are the margins of victory in the football matches of a league.
1, 3, 2, 5, 1, 4, 6, 2, 5, 2, 2, 2, 4, 1, 2, 3, 1, 1, 2, 3, 2, 6, 4, 3, 2, 1, 1, 4, 2, 1, 5, 3, 3, 2, 3, 2, 4, 2, 1, 2.
What is the mode of this data?
(a) 1 (b) 2
(c) 3 (d) 4

24. The scores in physics test (out of 100) of 15 students is as follows: 19, 42, 68, 27, 36, 48, 78, 38, 12, 17, 61, 65, 47, 84, 39. What is the median of this data?

(a) 39 (b) 42
(c) 47 (d) 48

25. What is the mode of this following data: 12, 14, 12, 16, 15, 13, 14, 18, 19, 12, 14, 15, 16, 15, 16, 16, 15. 17, 13, 16, 16, 15, 15, 13, 15, 17, 15, 14, 15, 13, 15, 14.
(a) 13 (b) 14
(c) 15 (d) 16

26. Find the arithmetic mean of 12 multiple of 8 which are greater than 100.
(a) 142 (b) 144
(c) 146 (d) 148

27. If the median of a given data is 13 and its mean is 13.28. what is its mode?
(a) 11.44 (b) 12.44
(c) 13.44 (d) None of these

28. If the mean and mode of a given data is 51 and 48 respectively. What is its median?
(a) 48 (b) 49
(c) 50 (d) 52

29. Find the difference of mean and median of the following data:

Daily wages (in Rs.)	100	125	150	175	200
No. of workers	6	8	9	12	10

(a) 5.66 (b) 6.66
(c) 3.66 (d) None of these

30. A student scored the following marks in an examination in Hindi 75, Mathematics 60, English 59 and Drawing 63. Find the weighted mean if the approved weightage of students in the above subjects are 2, 4, 1 and 3 respectively.
(a) 61.8 marks (b) 60.1 marks
(c) 62.8 marks (d) 63.8 marks

Data Handling

HOTS

1. In a Mathematics test following marks were obtained by 40 students of class VI. Arrange these marks in a table using, tally marks.

8	1	3	7	6	5	5	4	4	2
4	9	5	3	7	1	6	5	2	7
7	3	8	4	2	6	9	5	8	6
7	4	5	6	9	6	4	4	6	6

   How many students obtained marks equal to or more than 7?
   (a) 10 (b) 24
   (c) 25 (d) 3

2. In a Mathematics test following marks were obtained by 40 students of class VI. Arrange these marks in a table using, tally marks.

8	1	3	7	6	5	5	4	4	2
4	9	5	3	7	1	6	5	2	7
7	3	8	4	2	6	9	5	8	6
7	4	5	6	9	6	4	4	6	6

   How many students obtained marks below 4?
   (a) 10 (b) 24
   (c) 11 (d) 14

3. If the heights of 5 persons are 140 cm, 150 cm, 152 cm, 158 cm and 161 cm respectively, the mean height will be:
   (a) 152.2 cm (b) 132.5 cm
   (c) 130.4 cm (d) 125.2 cm

4. The mean of first 10 even natural numbers:
   (a) 13 (b) 10
   (c) 11 (d) 12

5. The following data gives the amount of manure (in thousand tonnes) manufactured by a company during some years:

Year	1992	1993	1994	1995	1996	1997
Manure (in thousand tonnes)	15	35	45	30	40	20

   The consecutive years during which there was maximum decrease in manure production are:
   (a) 1994 and 1995 (b) 1992 and 1993
   (c) 1996 and 1997 (d) 1995 and 1996

SUBJECTIVE QUESTIONS

1. Define the following terms:
   (i) Observations
   (ii) Data
   (iii) Frequency of an observation
   (iv) Frequency distribution
   Answer:
   (i) Observation is the activity of paying close attention to someone or something in order to get information in numerical form.
   (ii) **Data:** The collection of observations is known as data.
   (iii) **Frequency of an observation:** The number of times an observation occurs in a given data is called the frequency of an observation.
   (iv) **Frequency distribution:** It is a method of presenting raw data in a form that can be easily understood.

2. The final marks in Mathematics of 30 students are as follows:
   53, 61, 48, 60, 78, 68, 55, 100, 67, 90
   75, 88, 77, 37, 84, 58, 60, 48, 62, 56
   44, 58, 52, 64, 98, 59, 70, 39, 50, 60
   (i) Arrange these marks in the ascending order. 30 to 39 one group, 40 to 49 second group, etc.
   (ii) What is the highest score?
   (iii) What is the lowest score?
   (iv) What is the range?
   (v) If 40 is the pass mark how many have failed?
   (vi) How many have scored 75 or more?

(vii) Which observations between 50 and 60 have not actually appealed?
(viii) How many have scored less than 50?

Answer:
(i) Ascending order of the numbers in groups:
(30 – 39): 37, 39
(40 – 49): 44, 48, 48
(50 – 59): 50, 52, 53, 55, 56, 58, 58, 59
(60 – 69): 60, 60, 60, 61, 62, 64, 67, 68
(70 – 79): 70, 75, 77, 78
(80 – 89): 84, 88
(90 – 99): 90, 98
(100-109): 100
(ii) The highest score is 100.
(iii) The lowest score is 37.
(iv) Range is = Maximum observation – Minimum observation.
= 100 – 37
= 63.
(v) If 40 is the pass mark, then only 2 students have failed.
(vi) 8 students have scored 75 or more.
(vii) 51, 54 and 57 are not there between 50 and 60.
(viii) 5 students scored less than 50.

3. The weights of new born babies (in kg) in a hospital on a particular day are as follows:

2.3, 2.2, 2.1, 2.7, 2.6, 3.0, 2.5, 2.9, 2.8, 3.1, 2.5, 2.8, 2.7, 2.9, 2.4

(i) Rearrange the weights in descending order.
(ii) Determine the highest weight.
(iii) Determine the lowest weight.
(iv) Determine the range.
(v) How many babies were born on that day?
(vi) How many babies weigh below 2.5 kg?
(vii) How many babies weigh more than 2.8?
(viii) How many babies weigh 2.8 kg?

Answer:
(i) Weights in descending order:
3.1, 3.0, 2.9, 2.9, 2.8, 2.8, 2.7, 2.7, 2.6, 2.5, 2.5, 2.4, 2.3, 2.2, 2.1
(ii) Highest weight: 3.1 Kg.
(iii) Lowest weight: 2.1 Kg.
(iv) Range = Maximum observation – Minimum observation

= (3.1-2.1) kg
= 1.0 Kg.
(v) A total of 15 babies were born on that day.
(vi) 4 babies weigh below 2.5 kg.
(vii) 4 babies weigh more than 2.8 kg.
(viii) 2 babies weigh 2.8 kg.

4. Following data gives the number of children in 40 families:
1, 2, 6, 5, 1, 5, 1, 3, 2, 6, 2, 3, 4, 2, 0, 0, 4, 4, 3, 2
2, 0, 0, 1, 2, 2, 4, 3, 2, 1, 0, 5, 1, 2, 4, 3, 4, 1, 6, 2
Represent it in the form of a frequency distribution.

Answer:
Required frequency table for given data is:

Number of Children	Frequency
0	5
1	7
2	11
3	5
4	6
5	3
6	3

5. Prepare a frequency table of the following scores obtained by 50 students in a test:

42	51	21	42	37	37	42	49	38	52
7	33	17	44	39	7	14	27	39	42
42	62	37	39	67	51	53	53	59	41
29	38	27	31	54	19	53	51	22	61
42	39	59	47	33	34	16	37	57	43

Answer:
Required frequency-distribution table for given data:

Marks	Number of Students
7	2
14	1
16	1
17	1
19	1

Data Handling

21	1		44	1
22	1		47	1
27	2		49	1
29	1		51	3
31	1		52	1
33	2		53	3
34	1		54	1
37	4		57	1
38	2		59	2
39	4		61	1
41	1		62	1
42	6		67	1
43	1			

Elementary Mensuration: Perimeter & Area   13

Learning Objectives : In this chapter, students will learn about:
- ✓ Fundamental concepts of Triangles
- ✓ Fundamental concepts of Quadrilaterals

CHAPTER SUMMARY

Fundamental Concepts
- The sum of angles of a triangle is 180°.
- The sum of any two sides of a triangle is greater than the third side.

Pythagoras Theorem:
- In a right-angled triangle,
- $(Hypotenuse)^2 = (Base)^2 + (Perpendicular)^2$.
- The line joining the mid-point of a side of a triangle to the positive vertex is called the **median**.
- The point where the three medians of a triangle meet is called **centroid**. The centroid divides each of the medians in the ratio 2 : 1.
- In an isosceles triangle, the altitude from the vertex bisects the base.
- The median of a triangle divides it into two triangles of the same area.
- The area of the triangle formed by joining the mid-points of the sides of a given triangle is one-fourth of the area of the given triangle.

Quadrilaterals
- The diagonals of a parallelogram bisect each other.
- Each diagonal of a parallelogram divides it into triangles of the same area.
- The diagonals of a rectangle are equal and bisect each other.
- The diagonals of a square are equal and bisect each other at right angles.
- The diagonals of a rhombus are unequal and bisect each other at right angles.
- A parallelogram and a rectangle on the same base and between the same parallels are equal in area.
- Of all the parallelograms of given sides, the parallelogram which is a rectangle has the greatest area.

TRIVIA
Two of the most powerful tools of geometry which helped in the advancement of subject which helped in construction of various lengths, angles and geometric shapes were Compass and Straight edge.

Important Formulae
- Area of a rectangle = (Length × Breadth)
- Perimeter of a rectangle = 2 (Length + Breadth)

- Area of a square = (side)^2 = $\frac{1}{2}$ (diagonal)^2
- Area of 4 walls of a room = 2 (Length + Breadth) × Height
- Area of a triangle = $\frac{1}{2}$ × Base × Height
- Area of a triangle
  = $\sqrt{s(s-a)(s-b)(s-c)}$
  where a, b, c are the sides of the triangle and $s = \frac{1}{2}(a+b+c)$
- Area of an equilateral triangle = $\frac{\sqrt{3}}{4}$ × (side)^2
- Radius of incircle of an equilateral triangle of side $a = \frac{a}{2\sqrt{3}}$
- Radius of circumcircle of an equilateral triangle of side $a = \frac{a}{\sqrt{3}}$
- Radius of incircle of a triangle of area Δ and semi-perimeter $s = \frac{\Delta}{s}$
- Area of parallelogram = (Base × Height).
- Area of a rhombus = $\frac{1}{2}$ × (Product of diagonals).
- Area of a trapezium = $\frac{1}{2}$ × (sum of parallel sides) × distance between them.
- Area of a circle = πR^2, where R is the radius.
- Circumference of a circle = $2\pi R$.
- Length of an arc = $2\pi R \times \frac{\theta}{360°}$, where θ is the central angle.
- Area of a sector = $\frac{1}{2}$ (arc × R) = $\frac{\pi R^2 \theta}{360°}$
- Circumference of a semi-circle = πR.
- Area of semi-circle = $\frac{\pi r^2}{2}$.

Example 1: The area of a square increases by.........., if its side increases by 30%.
(a) 71%   (b) 60%
(c) 69%   (d) 30%

Solution: Option (c) is correct.
Let the side of the square be 10
Then area = $(10)^2$ = 100
New side = 10 × 1.3 = 13
New area = $(13)^2$ = 169
∴ % increase in area = 169 – 100 = 69%

Example 2: A circular track is 14 cm wide and its inner circumference is 440 cm. The diameter of the outer circle of the track is
(a) 84 cm   (b) 77 cm
(c) 168 cm   (d) 336 cm

Solution: Option (c) is correct.
Let radius of the inner track = r
Then, $2\pi r$ = 440 cm
$\Rightarrow r = \frac{440 \times 7}{22 \times 2} = 70$ cm
∵ Track is 14 cm wide; so radius of outer circle of the track is 70 + 14 = 84 cm
So diameter = 2 × 84 = 168 cm

MUST REMEMBER

- The line joining the mid-point of a side of a triangle to the positive vertex is called the median.
- The point where the three medians of a triangle meet is called centroid.
- Each diagonal of a parallelogram divides it into triangles of the same area.
- The diagonals of a rectangle are equal and bisect each other.
- A parallelogram and a rectangle on the same base and between the same parallels are equal in area.

MULTIPLE CHOICE QUESTIONS

1. The ratio between the length and the breadth of a rectangular park is 3 : 2. If a man cycling along the boundary of the park at the speed of 12 km/hr completes one round in 8 minutes, then the area of the park (in sq. m) is:
   (a) 15360
   (b) 153600
   (c) 30720
   (d) 307200

2. An error 2% in excess is made while measuring the side of a square. The percentage of error in the calculated area of the square is:
   (a) 2%
   (b) 2.02%
   (c) 4%
   (d) 4.04%

3. The ratio between the perimeter and the breadth of a rectangle is 5 : 1. If the area of the rectangle is 216 sq. cm, what is the length of the rectangle?
   (a) 16 cm
   (b) 18 cm
   (c) 24 cm
   (d) Data inadequate

4. The percentage increase in the area of a rectangle, if each of its sides is increased by 20%, is:
   (a) 40%
   (b) 42%
   (c) 44%
   (d) 46%

5. A rectangular park 60 m long and 40 m wide has two concrete crossroads running in the middle of the park and rest of the park has been used as a lawn. If the area of the lawn is 2109 sq. m, then what is the width of the road?
   (a) 2.91 m
   (b) 3 m
   (c) 5.82 m
   (d) None of these

6. The diagonal of the floor of a rectangular closet is 7.5 feet. The shorter side of the closet is 4.5 feet. What is the area of the closet in square feet?
   (a) 5
   (b) 13
   (c) 27
   (d) 37

7. A towel, when bleached, was found to have lost 20% of its length and 10% of its breadth. The percentage of decrease in area is:
   (a) 10%
   (b) 10.08%
   (c) 20%
   (d) 28%

8. A man walked diagonally across a square plot. Approximately, what is the percent saved by not walking along the edges?
   (a) 20
   (b) 24
   (c) 30
   (d) 33

9. The diagonal of a rectangle is 41 cm and its area is 20 sq. cm. The perimeter of the rectangle must be:
   (a) 9 cm
   (b) 18 cm
   (c) 20 cm
   (d) 41 cm

10. What is the least number of squares tiles required to pave the floor of a room 15 m 17 cm long and 9 m 2 cm broad?
    (a) 814
    (b) 820
    (c) 840
    (d) 844

11. The difference between the length and breadth of a rectangle is 23 m. If its perimeter is 206 m, then its area is:
    (a) $1520 \, m^2$
    (b) $2420 \, m^2$
    (c) $2480 \, m^2$
    (d) $2520 \, m^2$

12. The length of a rectangle is halved, while its breadth is tripled. What is the percentage change in area?
    (a) 25% increase
    (b) 50% increase
    (c) 50% decrease
    (d) 75% decrease

13. The length of a rectangular plot is 20 metres more than its breadth. If the cost of fencing the plot @ 26.50 per metre is ₹ 5300, what is the length of the plot in metres?
    (a) 40
    (b) 50
    (c) 120
    (d) None of these

14. A rectangular field is to be fenced on three sides leaving a side of 20 feet uncovered. If the area of the field is 680 sq. feet, how many feet of fencing will be required?
    (a) 34
    (b) 40
    (c) 68
    (d) 88

15. A tank is 25 m long, 12 m wide and 6 m deep. The cost of plastering its walls and bottom at 75 paise per sq. m, is:
    (a) ₹ 456
    (b) ₹ 458
    (c) ₹ 558
    (d) ₹ 568

16. The area of playground is 1600 m². What is the perimeter?
    I. It is a perfect square playground.
    II. It costs ₹ 3200 to put a fence around the playground at the rate of ₹ 20 per metre.
    (a) I alone sufficient while II alone not sufficient to answer
    (b) II alone sufficient while I alone not sufficient to answer
    (c) Either I or II alone sufficient to answer
    (d) Both I and II are not sufficient to answer

17. The area of a rectangle is equal to the area of a right-angled triangle. What is the length of the rectangle?
    I. The base of the triangle is 40 cm.
    II. The height of the triangle is 50 cm.
    (a) I alone sufficient while II alone not sufficient to answer
    (b) II alone sufficient while I alone not sufficient to answer
    (c) Either I or II alone sufficient to answer
    (d) Both I and II are not sufficient to answer

18. What is the height of the triangle?
    I. The area of the triangle is 20 times its base.
    II. The perimeter of the triangle is equal to the perimeter of a square of side 10 cm.
    (a) I alone sufficient while II alone not sufficient to answer
    (b) II alone sufficient while I alone not sufficient to answer
    (c) Either I or II alone sufficient to answer
    (d) Both I and II are not sufficient to answer

19. What will be the cost of painting the inner walls of a room if the rate of painting is ₹ 20 per square foot?
    I. Circumference of the floor is 44 feet.
    II. The height of the wall of the room is 12 feet.
    (a) I alone sufficient while II alone not sufficient to answer
    (b) II alone sufficient while I alone not sufficient to answer
    (c) Either I or II alone sufficient to answer
    (d) Both I and II are necessary to answer

20. What is the area of the hall?
    I. Material cost of flooring per square metre is ₹ 2.50.
    II. Labour cost of flooring the hall is ₹ 3500.
    III. Total cost of flooring the hall is ₹ 14,500.
    (a) I and II only
    (b) II and III only
    (c) All I, II and III
    (d) Any two of the three

21. What is the area of a right-angled triangle?
    I. The perimeter of the triangle is 30 cm.
    II. The ratio between the base and the height of the triangle is 5 : 12.
    III. The area of the triangle is equal to the area of a rectangle of length 10 cm.
    (a) I and II only
    (b) II and III only
    (c) I and III only
    (d) III, and either I or II only

22. What is the area of rectangular field?
    I. The perimeter of the field is 110 metres.
    II. The length is 5 metres more than the width.
    III. The ratio between length and width is 6 : 5 respectively.
    (a) I and II only
    (b) Any two of the three
    (c) All I, II and III
    (d) I, and either II or III only

Elementary Mensuration: Perimeter & Area

23. What is the area of the given rectangle?
    I. Perimeter of the rectangle is 60 cm.
    II. Breadth of the rectangle is 12 cm.
    III. Sum of two adjacent sides is 30 cm.
    (a) I only
    (b) II only
    (c) I and II only
    (d) II and either I or III

24. What is the cost of painting the two adjacent walls of a hall at ₹ 5 per m², which has no windows or doors?
    I. The area of the hall is 24 sq. m.
    II. The breadth, length and height of the hall are in the ratio of 4 : 6 : 5 respectively.
    III. Area of one wall is 30 sq. m.
    (a) I only
    (b) II only
    (c) III only
    (d) Both I and II

25. Find the area of the largest circle that can be drawn in a square of side 14 cm.
    (a) 154 cm²
    (b) 144 cm²
    (c) 136 cm²
    (d) 121 cm²

26. In a quadrilateral, the length of one of its diagonal is 23 cm and the perpendiculars drawn on this diagonal from other two vertices measure 17 cm and 7 cm respectively. Find the area of the quadrilateral.
    (a) 225 cm²
    (b) 149 cm²
    (c) 276 cm²
    (d) 136 cm²

27. The circumference of a circle is 100 cm. Find the side of the square inscribed in the circle.
    (a) $\sqrt{2} \times \dfrac{50}{\pi}$
    (b) $\sqrt{2} \times \dfrac{60}{\pi}$
    (c) $\sqrt{3} \times \dfrac{60}{\pi}$
    (d) $\sqrt{3} \times \dfrac{30}{\pi}$

28. If the radius of a circle is increased by 5%, find the percentage increase in its area.
    (a) 10%
    (b) 10.25%
    (c) 10.75%
    (d) 11%

29. If all sides of a hexagon is increased by 2%, find the percentage increase in its area.
    (a) 6.06%
    (b) 4.04%
    (c) 10.05%
    (d) 5.80%

30. If diameter of a circle is increased by 12%, find the percentage increase in its circumference.
    (a) 6%
    (b) 12%
    (c) 18%
    (d) 9%

HOTS

1. The area of playground is 1600 m². What is the perimeter?
    I. It is a perfect square playground.
    II. It costs ₹ 3200 to put a fence around the playground at the rate of ₹ 20 per metre.
    (a) I alone sufficient while II alone not sufficient to answer
    (b) II alone sufficient while I alone not sufficient to answer
    (c) Either I or II alone sufficient to answer
    (d) Both I and II are not sufficient to answer

2. The area of a rectangle is equal to the area of a right-angled triangle. What is the length of the rectangle?
    I. The base of the triangle is 40 cm.
    II. The height of the triangle is 50 cm.
    (a) I alone sufficient while II alone not sufficient to answer
    (b) II alone sufficient while I alone not sufficient to answer
    (c) Either I or II alone sufficient to answer
    (d) Both I and II are not sufficient to answer

3. What is the height of the triangle?
    I. The area of the triangle is 20 times its base.
    II. The perimeter of the triangle is equal to the perimeter of a square of side 10 cm.
    (a) I alone sufficient while II alone not sufficient to answer
    (b) II alone sufficient while I alone not sufficient to answer

(c) Either I or II alone sufficient to answer
(d) Both I and II are not sufficient to answer

4. What will be the cost of painting the inner walls of a room if the rate of painting is ₹ 20 per square foot?
   I. Circumference of the floor is 44 feet.
   II. The height of the wall of the room is 12 feet.
   (a) I alone sufficient while II alone not sufficient to answer
   (b) II alone sufficient while I alone not sufficient to answer
   (c) Either I or II alone sufficient to answer
   (d) Both I and II are necessary to answer

5. What is the area of the hall?
   I. Material cost of flooring per square metre is ₹ 2.50.
   II. Labour cost of flooring the hall is ₹ 3500.
   III. Total cost of flooring the hall is ₹ 14,500.
   (a) I and II only
   (b) II and III only
   (c) All I, II and III
   (d) Any two of the three

6. What is the area of a right-angled triangle?
   I. The perimeter of the triangle is 30 cm.
   II. The ratio between the base and the height of the triangle is 5 : 12.
   III. The area of the triangle is equal to the area of a rectangle of length 10 cm.
   (a) I and II only
   (b) II and III only
   (c) I and III only
   (d) III, and either I or II only

7. What is the area of rectangular field?
   I. The perimeter of the field is 110 metres.
   II. The length is 5 metres more than the width.
   III. The ratio between length and width is 6 : 5 respectively.
   (a) I and II only
   (b) Any two of the three
   (c) All I, II and III
   (d) I, and either II or III only

8. What is the area of the given rectangle?
   I. Perimeter of the rectangle is 60 cm.
   II. Breadth of the rectangle is 12 cm.
   III. Sum of two adjacent sides is 30 cm.
   (a) I only
   (b) II only
   (c) I and II only
   (d) II and either I or III

9. What is the cost of painting the two adjacent walls of a hall at ₹ 5 per m^2, which has no windows or doors?
   I. The area of the hall is 24 sq. m.
   II. The breadth, length and height of the hall are in the ratio of 4 : 6 : 5 respectively.
   III. Area of one wall is 30 sq. m.
   (a) I only (b) II only
   (c) III only (d) Both I and III

10. What is the volume of a 32 metre high cylindrical tank?
    I. The area of its base is 154 m^2.
    II. The diameter of the base is 14 m.
    (a) I alone sufficient while II alone not sufficient to answer
    (b) II alone sufficient while I alone not sufficient to answer
    (c) Either I or II alone sufficient to answer
    (d) Both I and II are not sufficient to answer

11. What is the height of this circular cone?
    I. The area of that cone is equal to the area of a rectangle whose length is 33 cm.
    II. The area of the base of that cone is 154 sq. cm.
    (a) I alone sufficient while II alone not sufficient to answer
    (b) II alone sufficient while I alone not sufficient to answer
    (c) Either I or II alone sufficient to answer
    (d) Both I and II are not sufficient to answer

12. What is the volume of a cube?
    I. The area of each face of the cube is 64 square metres.
    II. The length of one side of the cube is 8 metres.

Elementary Mensuration: Perimeter & Area

(a) I alone sufficient while II alone not sufficient to answer
(b) II alone sufficient while I alone not sufficient to answer
(c) Either I or II alone sufficient to answer
(d) Both I and II are not sufficient to answer

13. What is the capacity of the cylindrical tank?
    I. The area of the base is 61,600 sq. cm.
    II. The height of the tank is 1.5 times the radius.
    III. The circumference of base is 880 cm.
    (a) Only I and II
    (b) Only II and III
    (c) Only I and III
    (d) Only II and either I or III

14. Find the number of lead balls of diameter 1 cm each that can be made from a sphere of diameter 16 m.
    (a) 4096   (b) 2050
    (c) 3016   (d) 5024

15. In a quadrilateral, the length of one of its diagonal is 23 cm and the perpendiculars drawn on this diagonal from other two vertices measure 17 cm and 7 cm respectively. Find the area of the quadrilateral.
    (a) 225 cm^2 (b) 149 cm^2
    (c) 276 cm^2 (d) 136 cm^2

SUBJECTIVE QUESTIONS

1. Find the area, in square metres, of a rectangle whose length = 5.5 m, breadth = 2.4 m.
   Answer:
   Given Length = 5.5 m, Breadth = 2.4 m
   We know that area of rectangle = Length × Breadth
   = 5.5 m × 2.4 m = 13.2 m^2

2. Find the area, in square centimetres, of a square whose side is 1.2 dm.
   Answer:
   Given side of the square = 1.2 dm
   = 1.2 × 10 cm = 12 cm [Since 1 dm = 10 cm]
   We know that area of the square = (Side)^2
   = (12 cm)^2
   = 144 cm^2

3. Find in square meters, the area of a square of side 16.5 dam.
   Answer:
   Given side of the square = 16.5 dam = 16.5 × 10 m = 165 m [Since 1 dam/dm (decametre) = 10 m]
   Area of the square = (Side)^2
   = (165 m)^2
   = 27225 m^2

4. Find the area of a rectangular field in acres whose sides are 200 m and 125 m.
   Answer:
   Given length of the rectangular field = 200 m
   Breadth of the rectangular field = 125 m
   We know that area of the rectangular field = Length × Breadth
   = 200 m × 125 m
   = 25000 m^2
   = 250 acres [Since 100 m^2 = 1 acre]

5. Find the area of a rectangular field in hectares whose sides are 125 m and 400 m.
   Answer:
   Given length of the rectangular field = 125 m
   Breadth of the rectangular field = 400 m
   We know that the area of the rectangular field
   = Length × Breadth
   = 125 m × 400 m
   = 50000 m^2
   = 5 hectares [Since 10000 m^2 = 1 hectare]

Visualizing Solid Shapes 14

Learning Objectives : In this chapter, students will learn about:
- ✓ Important formulas for different geometrical shapes

CHAPTER SUMMARY

Important Formulas

- **Cuboid**

    Let length = l, breadth = b and height = h units. Then
    i. Volume = $(l \times b \times h)$ cubic units.
    ii. Surface area = $2(lb + bh + lh)$ sq. units.
    iii. Diagonal = $\sqrt{l^2 + b^2 + h^2}$ units.

- **Cube**

    Let each edge of a cube be of length a. Then,
    i. Volume = a^3 cubic units.
    ii. Surface area = $6a^2$ sq. units.
    iii. Diagonal = $\sqrt{3}a$ units.

- **Cylinder**

    Let radius of base = r and Height (or length) = h. Then,
    i. Volume = $(\pi r^2 h)$ cubic units.
    ii. Curved surface area = $(2\pi rh)$ sq. units.
    iii. Total surface area = $2\pi r(h + r)$ sq. units.

- **Cone**

    Let radius of base = r and Height = h. Then,
    i. Slant height, $l = \sqrt{h^2 + r^2}$ units.
    ii. Volume = $\dfrac{1}{3}\pi r^2 h$ cubic units.
    iii. Curved surface area = (πrl) sq. units.
    iv. Total surface area = $(\pi rl + \pi r^2)$ sq. units.

- **Sphere**

    Let the radius of the sphere be r. Then,
    i. Volume = $\dfrac{4}{3}\pi r^3$ cubic units.
    ii. Surface area = $(4\pi r^2)$ sq. units.

- **Hemisphere**

    Let the radius of a hemisphere be r. Then,
    i. Volume = $\dfrac{2}{3}\pi r^3$ cubic units.
    ii. Curved surface area = $(2\pi r^2)$ sq. units.
    iii. Total surface area = $(3\pi r^2)$ sq. units.

Note: 1 litre = 1000 cm^3.

TRIVIA

In Renaissance period of Projective Geometry, artists like Leonardo Da Vinci and Durer discovered methods to represent 3D objects on 23 surfaces.

Important Formulas related to Pipes and Cistern

- **Inlet:**

  A pipe connected with a tank or a cistern or a reservoir, that fills it, is known as an inlet.

- **Outlet:**

  A pipe connected with a tank or cistern or reservoir, emptying it, is known as an outlet.

  ☞ If a pipe can fill a tank in x hours, then:

  part filled in 1 hour $= \dfrac{1}{x}$

  ☞ If a pipe can empty a tank in y hours, then:

  part emptied in 1 hour $= \dfrac{1}{y}$

  ☞ If a pipe can fill a tank in x hours and another pipe can empty the full tank in y hours (where y > x), then on opening both the pipes, the net part filled in 1 hour $= (\dfrac{1}{x} - \dfrac{1}{y})$

  ☞ If a pipe can fill a tank in x hours and another pipe can empty the full tank in y hours (where y < x), then on opening both the pipes, the net part emptied in 1 hour $= (\dfrac{1}{y} - \dfrac{1}{x})$

Example 1: A rectangular block 6 cm by 12 cm by 15 cm is cut into exact number of equal cubes. The least possible number of cubes will be:
(a) 6 (b) 11
(c) 33 (d) 40

Solution: Option (d) is correct.
Volume of block $= 6 \times 12 \times 15$
$= 1080$ cm^3
The side of largest cube
$= (3 \times 3 \times 3)$ cm^3
$= 27$ cm^3
Number of cubes $= 1080/27 = 40$

Example 2: The percentage increase in the surface area of cube when each side is doubled, is:
(a) 25% (b) 50%
(c) 150% (d) 300%

Solution: Option (d) is correct.
Let the side of the cube be a,
Then surface area $= 6a^2$
If side is $2a$, then surface area
$= 6(2a)^2 = 24a^2$
So % increase in surface area
$= \left(\dfrac{24a^2 - 6a^2}{6a^2}\right) \times 100\% = 300\%$

Example 3: The volume of a cube is V. The total length of its edges is:
(a) $6V^{2/3}$ (b) $8\sqrt{V}$
(c) $12V^{2/3}$ (d) $12V^{1/3}$

Solution: Option (d) is correct.
Let the edge of cube be a.
Then, $a^3 = V$
$\Rightarrow a = \sqrt[3]{V}$
Total length of edge $= 12 \times (V)^{1/3}$ as there are 12 edges.

MUST REMEMBER

➡ A pipe connected with a tank or a cistern or a reservoir, that fills it, is known as an inlet.

➡ A pipe connected with a tank or cistern or reservoir, emptying it, is known as an outlet.

MULTIPLE CHOICE QUESTIONS

1. A right triangle with sides 3 cm, 4 cm and 5 cm is rotated along the side of 3 cm to form a cone. The volume of the cone so formed is:
   (a) 12π cm^3 (b) 15π cm^3
   (c) 16π cm^3 (d) 20π cm^3

2. In a shower, 5 cm of rain falls. The volume of water that falls on 1.5 hectares of ground is:
   (a) 75 cu. m   (b) 750 cu. m
   (c) 7500 cu. m   (d) 75000 cu. m

3. A hall is 15 m long and 12 m broad. If the sum of the areas of the floor and the ceiling is equal to the sum of the areas of four walls, the volume of the hall is:
   (a) 720 m^3 (b) 900 m^3
   (c) 1200 m^3 (d) 1800 m^3

4. 66 cubic centimetres of silver is drawn into a wire 1 mm in diameter. The length of the wire in metres will be:
   (a) 84 m   (b) 90 m
   (c) 168 m   (d) 336 m

5. A hollow iron pipe is 21 cm long and its external diameter is 8 cm. If the thickness of the pipe is 1 cm and iron weighs 8 g/cm^3, then the weight of the pipe is:
   (a) 3 kg   (b) 3.696 kg
   (c) 36 kg   (d) 36.9 kg

6. A boat having a length 3 m and breadth 2 m is floating on a lake. The boat sinks by 1 cm when a man gets on it. The mass of the man is:
   (a) 12 kg   (b) 60 kg
   (c) 72 kg   (d) 96 kg

7. 50 men took a dip in a water tank 40 m long and 20 m broad on a religious day. If the average displacement of water by a man is 4 m^3, then the rise in the water level in the tank will be:
   (a) 20 cm   (b) 25 cm
   (c) 35 cm   (d) 50 cm

8. The slant height of a right circular cone is 10 m and its height is 8 m. Find the area of its curved surface.
   (a) 30π m^2 (b) 40π m^2
   (c) 60π m^2 (d) 80π m^2

9. A cistern 6m long and 4 m wide contains water up to a depth of 1 m 25 cm. The total area of wet surface is:
   (a) 49 m^2 (b) 50 m^2
   (c) 53.5 m^2 (d) 55 m^2

10. A metallic sheet is of rectangular shape with dimensions 48 m × 36 m. From each of its corners, a square is cut off so as to make an open box. If the length of the square is 8 m, the volume of the box (in m^3) is:
    (a) 4830   (b) 5120
    (c) 6420   (d) 8960

11. The curved surface area of a cylindrical pillar is 264 m^2 and its volume is 924 m^3. Find the ratio of its diameter to its height.
    (a) 3 : 7   (b) 7 : 3
    (c) 6 : 7   (d) 7 : 6

12. A cistern of capacity 8000 litres measures externally 3.3 m by 2.6 m by 1.1 m and its walls are 5 cm thick. The thickness of the base is:
    (a) 90 cm   (b) 1 dm
    (c) 1 m   (d) 1.1 cm

13. What is the total surface area of a right circular cone of height 14 cm and base radius 7 cm?
    (a) 344.35 cm^2 (b) 462 cm^2
    (c) 498.35 cm^2 (d) None of these

14. A large cube is formed from the material obtained by melting three smaller cubes of sides 3, 4 and 5 cm. What is the ratio of the total surface areas of the smaller cubes and the large cube?
    (a) 2 : 1   (b) 3 : 2
    (c) 25 : 18   (d) 27 : 20

15. How many bricks, each measuring 25 cm × 11.25 cm × 6 cm, will be needed to build a wall of 8 m × 6 m × 22.5 cm?
    (a) 5600   (b) 6000
    (c) 6400   (d) 7200

Visualizing Solid Shapes

16. What is the volume of a 32 metre high cylindrical tank?
    I. The area of its base is 154 m².
    II. The diameter of the base is 14 m.
    (a) I alone sufficient while II alone not sufficient to answer
    (b) II alone sufficient while I alone not sufficient to answer
    (c) Either I or II alone sufficient to answer
    (d) Both I and II are not sufficient to answer

17. Is the given rectangular block a cube?
    I. At least 2 faces of the rectangular block are squares.
    II. The volume of the block is 64.
    (a) I alone sufficient while II alone not sufficient to answer
    (b) II alone sufficient while I alone not sufficient to answer
    (c) Either I or II alone sufficient to answer
    (d) Both I and II are not sufficient to answer

18. What is the capacity of this cylindrical tank?
    I. Radius of the base is half of its height which is 28 metres.
    II. Area of the base is 616 sq. metres and its height is 28 metres.
    (a) I alone sufficient while II alone not sufficient to answer
    (b) II alone sufficient while I alone not sufficient to answer
    (c) Either I or II alone sufficient to answer
    (d) Both I and II are not sufficient to answer

19. What is the height of this circular cone?
    I. The area of that cone is equal to the area of a rectangle whose length is 33 cm.
    II. The area of the base of that cone is 154 sq. cm.
    (a) I alone sufficient while II alone not sufficient to answer
    (b) II alone sufficient while I alone not sufficient to answer
    (c) Either I or II alone sufficient to answer
    (d) Both I and II are not sufficient to answer

20. What is the volume of a cube?
    I. The area of each face of the cube is 64 square metres.
    II. The length of one side of the cube is 8 metres.
    (a) I alone sufficient while II alone not sufficient to answer
    (b) II alone sufficient while I alone not sufficient to answer
    (c) Either I or II alone sufficient to answer
    (d) Both I and II are not sufficient to answer

21. What is the capacity of the cylindrical tank?
    I. The area of the base is 61,600 sq. cm.
    II. The height of the tank is 1.5 times the radius.
    III. The circumference of base is 880 cm.
    (a) Only I and II
    (b) Only II and III
    (c) Only I and III
    (d) Only II and either I or III

22. Three pipes A, B and C can fill an empty tank fully in 30 minutes, 20 minutes, and 10 minutes respectively. When the tank is empty, all the three pipes are opened. A, B and C discharge chemical solutions P, Q and R respectively. What is the proportion of the solution R in the liquid in the tank after 3 minutes?
    (a) 5/11   (b) 6/11
    (c) 7/11   (d) 8/11

23. Pipes A and B can fill a tank in 5 and 6 hours respectively. Pipe C can empty it in 12 hours. If all the three pipes are opened together, then the tank will be filled in:
    (a) $1\frac{13}{17}$ hours   (b) $2\frac{8}{11}$ hours
    (c) $3\frac{9}{17}$ hours   (d) $4\frac{1}{2}$ hours

24. A pump can fill a tank with water in 2 hours. Because of a leak, it took $2\frac{1}{3}$ hours to fill the tank. The leak can drain all the water of the tank in:
    (a) 4 hours   (b) 7 hours
    (c) 8 hours   (d) 14 hours

25. Two pipes A and B can fill a cistern in 37.5 minutes and 45 minutes respectively. Both pipes are opened. The cistern will be filled in just half an hour, if B is turned off after:
    (a) 5 min.   (b) 9 min.
    (c) 10 min.   (d) 15 min.

26. A tank is filled by three pipes with uniform flow. The first two pipes operating simultaneously fill the tank in the same time during which the tank is filled by the third pipe alone. The second pipe fills the tank 5 hours faster than the first pipe and 4 hours slower than the third pipe. The time required by the first pipe is:
    (a) 6 hours   (b) 10 hours
    (c) 15 hours   (d) 30 hours

27. Two pipes can fill a tank in 20 and 24 minutes respectively and a waste pipe can empty 3 gallons per minute. All the three pipes working together can fill the tank in 15 minutes. The capacity of the tank is:
    (a) 60 gallons   (b) 100 gallons
    (c) 120 gallons   (d) 180 gallons

28. A tank is filled in 5 hours by three pipes A, B and C. The pipe C is twice as fast as B and B is twice as fast as A. How much time will pipe A alone take to fill the tank?
    (a) 20 hours
    (b) 25 hours
    (c) 35 hours
    (d) Cannot be determined

29. Two pipes A and B together can fill a cistern in 4 hours. Had they been opened separately, then B would have taken 6 hours more than A to fill the cistern. How much time will be taken by A to fill the cistern separately?
    (a) 1 hour   (b) 2 hours
    (c) 6 hours   (d) 8 hours

30. Two pipes A and B can fill a tank in 20 and 30 minutes respectively. If both the pipes are used together, then how long will it take to fill the tank?
    (a) 12 min   (b) 15 min
    (c) 25 min   (d) 50 min

31. Two pipes A and B can fill a tank in 15 minutes and 20 minutes respectively. Both the pipes are opened together but after 4 minutes, pipe A is turned off. What is the total time required to fill the tank?
    (a) 10 min. 20 sec.   (b) 11 min. 45 sec.
    (c) 12 min. 30 sec.   (d) 14 min. 40 sec.

32. One pipe can fill a tank three times as fast as another pipe. If together the two pipes can fill the tank in 36 minutes, then the slower pipe alone will be able to fill the tank in:
    (a) 81 min.   (b) 108 min.
    (c) 144 min.   (d) 192 min.

33. A large tanker can be filled by two pipes A and B in 60 minutes and 40 minutes respectively. How many minutes will it take to fill the tanker from empty state if B is used for half the time and A and B fill it together for the other half?
    (a) 15 min   (b) 20 min
    (c) 27.5 min   (d) 30 min

34. A tap can fill a tank in 6 hours. After half the tank is filled, three more similar taps are opened. What is the total time taken to fill the tank completely?
    (a) 3 hrs 15 min   (b) 3 hrs 45 min
    (c) 4 hrs   (d) 4 hrs 15 min

35. Three taps A, B and C can fill a tank in 12, 15 and 20 hours respectively. If A is open all the time and B and C are open for one hour each alternately, the tank will be full in:
    (a) 6 hours   (b) 6.5 hours
    (c) 7 hours   (d) 7.5 hours

36. Three pipes A, B and C can fill a tank in 6 hours. After working at it together for 2 hours, C is closed and A and B can fill the remaining part in 7 hours. The number of hours taken by C alone to fill the tank is:
    (a) 10   (b) 12
    (c) 14   (d) 16

37. How much time will the leak take to empty the full cistern?
    I. The cistern is normally filled in 9 hours.
    II. It takes one hour more than the usual time to fill the cistern because of a leak in the bottom.
    (a) I alone sufficient while II alone not sufficient to answer
    (b) II alone sufficient while I alone not sufficient to answer
    (c) Either I or II alone sufficient to answer
    (d) Both I and II are necessary to answer

38. How long will it take to empty the tank if both the inlet pipe A and the outlet pipe B are opened simultaneously?
    I. A can fill the tank in 16 minutes.
    II. B can empty the full tank in 8 minutes.
    (a) I alone sufficient while II alone not sufficient to answer
    (b) II alone sufficient while I alone not sufficient to answer
    (c) Either I or II alone sufficient to answer
    (d) Both I and II are necessary to answer

39. If both the pipes are opened, how many hours will be taken to fill the tank?
    I. The capacity of the tank is 400 litres.
    II. The pipe A fills the tank in 4 hours.
    III. The pipe B fills the tank in 6 hours.
    (a) Only I and II
    (b) Only II and III
    (c) All I, II and III
    (d) Any two of the three

40. Find the number of lead balls of diameter 1 cm each that can be made from a sphere of diameter 16 m.
    (a) 4096   (b) 2050
    (c) 3016   (d) 5024

HOTS

1. Is the given rectangular block a cube?
    I. At least 2 faces of the rectangular block are squares.
    II. The volume of the block is 64.
    (a) I alone sufficient while II alone not sufficient to answer
    (b) II alone sufficient while I alone not sufficient to answer
    (c) Either I or II alone sufficient to answer
    (d) Both I and II are not sufficient to answer

2. What is the capacity of this cylindrical tank?
    I. Radius of the base is half of its height which is 28 metres.
    II. Area of the base is 616 sq. metres and its height is 28 metres.
    (a) I alone sufficient while II alone not sufficient to answer
    (b) II alone sufficient while I alone not sufficient to answer
    (c) Either I or II alone sufficient to answer
    (d) Both I and II are not sufficient to answer

3. How much time will the leak take to empty the full cistern?
    I. The cistern is normally filled in 9 hours.
    II. It takes one hour more than the usual time to fill the cistern because of a leak in the bottom.
    (a) I alone sufficient while II alone not sufficient to answer
    (b) II alone sufficient while I alone not sufficient to answer
    (c) Either I or II alone sufficient to answer
    (d) Both I and II are necessary to answer

4. How long will it take to empty the tank if both the inlet pipe A and the outlet pipe B are opened simultaneously?
    I. A can fill the tank in 16 minutes.
    II. B can empty the full tank in 8 minutes.
    (a) I alone sufficient while II alone not sufficient to answer
    (b) II alone sufficient while I alone not sufficient to answer
    (c) Either I or II alone sufficient to answer
    (d) Both I and II are necessary to answer

5. If both the pipes are opened, how many hours will be taken to fill the tank?
   I. The capacity of the tank is 400 litres.
   II. The pipe A fills the tank in 4 hours.
   III. The pipe B fills the tank in 6 hours.

   (a) Only I and II
   (b) Only II and III
   (c) All I, II and III
   (d) Any two of the three

SUBJECTIVE QUESTIONS

1. Give two examples from our daily life which are in the form of
   (i) A cone   (ii) A sphere
   (iii) A cuboid   (iv) A cylinder
   (v) A pyramid.

   Answer:
   (i) Examples for Cone: Ice-cream cone, birthday cap
   (ii) Examples of Sphere: Football, a round apple, an orange
   (iii) Examples of Cuboid: dice, duster, book, rectangular box
   (iv) Examples of Cylinder: circular pipe, glass, circular pole, gas cylinder
   (v) Examples for Pyramid: Christmas tree, prism

2. For the solids given below sketch the front, side and top view

   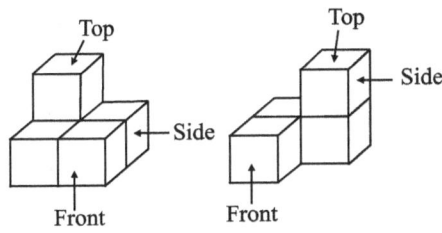

   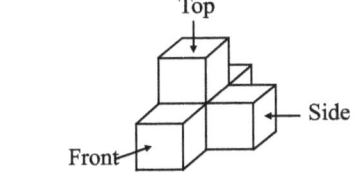

   Answer:
   (i)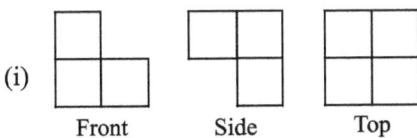

   (ii)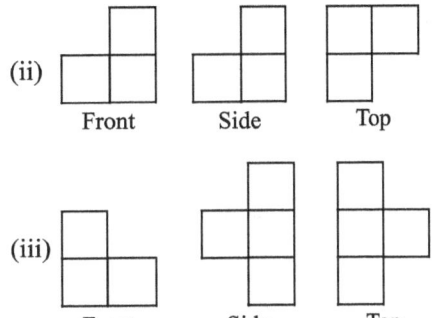

   (iii)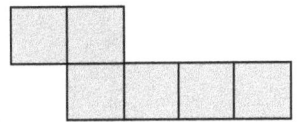

3. Identify the nets which can be used to make cubes (cut-out the nets and try it):

   (i)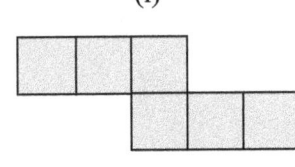

   (ii)

   (iii)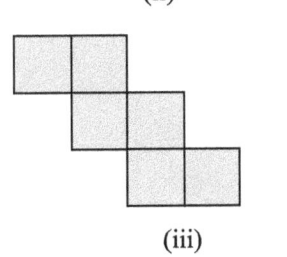

Visualizing Solid Shapes

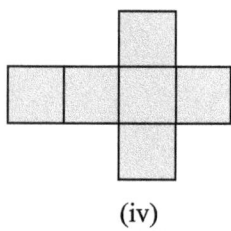

(iv)

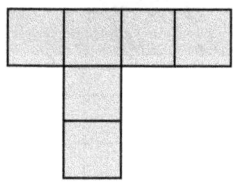

(v)

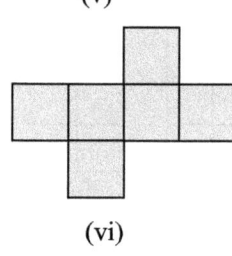

(vi)

Answer:

Only (ii), (iv) and (vi) form a cube.

4. Can the following be a net for a die? Explain your answer.

Answer:

We know that in a die, the sum of the number of opposite faces of a die is 7. In the given figure, it is not possible to get the sum as 7. Hence the given net is not suitable for a die.

Mathematical Reasoning   15

Learning Objectives : In this chapter, students will learn about:
- ✓ Solving questions related to mathematical reasoning

CHAPTER SUMMARY

The problems related to mathematical reasoning are based on arithmetic problems like unitary method, percentage, profit-loss, problems on age, linear equations and mathematical operations. The various examples given below show the various type of problems.

Example 1: In an examination, Ramesh scores 4 marks for every correct answer and loses 1 mark for every wrong answer. If Ramesh attempts all 60 questions and scores 130 marks, what is the number of questions he attempts correctly?

(a) 36 (b) 38
(c) 42 (d) 44

Solution: (b) Let the no. of questions attempted correctly be x.

∴ No. of incorrect ones = $(60 - x)$

A/Q, $4x - 1(60 - x) = 130$

$\Rightarrow \quad 4x - 60 + x = 130$

$\Rightarrow \quad 5x = 190$

$\Rightarrow \quad x = \dfrac{190}{5} = 38$

Example 2: If the cost price of 6 pencils is equal to the selling price of 5 pencils, what is the gain percent?

(a) 10% (b) 20%
(c) 30% (d) None of these

Solution: (b) Let the cost price of each pencil be ₹ 1.

C.P. of 5 pencils = ₹ 5.

S.P. of 5 pencils = C.P. of 6 pencils = ₹ 6.

Gain = $6 - 5$ = ₹ 1

Gain % = $\dfrac{1}{5} \times 100$ = 20%

Example 3: A father is 30 years older than his son. In 12 years, the man will be three times as old as his son. What is the present age of son?

(a) 2 years (b) 3 years
(c) 4 years (d) 5 years

Solution: (b) Let son's age be x years.

Father's age = $x + 30$

A/Q, $x + 30 + 12 = 3(x + 12)$

$\Rightarrow \quad x + 42 = 3x + 36$

$\Rightarrow \quad 3x - x = 42 - 36$

$\Rightarrow \quad 2x = 6$

$\Rightarrow \quad x = 3$ years

TRIVIA

There are exactly 8! (eight factorial) minutes in four weeks.
This is calculated as follows: $4 \times 7 \times 24 \times 60$
$= 8 \times 7 \times 6 \times 5 \times 4 \times 3 \times 2 \times 1$
$= 8!$

Example 4: If 36 men can finish a work in 25 days in how many days can 15 men finish it?

(a) 45 days (b) 60 days
(c) 35 days (d) None of these

Solution: (b) Required no. of days = $\dfrac{25 \times 36}{15} = 60$ days

Example 5: $\dfrac{2}{3}$ of a number is less than the original number by 20. What is that number?
(a) 60   (b) 40
(c) 50   (d) 80

Solution: (a) Let the number be x.
$\therefore x - \dfrac{2x}{3} = 20 \Rightarrow \dfrac{3x - 2x}{3} = 20$
$\Rightarrow x = 3 \times 20 = 60$

Example 6: If + means ×, × means – ; ÷ means + and – means ÷, what is the value of
$96 - 32 \times 7 + 3 \div 29$
(a) 11   (b) 12
(c) 13   (d) 14

Solution: (a) $96 \div 32 - 7 \times 3 + 29 = 3 - 21 + 29$
$= 32 - 21 = 11$

MULTIPLE CHOICE QUESTIONS

1. Ravi got twice as many sums wrong as he got correct. If he attempted 96 sums in all, how many sums did he solve correctly.
   (a) 16 (b) 32
   (c) 44 (d) 48

2. In the numbers from 1 to 100, how many times does 7 occur?
   (a) 17 (b) 18
   (c) 19 (d) 20

3. If 100 workers can finish a work in 100 days, then 40 workers can finish the work in how many days?
   (a) 40 (b) 120
   (c) 250 (d) 240

4. A group of students decided to go on a picnic and decided to spend ₹ 96 on eatables. Four of them did not turn up, after that the remaining students had to contribute extra ₹ 4 each. What was the number of students in the beginning?
   (a) 4 (b) 6
   (c) 8 (d) 12

5. A bus starts from city A. The number of women in the bus is half the number of men. In city B, 10 men leave the bus and 5 women enters. Now number of men and women is equal. What is the number of passengers in the beginning?
   (a) 35 (b) 45
   (c) 60 (d) 75

6. What is the least number of ducks that can swim in a way such that two ducks to front of a duck, two ducks behind a duck and a duck between two ducks?
   (a) 3 (b) 4
   (c) 5 (d) 6

7. If a clock takes seven seconds to strike seven, how long will it take to strike 10?
   (a) 10 seconds (b) 9 seconds
   (c) $10\frac{1}{2}$ seconds (d) None of these

8. The total of present ages of Mihir, Sonu and Ritesh is 86 years. What will be the total age of these three after 2 years?
   (a) 89 years (b) 91 years
   (c) 92 years (d) 94 years

9. In a caravan, in addition to 50 hens, there are 45 goats and 8 camels with some keepers. If the total number of feet is 224 more than the number of heads in the caravan, what is the number of keepers?
   (a) 5 (b) 10
   (c) 15 (d) 20

10. Out of 450 students, 270 students passed. What is the percentage of students who did not pass?
    (a) 50% (b) 60%
    (c) 40% (d) None of these

11. What will be the number which when added to itself 13 times, gives 112?
    (a) 8 (b) 6
    (c) 9 (d) 12

12. In a family, each daughter has the same number of brothers as she has sisters and each son has twice as many sisters as he has brothers. How many sons are there in the family?
    (a) 1 (b) 2
    (c) 3 (d) 4

13. The total of present ages of Ram, Shyam & Mohan is 96 years. What was the total of their ages three years ago?
    (a) 93 years (b) 92 years
    (c) 89 years (d) 87 years

14. Mr. Sharma is three times as old as his son. Five years back, he was four times as old as his son. What is the age of Mr. Sharma?
    (a) 30 years (b) 45 years
    (c) 48 years (d) 63 years

Mathematical Reasoning

15. A train is moving at the speed of 72 km/hr In how many seconds will it cross an electric pole if the length of the train is 360m?
    (a) 12 sec.   (b) 15 sec.
    (c) 18 sec.   (d) 21sec.

16. By selling an item at ₹. 720, Manish gains 20%. What is its cost price?
    (a) 560   (b) 600
    (c) 620   (d) 650

17. Manoj is twice as old as Monu. 3 years ago Manoj was three times as old as Monu. What is the present age of Manoj?
    (a) 6 years   (b) 12 years
    (c) 18 years   (d) 24 years

18. What is the product of all the numbers in the dial of a telephone?
    (a) 158460   (b) 158480
    (c) 159480   (d) None of these

19. At the end of a meeting, ten people present shake hands with each other once. What is the total number of handshakes?
    (a) 45   (b) 55
    (c) 60   (d) 65

Direction (20 to 25) : If + means ×, × means –, ÷ means + and '–' means ÷, then find the value in each of the following

20. $175 - 25 \div 5 + 20 \times 3 + 10 = ?$
    (a) 75   (b) 76
    (c) 77   (d) 78

21. $225 - 15 + 9 \times 15 \div 3 = ?$
    (a) 123   (b) 255
    (c) 120   (d) 155

22. $23 \div 107 \times 135 - 5 + 3 = ?$
    (a) 47   (b) 49
    (c) 59   (d) 57

23. $297 \times 57 \times 345 - 15 + 11 \div 18$
    (a) 5   (b) 15
    (c) 25   (d) 35

24. $78 - 13 + 7 \times 6 \div 17 + 3$
    (a) 67   (b) 87
    (c) 77   (d) 97

25. $123 \times 4 + 7 \div 76 - 19 + 7$
    (a) 123   (b) 861
    (c) 128   (d) None of these

HOTS

1. Ravi got twice as many sums wrong as he got correct. If he attempted 96 sums in all, how many sums did he solve correctly.
   (a) 16   (b) 32
   (c) 44   (d) 48

2. If 100 workers can finish a work in 100 days, then 40 workers can finish the work in how many days?
   (a) 40   (b) 120
   (c) 250   (d) 240

3. A group of students decided to go on a picnic and decided to spend ₹ 96 on eatables. Four of them did not turn up, after that the remaining ones had to contribute ₹ 4 each extra. What was the number of students in the beginning?
   (a) 4   (b) 6
   (c) 8   (d) 12

4. A bus starts from city A. The number of women in the bus is half the number of men. In city B, 10 men leave the bus and 5 women enters. Now number of men and women is equal. What is the number of passengers in the beginning?
   (a) 35   (b) 45
   (c) 60   (d) 75

5. What is the least number of ducks that can swim in a way such that two ducks to front of a duck, two ducks behind a duck and a duck between two ducks?
   (a) 3   (b) 4
   (c) 5   (d) 6

6. If a clock takes seven seconds to strike seven, how long will it take to strike 10?
   (a) 10 sec.
   (b) 9 sec.
   (c) $10\frac{1}{2}$ sec.
   (d) None of these

7. The total of present ages of Mihir, Sonu and Ritesh is 86 years. What will be the total age of these three after 2 years?
   (a) 89 years
   (b) 91 years
   (c) 92 years
   (d) 94 years

8. In a caravan, in addition to 50 hens, there are 45 goats and 8 camels with some keepers. If the total number of feet is 224 more than the number of heads in the caravan, what is the number of keepers?
   (a) 5
   (b) 10
   (c) 15
   (d) 20

9. In a family, each daughter has the same number of brothers as she has sisters and each son has twice as many sisters as he has brothers. How many sons are there in the family?
   (a) 1
   (b) 2
   (c) 3
   (d) 4

10. The total of present ages of Ram, Shyam & Mohan is 96 years. What was the total of their ages three years ago?
    (a) 93 years
    (b) 92 years
    (c) 89 years
    (d) 87 years

11. Mr. Sharma is three times as old as his son. Five years back, he was four times as old as his son. What is the age of Mr. Sharma?
    (a) 30 years
    (b) 45 years
    (c) 48 years
    (d) 63 years

12. A train is moving at the speed of 72 km/hr In how many seconds will it cross an electric pole if the length of the train is 360m?
    (a) 12 sec.
    (b) 15 sec.
    (c) 18 sec.
    (d) 21 sec.

13. Manoj is twice as old as Monu. 3 years ago Manoj was three times as old as Monu. What is the present age of Manoj?
    (a) 6 years
    (b) 12 years
    (c) 18 years
    (d) 24 years

14. At the end of a meeting the ten people present shake hands with each other once. What is the total number of handshakes?
    (a) 45
    (b) 55
    (c) 60
    (d) 65

15. If Raju runs a distance of 7 km 800 m in going round a rectangular stadium ground three times then what is the length of the ground if its width is 330 m?
    (a) 930 m
    (b) 950 m
    (c) 960 m
    (d) 970 m

Mathematical Reasoning

SECTION 2
LOGICAL REASONING

Pattern

Learning Objectives : In this chapter, students will learn about:
- ✓ Solving questions related to patterns

CHAPTER SUMMARY

In thes types of questions, a figure, set of figures or matrix is given. There are numbers which are arranged according to a particular rule or pattern. We have to study the pattern and find the way in which the numbers are arranged.

Direction (1 to 5): Choose the appropriate number which follows the given pattern.

Example 1:

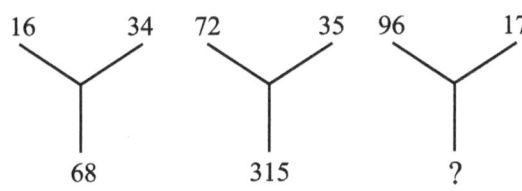

(a) 204   (b) 206
(c) 208   (d) 202

Solution: (a)

$$\frac{16 \times 34}{8} = 68$$

$$\frac{72 \times 35}{8} = 315$$

$$\frac{96 \times 17}{8} = 204$$

Example 2:

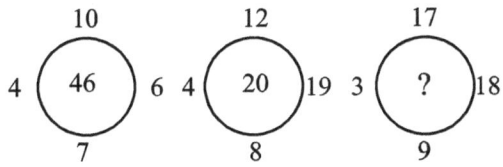

(a) 89   (b) 99
(c) 109   (d) 100

Solution: (b)

$(10 \times 7) - (4 \times 6) = 70 - 24 = 46$

$(12 \times 8) - (4 \times 19) = 96 - 76 = 20$

$(17 \times 9) - (3 \times 18) = 153 - 54 = 99$

Example 3:

11	168	17
9	115	14
13	?	19

(a) 172   (b) 182
(c) 192   (d) 194

Solution: (c)

$(17)2 - (11)2 = 168$

$(14)2 - (9)2 = 115$

$(19)2 - (13)2 = 192$

Example 4:

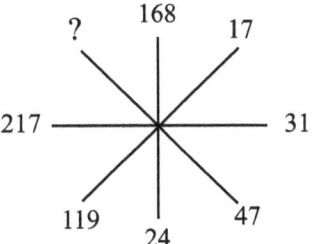

(a) 319   (b) 329
(c) 339   (d) 349

Solution: (b)

$17 \times 7 = 119$

$24 \times 7 = 168$

$31 \times 7 = 217$
$47 \times 7 = 329$

Example 5:

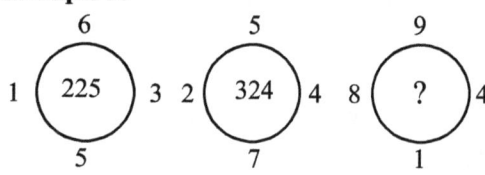

(a) 484 (b) 384
(c) 480 (d) None of these

Solution: (a)

$1 + 5 + 3 + 6 = 15 \rightarrow 15^2 = 225$
$2 + 7 + 4 + 5 = 18 \rightarrow 18^2 = 324$
$8 + 1 + 4 + 9 = 22 \rightarrow 22^2 = 484$

MULTIPLE CHOICE QUESTIONS

Direction (1 to 30): Choose the appropriate number which follows the given pattern.

1.
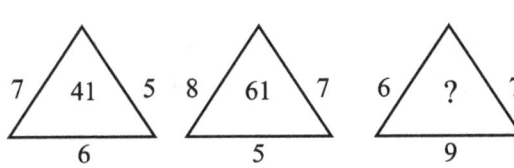
(a) 61 (b) 71
(c) 51 (d) 59

2.
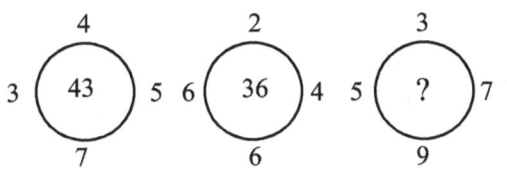
(a) 62 (b) 52
(c) 72 (d) 82

3.
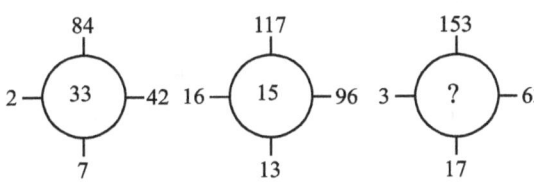
(a) 28 (b) 30
(c) 31 (d) 32

4.
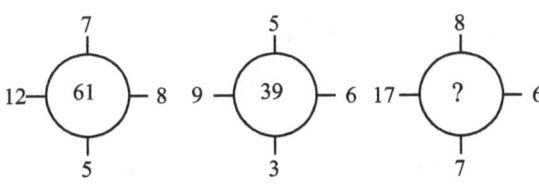
(a) 36 (b) 46
(c) 56 (d) 66

5.
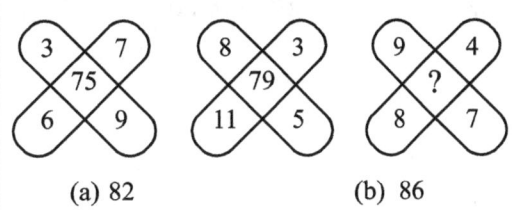
(a) 82 (b) 86
(c) 92 (d) 93

6.
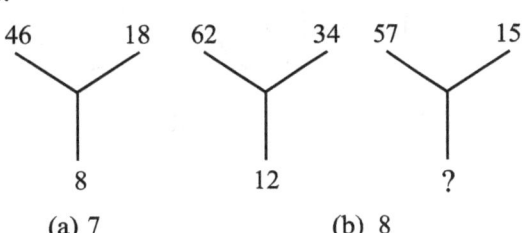
(a) 7 (b) 8
(c) 9 (d) 6

7.
	7				8				5	
13	80	3		23	85	1		25	?	2
	5				17				12	

(a) 172 (b) 174
(c) 176 (d) 178

8.
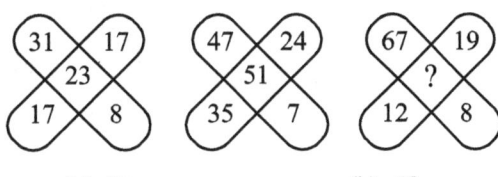
(a) 52 (b) 53
(c) 42 (d) 54

Pattern

9.

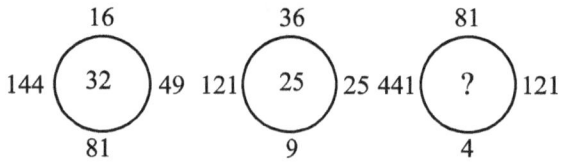

(a) 41 (b) 42
(c) 43 (d) 44

10.

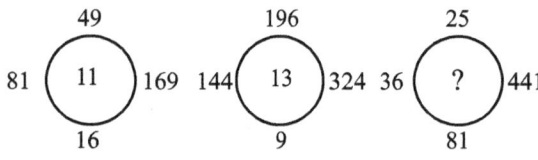

(a) 12 (b) 13
(c) 14 (d) 15

11.

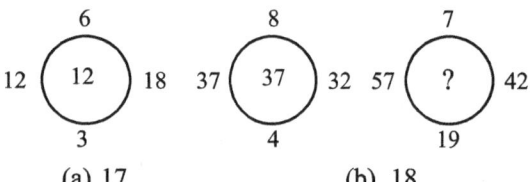

(a) 17 (b) 18
(c) 21 (d) 24

12.

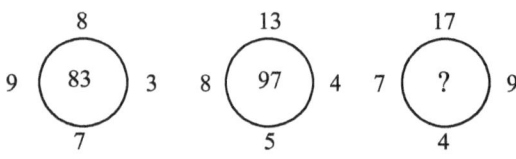

(a) 121 (b) 131
(c) 133 (d) 123

13.

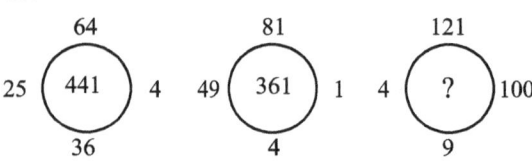

(a) 625 (b) 676
(c) 576 (d) None of these

14.

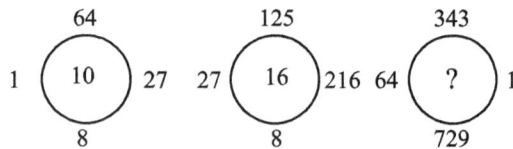

(a) 19 (b) 20
(c) 21 (d) 22

15.

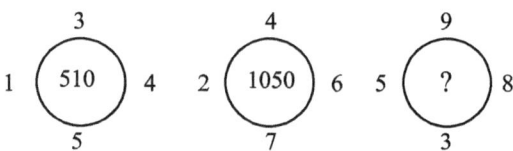

(a) 1760 (b) 1770
(c) 1780 (d) 1790

16.

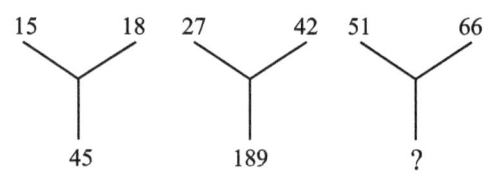

(a) 561 (b) 562
(c) 563 (d) 564

17.

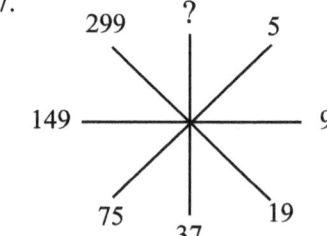

(a) 598 (b) 597
(c) 596 (d) 599

18.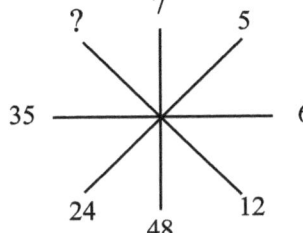
(a) 144 (b) 145
(c) 143 (d) 142

19.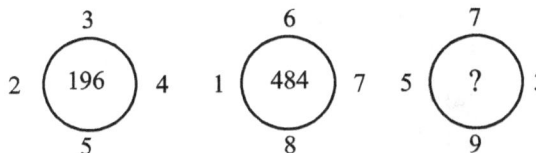
(a) 576 (b) 676
(c) 636 (d) None of these

20.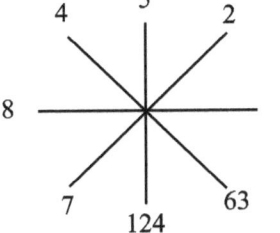
(a) 512 (b) 511
(c) 513 (d) 514

21.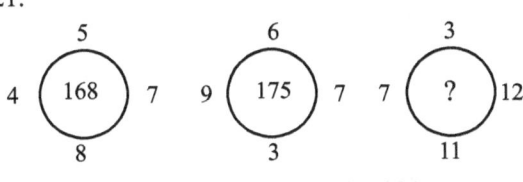
(a) 131 (b) 231
(c) 241 (d) 243

22.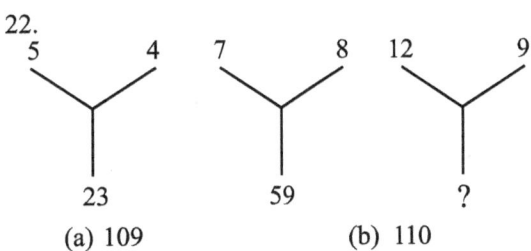
(a) 109 (b) 110
(c) 111 (d) 112

23.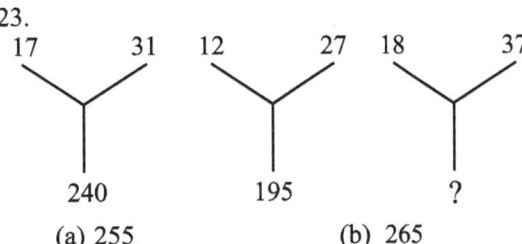
(a) 255 (b) 265
(c) 275 (d) 285

24.
18	272	16
25	504	21
47	?	28

(a) 1188 (b) 1288
(c) 1268 (d) 1278

25.
29	360	12
37	532	14
43	?	15

(a) 645 (b) 650
(c) 655 (d) 660

26.
48	55	43
67	66	61
78	?	70

(a) 77 (b) 88
(c) 99 (d) None of these

Pattern

27.

2	5	3
12	17	11
140	264	?

(a) 372 (b) 374
(c) 376 (d) None of these

28.

979	7	864
465	5	712
856	?	324

(a) 10 (b) 11
(c) 12 (d) 13

29.

157	428	264
436	324	517
639	?	718

(a) 314 (b) 316
(c) 318 (d) 321

30.

3	8	121
7	12	361
9	13	?

(a) 441 (b) 461
(c) 484 (d) None of these

Number Series

Learning Objectives : In this chapter, students will learn about:
- ✓ Solving questions related to number series

CHAPTER SUMMARY

Number Series

A number series can be considered as a collection of numbers in which all the terms are formed according to some particular rule or all the terms follow a particular pattern. The relation of any term to its preceding term will be same throughout the series.

In the questions based on number series a student has to find out the rule in which the terms of the series are selected and depending on that rule he/she has to find out the missing number. There is no definite rule for the series.

Solved Examples

Direction to Solve:
Choose the correct alternative that will continue the same pattern and replace the question mark in the given series.

Example 1: 2, 3, 3, 5, 10, 13, ?, 43, 172, 177
    (a) 23   (b) 38
    (c) 39   (d) 40

Solution: Option (c) is correct.

Explanation: The pattern is + 1, × 1, + 2, × 2, + 3, × 3, + 4, × 4, + 5.

So, missing term = 13 × 3 = 39.

Example 2: Which of the following will not be a number of the series 1, 8, 27, 64, 125,.....?
    (a) 256   (b) 512
    (c) 729   (d) 1000

Solution: Option (a) is correct.

Explanation: The given series consists of cubes of natural numbers only. 256 is not the cube of any natural number.

Example 3: 2, 1, 2, 4, 4, 5, 6, 7, 8, 8, 10, 11, ?
    (a) 9   (b) 10
    (c) 11   (d) 12

Solution: Option (b) is correct.

Explanation: The given sequence is a combination of three series :

    I. 1st, 4th, 7th, 10th, 13th terms i.e. 2, 4, 6, 8, ?
    II. 2nd, 5th, 8th, 11th terms i.e. 1, 4, 7, 10
    III. 3rd, 6th, 9th, 12th terms i.e. 2, 5, 8, 11
    Clearly, I consists of consecutive even numbers. So, the missing term is 10.

MULTIPLE CHOICE QUESTIONS

Direction (1 to 25): In each of the following questions, a number series is given with one missing term. Choose correct alternative that will continue the same pattern and fill in the blank spaces.

1. 1000, 200, 40, __
   (a) 8 (b) 10
   (c) 15 (d) 20

2. 5.2, 4.8, 4.4, 4, __
   (a) 3 (b) 3.3
   (c) 3.5 (d) 3.6

3. 2, 6, 18, 54, __
   (a) 108 (b) 148
   (c) 162 (d) 216

4. 80, 10, 70, 15, 60, __
   (a) 20 (b) 25
   (c) 30 (d) 50

5. 8, 43, 11, 41, __, 39, 17
   (a) 8 (b) 14
   (c) 43 (d) 44

6. 70, 71, 76, __, 81, 86, 70, 91
   (a) 70 (b) 71
   (c) 80 (d) 96

7. V, VIII, XI, XIV, __, XX,
   (a) IX (b) XXIII
   (c) XV (d) XVII

8. U32, V29, __, X23, Y20
   (a) W26 (b) W17
   (c) Z17 (d) Z26

9. 0.15, 0.3, ____, 1.2, 2.4
   (a) 4.8 (b) 0.006
   (c) 0.6 (d) 0.9

10. XXIV, XX, __, XII, VIII
    (a) XXII (b) XIII
    (c) XVI (d) IV

11. 4, 7, 25, 10, __, 20, 16, 19, What number should fill the blank?
    (a) 13 (b) 15
    (c) 20 (d) 28

12. J14, L16, __, P20, R22
    (a) S24 (b) N18
    (c) M18 (d) T24

13. VI, 10, V, 11, __, 12, III
    (a) II (b) IV
    (c) IX (d) 14

14. (1/9), (1/3), 1, __ , 9
    (a) 2/3 (b) 3
    (c) 6 (d) 27

15. 15, __, 27, 27, 39, 39
    (a) 51 (b) 39
    (c) 23 (d) 15

16. 72, 76, 73, 77, 74, __, 75
    (a) 70 (b) 71
    (c) 75 (d) 78

17. 10, 100, 200, 310, __
    (a) 400 (b) 410
    (c) 420 (d) 430

18. 11, 10, __, 100, 1001, 1000, 10001
    (a) 101 (b) 110
    (c) 111 (d) None of these

19. 2, 7, 27, 107, 427, __
    (a) 1262 (b) 1707
    (c) 4027 (d) 4207

20. 2, 3, 8, 27, 112, __
    (a) 226 (b) 339
    (c) 452 (d) 565

21. 6, 17, 39, 72, __
    (a) 83 (b) 94
    (c) 116 (d) 127

22. 20, 20, 19, 16, 17, 13, 14, 11, __, __
    (a) 10, 10 (b) 10, 11
    (c) 13, 14 (d) 13, 16

23. 24, 60, 120, 210, __
    (a) 300 (b) 336
    (c) 420 (d) 525

24. 625, 5, 125, 25, 25, __, 5
    (a) 5 (b) 25
    (c) 125 (d) 625

25. 240, __, 120, 40, 10, 2
    (a) 180 (b) 240
    (c) 420 (d) 480

Alphabetical Series

Learning Objectives : In this chapter, students will learn about:
- ✓ Solving questions related to alphabetical series

CHAPTER SUMMARY

Alphabetical Series form an important part of the reasoning section in various competitive examinations.

Solved Examples

Example 1: In the following letter series, some of the letters are missing, which are given in such order as one of the alternatives below it. Choose the correct alternative.

_ tu _ rt _ s _ _ usrtu _

(a) rtusru (b) rsutrr
(c) rsurtr (d) rsurts

Solution: Option (d) is correct.

Explanation: The series rtus/rtus/rtus/rtus. Thus, the pattern 'rtus' is repeated.

Directions

In each of the following questions, various terms of an alphabet series are given with one or more terms missing as shown by (?). Choose the missing terms out of the given alternatives.

Example 2: A, G, L, P, S, ?

(a) U (b) W
(c) X (d) Y

Solution: Option (a) is correct.

Explanation:

A $\xrightarrow{+6}$ G $\xrightarrow{+5}$ L $\xrightarrow{+4}$ P $\xrightarrow{+3}$ S $\xrightarrow{+2}$ U

Example 3: ajs, gpy, ?, sbk, yhq

(a) dmv (b) mve
(c) oua (d) qzi

Solution: Option (b) is correct.

Explanation:

1st letter : a $\xrightarrow{+6}$ g $\xrightarrow{+6}$ (m) $\xrightarrow{+6}$ s $\xrightarrow{+6}$ y

2nd letter : j $\xrightarrow{+6}$ p $\xrightarrow{+6}$ (v) $\xrightarrow{+6}$ b $\xrightarrow{+6}$ h

3rd letter : s $\xrightarrow{+6}$ y $\xrightarrow{+6}$ (e) $\xrightarrow{+6}$ k $\xrightarrow{+6}$ q

Example 4: AB, DEF, HIJK, ?, STUVWX

(a) LMNO (b) LMNOP
(c) MNOPQ (d) QRSTU

Solution: Option (c) is correct.

Explanation: The number of letters in terms of the given series increases by one at each step.

The first letter of each term is two steps ahead of the last letter of the preceding term.

However, each term consists of consecutive letters in order.

Example 5: Y, B, T, G, O, ?

(a) N (b) M
(c) L (d) K

Solution: Option (c) is correct.

Explanation: The given sequence is a combination of two series :

I. Y, T, O and II. B, G, ?

I consists of 2nd, 7th and 12th letters from the end of the English alphabet

II consists of 2nd, 7th and 12th letters from the beginning of the English alphabet.

So, the missing letter in II is the 12th letter from the beginning of the English alphabet, which is L.

MULTIPLE CHOICE QUESTIONS

Direction (1 to 10): In each of the following letter series, some of the letters are missing, which are given in such order as one of the alternatives below it. Choose the correct alternative.

1. _ op _ mo _ n _ _ pnmop _ .
   (a) mnpmon
   (b) mpnmop
   (c) mnompn
   (d) mnpomn

2. _bcc _ ac _ aabb _ ab _ cc
   (a) aabca
   (b) abaca
   (c) bacab
   (d) bcaca

3. m _ nm _ n _ an _ a _ ma _
   (a) aamnan
   (b) ammanm
   (c) aammnn
   (d) amammn

4. ab _ _ d _ aaba _ na _ badna _ b
   (a) andaa
   (b) babda
   (c) badna
   (d) dbanb

5. bca _ b _ aabc _ _ a _ caa
   (a) acab
   (b) bcbb
   (c) cbab
   (d) ccab

6. ab _ _ baa _ _ ab _
   (a) aaaaa
   (b) aabaa
   (c) aabab
   (d) baabb

7. _ bc _ ca _ aba _ c _ ca
   (a) abcbb
   (b) bbbcc
   (c) bacba
   (d) abbcc

8. ba _ cb _ b _ bab _
   (a) acbb
   (b) bacc
   (c) bcaa
   (d) cabb

9. c _ bba _ cab _ ac _ ab _ ac
   (a) abcbc
   (b) acbcb
   (c) babcc
   (d) bcacb

10. _ aa _ ba _ bb _ ab _ aab
    (a) aaabb
    (b) babab
    (c) bbaab
    (d) bbbaa

Direction (11 to 25): In each of the following questions, an alphabet series is given with one missing term. Choose correct alternative that will continue the same pattern and fill in the blank spaces.

11. QAR, RAS, SAT, TAU, _____
    (a) UAV
    (b) UAT
    (c) TAS
    (d) TAT

12. DEF, DEF$_2$, DE$_2$F$_2$, _____, D$_2$E$_2$F$_3$
    (a) DEF$_3$
    (b) D$_3$EF$_3$
    (c) D$_2$E$_3$F
    (d) D$_2$E$_2$F$_2$

13. P$_5$QR, P$_4$QS, P$_3$QT, _____, P$_1$QV
    (a) PQW
    (b) PQV$_2$
    (c) P$_2$QU
    (d) PQ$_3$U

14. FAG, GAF, HAI, IAH, _____
    (a) JAK
    (b) HAL
    (c) HAK
    (d) JAI

15. CMM, EOO, GQQ, _____, KUU
    (a) GRR
    (b) GSS
    (c) ISS
    (d) ITT

16. ELFA, GLHA, ILJA, _____, MLNA
    (a) OLPA
    (b) KLMA
    (c) LLMA
    (d) KLLA

17. ejo tyd ins xch ?
    (a) nrw
    (b) mrw
    (c) msx
    (d) nsx

18. JAK, KBL, LCM, MDN, _____
    (a) OEP
    (b) NEO
    (c) MEN
    (d) PFQ

19. BCB, DED, FGF, HIH, ___
    (a) JKJ
    (b) HJH
    (c) IJI
    (d) JHJ

20. A, B, N, C, D, O, E, F, P, ?, ?, ?
    (a) G, H, I
    (b) G, H, J
    (c) G, H, Q
    (d) J, K, L

21. A, B, B, D, C, F, D; H, E, ?, ?
    (a) E, F
    (b) F, G
    (c) F, I
    (d) J, F

22. AB, DEF, HIJK, ?, STUVWX
    (a) LMNO
    (b) LMNOP
    (c) MNOPQ
    (d) QRSTU

23. Y, B, T, G, O, ?
    (a) N
    (b) M
    (c) L
    (d) K

24. b e d f ? h j ? l
    (a) i m
    (b) m i
    (c) i n
    (d) j m

25. ZA$_5$, Y$_4$B, XC$_6$, W$_3$D, _____
    (a) E$_7$V
    (b) V$_2$E
    (c) VE$_5$
    (d) VE$_7$

Alphabetical Series

Odd One Out   4

Learning Objectives : In this chapter, students will learn about:
✓ Solving questions related to odd one out concept

CHAPTER SUMMARY

Verbal Classification tests, also known as 'Odd One Out' consist of a list of 4 – 5 items. These items could be either words, group of letters, or figures (digits). Out of the given 4 – 5 items, one of them is different from the others. In other words, except one, all of them have some sort of similarity. You are required to study the given list of items, determine the similarity between them and pick out the one that does not bear the same characteristics as the others in the list. These questions test your ability to observe differences and similarities among various objects.

Example 1: Find the odd one among the following.
(a) Mercury (b) Moon
(c) Jupiter (d) Saturn

Solution: Option (b) is correct.

Explanation: All others except Moon are planets whereas Moon is a satellite.

Example 2: Find the odd one among the following.
(a) SORE (b) SOTLU
(c) NORGAE (d) MEJNIAS

Solution: Option (c) is correct.

Explanation: The letters in the words are jumbled. The actual words are ROSE, LOTUS, ORANGE and JASMINE. All, except ORANGE, are flowers whereas ORANGE is a fruit.

Example 3: Find the odd one among the following.
(a) Different (b) Separate
(c) Distinct (d) Similar
(e) Distinguishable

Solution: Option (d) is correct.

Explanation: Except option (d) all the other words are synonyms.

MULTIPLE CHOICE QUESTIONS

Direction (1 to 20): Find the odd one out.

1. 3, 5, 7, 12, 17, 19
   - (a) 19
   - (b) 17
   - (c) 5
   - (d) 12

2. 41, 43, 47, 53, 61, 71, 73, 81
   - (a) 61
   - (b) 71
   - (c) 73
   - (d) 81

3. 835, 734, 642, 751, 853, 981, 532
   - (a) 751
   - (b) 853
   - (c) 981
   - (d) 532

4. 331, 482, 551, 263, 383, 362, 284
   - (a) 263
   - (b) 383
   - (c) 331
   - (d) 551

5. 16, 25, 36, 72, 144, 196, 225
   - (a) 36
   - (b) 72
   - (c) 196
   - (d) 225

6. 2, 5, 10, 17, 26, 37, 50, 64
   - (a) 50
   - (b) 26
   - (c) 37
   - (d) 64

7. 582, 605, 588, 611, 634, 617, 600
   - (a) 634
   - (b) 611
   - (c) 605
   - (d) 600

8. 56, 72, 90, 110, 132, 150
   - (a) 72
   - (b) 110
   - (c) 132
   - (d) 150

9. 36, 54, 18, 27, 9, 18.5, 4.5
   - (a) 4.5
   - (b) 18.5
   - (c) 54
   - (d) 18

10. 6, 13, 18, 25, 30, 37, 40
    - (a) 25
    - (b) 30
    - (c) 37
    - (d) 40

11. 46080, 3840, 384, 48, 24, 2, 1
    - (a) 1
    - (b) 2
    - (c) 24
    - (d) 384

12. 7, 8, 18, 57, 228, 1165, 6996
    - (a) 8
    - (b) 18
    - (c) 57
    - (d) 228

13. 190, 166, 145, 128, 112, 100, 91
    - (a) 100
    - (b) 166
    - (c) 145
    - (d) 128

14. 445, 221, 109, 46, 25, 11, 4
    - (a) 221
    - (b) 109
    - (c) 46
    - (d) 25

15. 196, 169, 144, 121, 100, 80, 64
    - (a) 169
    - (b) 144
    - (c) 144
    - (d) 80

16. 3, 7, 15, 27, 63, 127, 255
    - (a) 7
    - (b) 15
    - (c) 27
    - (d) 63

17. 2880, 480, 92, 24, 8, 4, 4
    - (a) 480
    - (b) 92
    - (c) 24
    - (d) 8

18. 10, 26, 74, 218, 654, 1946, 5834
    - (a) 26
    - (b) 74
    - (c) 218
    - (d) 654

19. 15, 16, 34, 105, 424, 2124, 12576
    - (a) 16
    - (b) 34
    - (c) 105
    - (d) 2124

20. 64, 71, 80, 91, 104, 119, 135, 155
    - (a) 71
    - (b) 80
    - (c) 104
    - (d) 135

21. Choose the word which is different from the rest.
    - (a) Curd
    - (b) Butter
    - (c) Oil
    - (d) Cheese

22. Choose the word which is different from the rest.
    - (a) Rigveda
    - (b) Yajurveda
    - (c) Atharvaveda
    - (d) Ayurveda

23. Choose the word which is different from the rest.
    - (a) Kiwi
    - (b) Eagle
    - (c) Emu
    - (d) Ostrich

24. Choose the word which is different from the rest.
    - (a) Wheat
    - (b) Paddy
    - (c) Jowar
    - (d) Mustard

25. Choose the word which is different from the rest.
    - (a) House
    - (b) Apartment
    - (c) Society
    - (d) Building

26. Choose the word which is different from the rest.
    (a) Reader   (b) Writer
    (c) Printer   (d) Publisher
27. Choose the word which is different from the rest.
    (a) Dog   (b) Horse
    (c) Goat   (d) Fox
28. Choose the word which is different from the rest.
    (a) House   (b) Cottage
    (c) School   (d) Palace
29. Choose the word which is different from the rest.
    (a) Travelled   (b) Sailed
    (c) Walked   (d) Rode
30. Choose the word which is different from the rest.
    (a) Fear   (b) Anger
    (c) Sober   (d) Love
31. Choose the word which is different from the rest.
    (a) Buffalo   (b) Stag
    (c) Camel   (d) Rhinoceros
32. Choose the word which is different from the rest.
    (a) Japan   (b) India
    (c) Sri Lanka   (d) New Zealand
33. Choose the word which is different from the rest.
    (a) Spectacles   (b) Goggles
    (c) Binoculars   (d) Microphone
34. Choose the word which is different from the rest.
    (a) Shehnai   (b) Bagpipe
    (c) Flute   (d) Sitar
35. Choose the word which is different from the rest.
    (a) Sheep   (b) Gazel
    (c) Ibex   (d) Shrew
36. Choose the word which is different from the rest.
    (a) Cheetah   (b) Lion
    (c) Bear   (d) Tiger
37. Choose the word which is different from the rest.
    (a) Producer   (b) Director
    (c) Investor   (d) Financier
38. Choose the word which is different from the rest.
    (a) Tricycle   (b) Trident
    (c) Trifle   (d) Tricolour
39. Choose the word which is different from the rest.
    (a) Chameleon   (b) Crocodile
    (c) Alligator   (d) Locust
40. Choose the word which is different from the rest.
    (a) Calendar   (b) Year
    (c) Date   (d) Month

Direction (41 to 60): In each of the following questions, some groups of letters are given, all of which, except one, share a common similarity while one is different.

41. Choose the odd one out.
    (a) HSRI   (b) MVUN
    (c) OLKP   (d) PJQX
42. Choose the odd one out.
    (a) YDWB   (b) TKRI
    (c) QNOM   (d) HLFJ
43. Choose the odd one out.
    (a) BdEg   (b) KmNp
    (c) PrSu   (d) TwXz
44. Choose the odd one out.
    (a) OUSF   (b) PIGS
    (c) TEPJ   (d) XLPA
45. Choose the odd one out.
    (a) ABDG   (b) IJLO
    (c) MNPS   (d) RSUY
46. Choose the odd one out.
    (a) PEAR   (b) TORE
    (c) REAP   (d) TEAR
47. Choose the odd one out.
    (a) BCDE   (b) PQRS
    (c) WXYZ   (d) STUW

48. Choose the odd one out.
    (a) AEIO   (b) BFJN
    (c) CGKO   (d) DHLP
49. Choose the odd one out.
    (a) CXGT   (b) EVBY
    (c) DXEY   (d) AZDW
50. Choose the odd one out.
    (a) ABpQ   (b) npRS
    (c) PQrT   (d) EFGh
51. Choose the odd one out.
    (a) AEGC   (b) HLNJ
    (c) OSVQ   (d) VZBX
52. Choose the odd one out.
    (a) ADGJ   (b) FILO
    (c) LORU   (d) ILMP
53. Choose the odd one out.
    (a) BFJM   (b) DEFG
    (c) JMPS   (d) PRTV
54. Choose the odd one out.
    (a) CegI   (b) FhjL
    (c) PrtV   (d) KnpR
55. Choose the odd one out.
    (a) OTP   (b) ABA
    (c) SZX   (d) UVB
56. Choose the odd one out.
    (a) FAA   (b) OFF
    (c) ATT   (d) IFF
57. Choose the odd one out.
    (a) HS   (b) MN
    (c) GT   (d) KO
58. Choose the odd one out.
    (a) CYX   (b) LPO
    (c) FVU   (d) FUT
59. Choose the odd one out.
    (a) AOT   (b) CPA
    (c) REB   (d) TIW
60. Choose the odd one out.
    (a) VRT   (b) RMP
    (c) YUW   (d) FBD

Odd One Out

Coding Decoding   5

 **Learning Objectives :** In this chapter, students will learn about:
- ✓ Concept of Coding and Decoding

CHAPTER SUMMARY

A code is a 'System of Signals.' Therefore, coding is a method of transmitting a message between the sender and the receiver without a third person knowing it.

The coding and decoding test is set up to judge the candidate's ability to decipher the rule that codes a particular word/message and break the code to decipher the message.

Letter Coding

Example 1: In a certain system of coding, the word STATEMENT is written as TNEMETATS. In the same system of coding, what should be the code for the word POLITICAL?

(a) OPILITACL   (b) TCATILIOP
(c) LACITILOP   (d) None of these

Solution: (c) The letters of the given word are written in reverse order to obtain the code. Reversing the order of letters in POLITICAL, we get LACITILOP, which is the required code.

Example 2: If in a certain language EXECUTIVE is coded as TCIEUXVEE, then how is MAUSOLEUM coded in that language?

(a) LSEUOAUMM
(b) AUUCOSLMM
(c) AUEUOSEMM
(d) SLUEOAUMM

Solution: (a) MAUSOLEUM → LSEUOAUMM
1 2 3 4 5 6 7 8 9
6 4 7 3 5 2 8 1 9

Direct Letter Coding

In this, letters are assigned codes according to a set pattern or rule concerning the movement or reordering of letters and one needs to detect this hidden rule to decode a message.

Example 3: If the word EARTH is written as QPMZS in coded form, how can HEART be written following the same coding?

(a) SQPMZ   (b) SPQZM
(c) SQPZM   (d) SQMPZ

Solution: (a)

Letter: E A R T H
Code: Q P M Z S

So, the code for HEART becomes SQPMZ.

Example 4: In a certain code, STOVE is written as FNBLK, then how will VOTES be written in the same code?

(a) LNBKF   (b) LKNBF
(c) LBNKF   (d) FLKBN

Solution: (c)

Letter: S T O V E
Code: F N B L K

The code for VOTES is LBNKF.

Number/Symbol Coding

Numerical code values are assigned to a word or alphabetical code letters are assigned to the numbers.

Example 5: If RED is coded as 6720, then how would GREEN be coded?

(a) 9207716 (b) 1677199
(c) 1677209 (d) 1677209

Solution: (c)

RED → DER → 4/5/18 → 6/7/20 → 6720
GREEN → NEERG
→ 14/5/5/18/7 → 16/7/7/20/9
→ 1677209

Example 6: If E = 5, PEN = 35, then PAGE = ?

(a) 27 (b) 29
(c) 36 (d) 28

Solution: (b)

Putting A = 1, B = 2, C = 3, D = 4, E = 5, …… M = 13, …….. X = 24, Y = 25, Z = 26
PEN = P + E + N = 16 + 5 + 14 = 35
PAGE = P + A + G + E = 16 + 1 + 7 + 5 = 29

MULTIPLE CHOICE QUESTIONS

1. In a certain language, SIGHT is written as FVTUC, how is REVEAL written in the same language?
   (a) ERIRNY
   (b) DQHQMX
   (c) FSJSOZ
   (d) YNRIRE

2. If in a certain language, MADRAS is coded as NBESBT, how is BOMBAY coded in that language?
   (a) CPNCBZ
   (b) CPNCBX
   (c) CPOCBZ
   (d) CQOCBZ

3. In a certain code, ROAD is written as URDG, how is SWAN written in that code?
   (a) VZCP
   (b) UXDQ
   (c) VZDQ
   (d) VXDQ

4. In a certain code, FAVOUR is written as EBUPTS, how is DRAGON written in that code?
   (a) CBFFDS
   (b) CBMHDS
   (c) CSZHNO
   (d) EBHHFS

5. If DELHI can be coded as CCIDD, how would you code KOLKATA?
   (a) AJMTVT
   (b) AMJXVS
   (c) JMIGVNT
   (d) WXYZAXT

6. If POND is coded as RSTL, how is DEAR written in that code?
   (a) GHIZ
   (b) FIGZ
   (c) JIGZ
   (d) GHIJ

7. In a certain code, KAVERI is written as VAKIRE, how is MYSORE written in that code?
   (a) SYMERO
   (b) SYMEOR
   (c) EROSYM
   (d) SMYERP

8. In a certain code, CALENDAR is written as CLANEADR. How is CIRCULAR written in that code?
   (a) CRIUCLRA
   (b) ICRCLUAR
   (c) CRIUCALR
   (d) ICCRLURA

9. In a certain code, CONDEMN is written as CNODMEN. How will TEACHER be written in that code?
   (a) TAECHER
   (b) TAECEHR
   (c) TCAEHER
   (d) TAEECHR

10. In a certain code language, HAND is written as SZMW then what will be the code for MILK?
    (a) ORNP
    (b) RNOP
    (c) NROP
    (d) PNRO

11. In a certain code language, BOARD is written as EQBNC. How will the word CLIMB be written in that language?
    (a) FNJRD
    (b) DKJLC
    (c) CLJKD
    (d) DNHMB

12. In a certain code, PLEADING is written as FMHCQMFB. How is SHOULDER written in that code?
    (a) KCDQTIPV
    (b) QDCKTIPV
    (c) QDCKVPIT
    (d) None of these

13. If in a certain language SHIFT is coded as RFFBO, which word would be coded as LKUMB?
    (a) KJTLA
    (b) MJVLC
    (c) MMXQG
    (d) MLVNC

14. In a certain code, JANUARY, is written as RYUAANJ. Which word will be written as ERMBCEDE in that code?
    (a) DECEMBER
    (b) SEPTEMBER
    (c) OCTOBER
    (d) AUGUST

15. In a certain code, REFRIGERATOR is coded as ROTAREGIRFER. Which word would be coded as NOITINUMMA?
    (a) ANMOMIUTNI
    (b) AMMUNITION
    (c) NMMUNITIOA
    (d) AMNTONI

16. In a certain code, O is written as D, A as F, M as I, S as O, N as P, E as M, I as C, P as Q and C as R, then how will COMPANIES be written in that code?
    (a) SMINCPAMO
    (b) SEIACPAMO
    (c) SEINMCIPAMO
    (d) RDIQFPCMO

17. If MINERAL is written as QRSTUVW and SOUND is written as ABCSD, then how will READER be written in the same code?
    (a) QDZCDQ
    (b) UTVDTU
    (c) TUDVUT
    (d) SBFEFS

18. If TEACHER is coded as LMKJNMP, then how will HEART be coded?
    (a) NMKPL
    (b) NPPKL
    (c) NPKML
    (d) NMAPL

19. If R is denoted by N, D is denoted by T, I by U, O by I, E by R, T by L, U by C, N by K and C by G, then how will the word INTRODUCE be written?
    (a) ULNITCGRK
    (b) UNIGRKTL
    (c) UKLNITCGR
    (d) UNICKIOR

20. If the word PORTER can be coded as MBNZQN, then how can REPORT be written?
    (a) NQBMNZ
    (b) NQMNBZ
    (c) NBQMNZ
    (d) NQMBNZ

21. If the word RASCALS can be coded as BNMZNTM, then how can SALSA be written?
    (a) MNTMN
    (b) TNMNM
    (c) MNTLT
    (d) TMNMT

22. If in a code language, ORGANISATION is written as CBDWLQJWYQCL and OPERATION is written as CXFBWYQCL, then how is SEPARATION coded?
    (a) QCLYWBFXJE
    (b) JFQYWBCXQL
    (c) JFXWBWYQCL
    (d) EJXEBEYQCL

23. In a code language, FACTORIAL is written as DODNGLCOH and DANCE is written as YOJDZ, how can EDUCATION be written in that code?
    (a) ZJDONCGJT
    (b) ZYMODCLNJ
    (c) ZYOMDCNJ
    (d) None of these

24. In a coding system, SHEEP is written as GAXXR and BLEAT as HPXTN. How can SLATE be written in this coding system?
    (a) PTGXN
    (b) GPXMT
    (c) GPTXN
    (d) GPTNX

25. In a code language, STARK is written as LBFMG and MOBILE is written as TNRSPJ. How is BLAME written in that code?
    (a) TSFGJ
    (b) TSFRJ
    (c) RPFTJ
    (d) NJFTP

26. If MACHINE is coded as 19 – 7 – 9 – 14 – 15 – 20 – 11, how will you code DANGER?
    (a) 11 – 7 – 20 – 16 – 11 – 24
    (b) 13 – 7 – 20 – 10 – 11 – 25
    (c) 13 – 7 – 20 – 9 – 11 – 25
    (d) 10 – 7 – 20 – 13 – 11 – 24

27. If A = 26, SUN = 27, then CAT = ?
    (a) 57
    (b) 27
    (c) 58
    (d) 24

28. If AT = 20, BAT = 40, then CAT will be equal to.
    (a) 70
    (b) 50
    (c) 30
    (d) 60

29. If DEER = 12215 and HIGH = 5645, how will you code HEEL?
    (a) 5229
    (b) 3449
    (c) 4337
    (d) 2328

30. If O = 16, FOR = 42, then what is FRONT equal to?
    (a) 78
    (b) 65
    (c) 73
    (d) 61

Coding Decoding

Alphabet Test 6

Learning Objectives : In this chapter, students will learn about:
- ✓ Letter word problems
- ✓ Alphabet Quibble

CHAPTER SUMMARY

In alphabet test the words are arranged in alphabetical order and choose the one that comes first according to dictionary.

Example 1:
- (a) Fungi
- (b) Fun
- (c) Fuse
- (d) Full

Solution: (d) Full, Fun, Fungi, Fuse.

Example 2:
- (a) Boutique
- (b) Bottle
- (c) Boat
- (d) Bottom

Solution: (c) Boat, Bottle, Bottom, Boutique.

Example 3:
- (a) Sandwich
- (b) Sandy
- (c) Saturn
- (d) Satisfy

Solution: (a) Sandwich, Sandy, Satisfy, Saturn.

Example 4:
- (a) Destroy
- (b) Determine
- (c) Delete
- (d) Democracy

Solution: (c) Delete, Democracy, Destroy, Determine.

Letter–Word Problems

Example 5: How many such letters are there in the word BACKLASH each of which is as far away from the beginning of the word as it is from the beginning of English alphabet.
- (a) One
- (b) Three
- (c) Four
- (d) Two

Solution: (d) Clearly, C and H are respectively the third and eight letters in the word BACKLASH as well as in the English alphabet. Thus, there are two such letters.

Example 6: How many such pairs of letters are there in word PRESENCE which has as many letters between them in the word as in alphabet series.
- (a) One
- (b) Two
- (c) Three
- (d) Four

Solution: (c)   PRES   PQRS
                    RESEN   RQPON
                    ENC   EDC

Rule–Detection

In each of the following questions, find out which of the letter – series follows the given rule

Example 7: Number of letters skipped in between adjacent letters of the series increases by one.
- (a) OIGDC
- (b) OMJFA
- (c) OMKIG
- (d) OMLKJ

Solution: (b)   [O] N   [M] L   K   [J] I
                    H   G   [F] E   D   C
                    B   [A]

Example 8: Number of letters skipped in between adjacent letters in the series decreases by three.
- (a) DMSXA
- (b) HUELO
- (c) HUELP
- (d) HVDKP

Solution: (c)

H	I	J	K	L	M	N	O
P	Q	R	S	T	U	V	W
X	Y	Z	A	B	C	D	E
F	G	H	I	J	K	L	M
N	O	P					

(Boxed: H, U, E, L, P)

Alphabetical Quibble

In this type of questions, generally, a letter series is given, be it the English alphabets from A to Z or a randomized sequence of letters. The candidates have to identify the option which satisfies the given condition.

Example 9: If each letter in the English alphabet is attached a value equal to its serial number in the alphabet, which among the following will have the highest sum of the values of all its letters?

(a) WIND (b) TONE

Solution: (b) Putting A = 1, B = 2, C = 3, D = 4, ..., Z = 26 we may calculate the sum of the values of the letters of each of the given words as follows:

(a) WIND → W + I + N + D = 23 + 9 + 14 + 4 = 50
(b) TONE → T + O + N + E = 20 + 15 + 14 + 5 = 54

MULTIPLE CHOICE QUESTIONS

Direction (1 to 5): Arrange the given words in alphabetical order and choose the one that comes first.

1.
   (a) Waving   (b) Watching
   (c) Waiting   (d) Wanting

2.
   (a) Lapse   (b) Leave
   (c) Leisure   (d) Laurel

3.
   (a) Protein   (b) Proverb
   (c) Property   (d) Project

4.
   (a) Dissect   (b) Dissociate
   (c) Distract   (d) Dissipate

5.
   (a) Page   (b) Pagan
   (c) Palate   (d) Pageant

Direction (6 to 10): Arrange the given words in alphabetical order and choose the one that comes last.

6.
   (a) Mink   (b) Music
   (c) Murder   (d) Murmer

7.
   (a) Maritime   (b) Marine
   (c) Marital   (d) Marigold

8.
   (a) Preview   (b) Premium
   (c) Previous   (d) Prevent

9.
   (a) Lattice   (b) Latent
   (c) Latitude   (d) Launch

10.
    (a) Barricading (b) Banishing
    (c) Backing   (d) Bathing

Direction (11 to 14): In each of the following questions find out how many such pairs of letters are there in the given word each of which has as many letters between them in the word as in the English alphabet.

11. PARADISE
    (a) One   (b) Three
    (c) Four   (d) Two

12. HORIZON
    (a) Four   (b) Three
    (c) Two   (d) One

13. LANGUISH
    (a) Two   (b) Three
    (c) One   (d) None of these

14. HACKLE
    (a) Four   (b) Two
    (c) One   (d) Three

15. Which letter in word CYBERNETICS occupies the same position as it does in the English alphabet?
    (a) C   (b) I
    (c) E   (d) T

Direction (16 to 25): In each of the following questions, find out which of the letter – series satisfies the given rule.

16. Number of letters skipped in between adjacent letters in the series is two.
    (a) ZEGKMPR   (b) SVZCGJN
    (c) MPSVYBE   (d) QSVYXCF

17. Number of letters skipped in between the adjacent letters in the series are consecutive even numbers.
    (a) GIMSZ   (b) ADIPY
    (c) CDFIM   (d) DFJPX

18. Number of letters skipped in between adjacent letters of the series increase by one.
    (a) OMJFA   (b) OMLKJ
    (c) OMKIG   (d) OIGDC

19. Number of letters skipped in between adjacent letters in the series decrease by two.
    (a) EPVAF   (b) XFMQV
    (c) UCJOP   (d) GPWBE

20. Number of letters skipped in between adjacent letters in the series doubles every time.
    (a) GJNSY (b) EGJOF
    (c) BDGLU (d) ADIPY

21. In the following series, the number of letters skipped in between the adjacent letters are in ascending order, i.e., 1, 2, 3, 4. Which one of the following letter groups does not obey this rule?
    (a) HJMPT (b) DFIMR
    (c) GILPU (d) CEHLQ

22. Number of letters skipped in between adjacent letters in the series is in the order of 2, 5, 7, 10.
    (a) SYBFP (b) FNKOT
    (c) CEGLT (d) QTZHS

23. The letters are not according to a general rule.
    (a) ZBDFHJ (b) MORTVX
    (c) PRTVXZ (d) CEGIKM

24. Number of letters skipped in between adjacent letters in the series is odd.
    (a) MPRUX (b) EIMQV
    (c) FIMRX (d) BDHLR

25. Number of letters skipped in between adjacent letters in the series increases by one.
    (a) BDEGI (b) ACFJO
    (c) BFILN (d) None of these

Direction (26 to 28): Study the following arrangement of the English alphabet and answer the questions given below:

26. Which of the following pairs of letters has as many letters between them in the given arrangement as there are between them in the English alphabet?
    (a) MO (b) MR
    (c) EL (d) AI.

27. How many T's are there in the following sequence which are immediately preceded by P but not immediately followed by S?

    S T P Q T S P T R P T S T P S T Q P T R P T M P T S

    (a) One (b) Two
    (c) Three (d) None of these

28. How many L's are there which do not have R preceding them and also do not have T following them?

    Z Q S T L R M N Q N R T U V X R L T A S L T Q R S L T

    (a) 4 (b) 3
    (c) 2 (d) 1

Direction (29 to 30): Each of following questions is based on the following alphabet series.

29. If 1st and 26th, 2nd and 25th, 3rd and 24th, and so on, letters of the English alphabet are paired, then which of the following pairs is correct?
    (a) IP (b) EV
    (c) GR (d) CW

30. Which letter should be ninth letter to the left of ninth letter from the right, if the first half of the English alphabet is reversed?
    (a) E (b) F
    (c) I (d) D

Alphabet Test   133

Blood Relation Test   7

Learning Objectives : In this chapter, students will learn about:
- ✓ Solving questions related to patterns

CHAPTER SUMMARY

Blood relation test mainly deals with the hierarchical structure of a family i.e. grandparents, parents and children etc. Different relationships between the family members of different generations are given. To answer the questions related to blood relations, the entire family tree has to be drawn by putting the various relationships.

In such problems, the aptitude of candidate is shown by the knowledge of the various blood relations. The typical relationships that are commonly used in blood relation problems are summarized as follows.

	Relations	
1	Grandfather's son	Father or Uncle
2	Grandmother's son	Father or Uncle
3	Grandfather's only son	Father
4	Grandmother's only son	Father
5	Mother's or father's mother	Grandmother
6	Son's wife	Daughter-in-Law
7	Daughter's husband	Son-in-Law
8	Husband's or wife's sister	Sister-in-Law
9	Brother's son	Nephew
10	Brother's daughter	Niece
11	Uncle or aunt's son or daughter	Cousin
12	Sister's husband	Brother-in-Law
13	Brother's wife	Sister-in-Law
14	Grandson's or granddaughter's daughter	Great grand daughter

Solved Examples

Example 1: If A + B means A is the mother of B; A − B means A is the brother of B; A % B means A is the father of B and A × B means A is the sister of B, which of the following shows that P is the maternal uncle of Q?

(a) Q − N + M × P
(b) P + S × N − Q
(c) P − M + N × Q
(d) Q − S % P

Solution: Option (c) is correct.

Explanation: P − M → P is the brother of M

M + N → M is the mother of N

N × Q → N is the sister of Q

Therefore, P is the maternal uncle of Q.

Example 2: If A is the brother of B; B is the sister of C; and C is the father of D, how D is related to A?

(a) Brother
(b) Sister
(c) Nephew
(d) Insufficient data

Solution: Option (d) is correct.

Explanation: If D is Male, the answer is Nephew.

If D is Female, the answer is Niece.

As the sex of D is not known, hence, the relation between D and A cannot be determined.

Note: Niece: A daughter of one's brother or sister, or of one's brother-in-law or sister-in-law.

Nephew: A son of one's brother or sister, or of one's brother-in-law or sister-in-law.

Example 3: Pointing to a photograph of a boy Suresh said, "He is the son of the only son of my mother." How is Suresh related to that boy?

(a) Brother
(b) Uncle
(c) Cousin
(d) Father

Solution: Option (d) is correct.

Explanation: The boy in the photograph is the only son of the son of Suresh's mother i.e., the son of Suresh. Hence, Suresh is the father of boy.

MULTIPLE CHOICE QUESTIONS

1. Pointing to a man on the stage, Ritu said, "He is the brother of the daughter of the wife of my husband." How is the man on the stage related to Ritu?
   (a) Husband (b) Cousin
   (c) Nephew (d) Son

2. A party consists of grandmother, father, mother, four sons and their wives and one son and two daughters to each of the sons. How many females are there in all?
   (a) 14 (b) 19
   (c) 12 (d) 25

3. Lata and Mona are Ravi's wives. Shalu is Mona's Step-daughter. How is Lata related to Shalu?
   (a) Sister (b) Mother-in-Law
   (c) Mother (d) Step-mother

4. Deepak has a brother Amit. Deepak is the son of Chaya. Binod is Chaya's father. In terms of relationship, what is Amit of Binod?
   (a) Son (b) Grandson
   (c) Brother (d) Grandfather

5. Disha's mother is the only daughter of Mona's father. How is Mona's husband related to Disha?
   (a) Uncle (b) Father
   (c) Grandfather (d) Brother

6. If
   (a) M is brother of N
   (b) B is brother of N
   (c) M is brother of D

   then which of the following statements is definitely true?
   (a) N is brother of B
   (b) N is brother of D
   (c) M is brother of B
   (d) D is brother of M

7. Daya is brother of Raj. Rita is sister of Amit. Raj is son of Rita. How is Daya related to Rita?
   (a) Son (b) Brother
   (c) Nephew (d) Father

8. A is B's sister. C is B's mother. D is C's father. E is D's mother. Then, how is A related to D?
   (a) Grandmother (b) Grandfather
   (c) Daughter (d) Grand daughter

9. Given that:
   (1) A is brother of B
   (2) C is father of A
   (3) D is brother of E
   (4) E is daughter of B

   The uncle of D is
   (a) A (b) B
   (c) C (d) E

10. Pointing to Lalit in the photograph, Rajan said, "His mother has only one grandchild whose mother is my sister." How is Rajan related to Lalit?
    (a) Brother
    (b) Brother-in-law
    (c) Father-in-law
    (d) Data inadequate

11. Deepak said to Nitin, "The boy playing with the football is the younger of the two brothers of the daughter of my father's wife." How is the boy playing football related to Deepak?
    (a) Cousin (b) Brother
    (c) Son (d) Brother-in-law

12. B is the brother of A, S is the sister of B, E is the brother of D, D is the daughter of A, and F is the father of S. Then, the uncle of E is:
    (a) A (b) B
    (c) F (d) D

13. Introducing a boy, a girl said, "He is the only son of my mother's mother". How is the girl related to that boy?
    (a) Aunt (b) Niece
    (c) Sister (d) Mother

14. If Y says that his mother is the only daughter of X's mother, How is X' related to Y?
    (a) Niece (b) Brother
    (c) Cousin (d) Maternal uncle

15. Pointing to Sagar in a photograph, Manjula said, "His brother's father is the only son of my grandfather. "How is Manjula related to Sagar?
    (a) Aunt (b) Sister
    (c) Mother (d) Niece

16. Sia introduced Raghav as the son of the only daughter of the father of her uncle. How is Raghav related to Sia?
    (a) Brother
    (b) Cousin
    (c) Nephew
    (d) Can't be determined

17. Amit said, "The girl is the wife of the grandson of my mother". Who is Amit to the girl?
    (a) Father   (b) Grandfather
    (c) Husband   (d) Father-in-law

18. Introducing a woman, Nisha said, 'She is the daughter-in-law of the grandmother of my father's only son." How is the woman related to Nisha?
    (a) Grandmother   (b) Sister-in-law
    (c) Sister   (d) Mother

19. If A is the mother of D, B is not the son of C, C is the father of D, D is the sister of B, then how is A related to B?
    (a) Mother   (b) Brother
    (c) Step son   (d) Sister

20. Showing the lady in the park, Adarsh said, "She is the daughter of my grand-father's only son." How is Adarsh related to that lady?
    (a) Brother   (b) Father-in-law
    (c) Maternal uncle   (d) Husband

21. Pointing to a girl Sandeep said, "She is the daughter of the only sister of my father." How is Sandeep related to the girl?
    (a) Uncle   (b) Cousin
    (c) Father   (d) Grandfather

22. Pointing to a boy in the photograph Reena said, "He is the only son of the only child of my grandfather." How Reena is related to that boy?
    (a) Mother
    (b) Sister
    (c) Aunt
    (d) Cannot be determined

23. A is the son of C; C and Q are sisters; Z is the mother of Q and P is the son of Z. Which of the following statements is true?
    (a) P and A are cousins
    (b) P is the maternal uncle of A
    (c) Q is the maternal grandfather of A
    (d) C and P are sisters

24. If P + Q means P is the brother of Q; P × Q means P is the wife of Q, and P % Q means P is the daughter of Q, then which of the following means D is the maternal uncle of A?
    (a) A % B × C + D
    (b) A × B + C % D
    (c) A + C % B × D
    (d) None of these

25. P is the mother of K; K is the sister of D; D is the father of J. How is P related to J?
    (a) Mother
    (b) Grandmother
    (c) Aunt
    (d) Data is inadequate

26. Sanjay introduces Ravi as the son of the only brother of his father's wife. How is Ravi related to Sanjay?
    (a) Cousin   (b) Son
    (c) Son-in-law   (d) Uncle

27. Praveen said to Nilesh, "That boy playing with the football is the younger of the brothers of the daughter of my father's wife". How is the boy playing football related to Praveen?
    (a) Son   (b) Brother
    (c) Cousin   (d) Nephew

28. Raj told Anil, "Yesterday I defeated the only brother of the daughter of my grandmother". Who did Raj defeat?
    (a) Nephew   (b) Cousin
    (c) Son   (d) Father

29. Ankit is the son of Zubin. Manju is the daughter of Anil. Sheela is the mother of Manju. Mohan is the brother of Manju. How is Mohan related to Sheela?
    (a) Brother   (b) Father
    (c) Son   (d) None of these

30. Prakash is the son of Pramod. Neha is the daughter of Abhishek. Ruchi is the mother of Neha. Awadhesh is the brother of Neha. How is Awadhesh related to Ruchi?
    (a) Brother
    (b) Father
    (c) Son
    (d) Cannot be determined

Direction Sense Test   8

Learning Objectives : In this chapter, students will learn about:
- Solving questions related to direction sense test

CHAPTER SUMMARY

Direction
There are four main directions - East, West, North and South as shown below:

There are four cardinal directions - North-East (N-E), North-West (N-W), South-East (S-E), and South-West (S-W) as shown below:

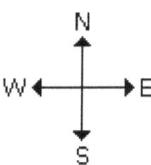

Some Important Points
1. At the time of sunrise if a man stands facing the east, his shadow will be towards west.
2. At the time of sunset the shadow of an object is always in the east.
3. If a man stands facing the North, at the time of sunrise his shadow will be towards his left and at the time of sunset it will be towards his right.
4. At 12:00 noon, the rays of the sun are vertically downward hence there will be no shadow.

Example 1: Siva starting from his house goes 5 km in the East, and then he turns to his left and goes 4 km. Finally he turns to his left and goes 5 km. Now how far is he from his house and in what direction?

Solution:

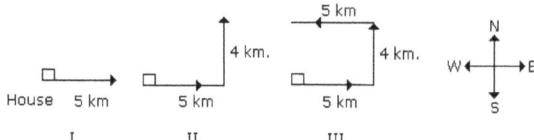

From third position it is clear he is 4 km from his house and is in North direction.

Example 2: Suresh starting from his house goes 4 km in the East, then he turns to his right and goes 3 km. What minimum distance will be covered by him to come back to his house?

Solution:

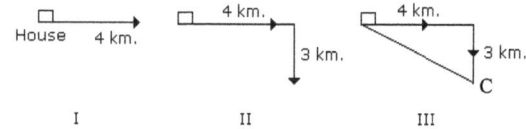

Minimum Distance

$$AC = \sqrt{(4)^2 + (3)^2}$$
$$= \sqrt{AB^2 + BC^2}$$

$$= \sqrt{16+9}$$
$$= \sqrt{25}$$
$$= 5 \text{ km}$$

Example 3: One morning after sunrise Juhi while going to school met Lalli at Boring road crossing. Lalli's shadow was exactly to the right of Juhi. If they were face to face, which direction was Juhi facing?

Solution: In the morning the sun rises in the East.

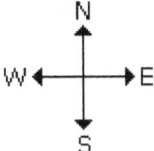

So in morning the shadow falls towards the West.

Now Lalli's shadow falls to the right of the Juhi. Hence Juhi is facing South.

MULTIPLE CHOICE QUESTIONS

1. From his house, Lokesh went 15 km to the North. Then he turned toward West and covered 10 km. Then he turned towards South and covered 5 km. Finally turning to the East, he covered 10 km. In which direction is he from his house?
   (a) East (b) West
   (c) North (d) South

2. Sachin walks 20 km towards North. He turns left and walks 40 km. He again turns left and walks 20 km. Finally he moves 20 km after turning to the left. How far is he from his starting position?
   (a) 20 km (b) 30 km
   (c) 50 km (d) 60 km

3. Sundar runs 20 m towards East and turns to right and runs 10 m. Then he turns to the right and runs 9 m. Again he turns to right and runs 5 m. After this he turns to left and runs 12 m and finally he turns to right and moves 6 m. Now to which direction is Sundar facing?
   (a) East (b) West
   (c) North (d) South

4. Radha moves a distance of 7 km towards South-East, then she moves towards West and travels a distance of 14 km. From here she moves towards North-West a distance of 7 km and finally she moves a distance of 4 km towards East. How far is she now from the starting point?
   (a) 3 km (b) 4 km
   (c) 10 km (d) 11 km

5. Village Q is to the North of the village P. The village R is in the East of village Q. The village S is to the left of the village P. In which direction is the village S with respect to village R?
   (a) East (b) South-West
   (c) South–East (d) North-West

6. Amit started walking positioning his back towards the sun. After some time, he turned left, then turned right and towards the left again. In which direction is he going now?
   (a) North or South (b) East or West
   (c) North or West (d) South or West

7. One morning after sunrise, Suresh was standing facing a pole. The shadow of the pole fell exactly to his right. To which direction was he facing?
   (a) East
   (b) South
   (c) West
   (d) Data is inadequate

8. A child went 90 m towards East to look for his father, then he turned right and went 20 m. After this he turned right and after going 30 m he reached his uncle's house. His father was not there. From there he went 100 m to his North and met his father. When he meet his father how for was he from the starting point?
   (a) 80 m (b) 100 m
   (c) 140 m (d) 260 m

9. Four friends A, B, C and D live in same locality. The house of B is in East of A's house but in the North of C's house. The house of C is in the West of D's house. D's house is in which direction of A's house?
   (a) South-East
   (b) North-East
   (c) East
   (d) Data is inadequate

10. After walking 6 km, I turned to the right and then walked 2 km. After that I turned to the left and walked 10 km. In the end, I was moving towards the North. From which direction did I start my journey?
    (a) North (b) South
    (c) East (d) West

11. Reena walked 10 feet from A to B towards East. Then she turned to the right and walked 3 feet. Again she turned to the right and walked 14 feet. How far is she from A?
    (a) 4 feet (b) 5 feet
    (c) 24 feet (d) 27 feet

12. If A × B means A is to the South of B; A + B means A is to the North of B; A % B means A is to the East of B; A - B means A is to the West of B; then in P % Q + R - S, S is in which direction with respect to Q?
    (a) South-West
    (b) South-East
    (c) North-East
    (d) North-West

13. One morning after sunrise, Vimal started to walk. During this walk he met Stephen who was coming from opposite direction. Vimal watched the shadow of Stephen to the right of him (Vimal). Which direction was Vimal facing?
    (a) East
    (b) West
    (c) South
    (d) Data inadequate

14. Golu started from his house towards North. After covering a distance of 8 km. he turned towards left and covered a distance of 6 km. What is the shortest distance now from his house?
    (a) 10 km
    (b) 16 km
    (c) 14 km
    (d) 2 km

15. P started from his house towards West. After walking a distance of 25 m, he turned to the right and walked 10 m. He then again turned to the right and walked 15 m. After this he is to turn right at 135° to his right and cover 30 m. In which direction should he go?
    (a) West
    (b) South
    (c) South-West
    (d) South-East

16. Rohit walked 25 m towards South. Then he turned to his left and walked 20 m. He then turned to his left and walked 25 m. He again turned to his right and walked 15 m. At what distance is he from the starting point and in which direction?
    (a) 35 m East
    (b) 35 m North
    (c) 30 m West
    (d) 45 m East

17. Umesh directly went from P to Q which is 9 feet distant. Then he turns to the right and walked 4 feet. After this he turned to the right and walked a distance which is equal from P to Q. Finally he turned to the right and walked 3 feet. How far is he now from P?
    (a) 6 feet
    (b) 5 feet
    (c) 1 feet
    (d) 0 feet

18. Ravi left home and cycled 10 km towards South, then turned right and cycled 5 km and then again turned right and cycled 10 km. After this he turned left and cycled 10 km. How many kilometers will he have to cycle to reach his home straight?
    (a) 10 km
    (b) 15 km
    (c) 20 km
    (d) 25 km

19. One morning after sunrise Nivedita and Niharika were talking to each other face to face at Dalphin crossing. If Niharika's shadow was exactly to the right of Nivedita, which direction was Niharika facing?
    (a) North
    (b) South
    (c) East
    (d) Data is inadequate

20. Shyam walks 5 km towards East and then turns left and walks 6 km. Again he turns right and walks 9 km. Finally he turns to his right and walks 6 km. How far is he from the starting point?
    (a) 26 km
    (b) 21 km
    (c) 14 km
    (d) 9 km

21. X started to walk straight towards South. After walking 5 m he turned to the left and walked 3 m. After this he turned to the right and walked 5 m. Now in which direction is X facing?
    (a) North-East
    (b) South
    (c) North
    (d) South-West

22. A boy rides his bicycle Northward, then turned left and rode 1 km and again turned left and rode 2 km. He found himself 1 km West of his starting point. How far did he ride Northward initially?
    (a) 1 km
    (b) 2 km
    (c) 3 km
    (d) 5 km

Direction Sense Test

Direction (23 to 25): Each of the following questions is based on the following information:

1. A # B means B is at 1 metre to the right of A.
2. A $ B means B is at 1 metre to the North of A.
3. A * B means B is at 1 metre to the left of A.
4. A @ B means B is at 1 metre to the south of A.
5. In each question the first person from the left is facing North.

23. According to X @ B * P, P is in which direction with respect to X?

(a) North (b) South
(c) North-East (d) South-West

24. According to M # N $ T, T is in which direction with respect to M?
(a) North-West (b) North-East
(c) South-West (d) South-East

25. According to P # R $ A * ; U in which direction with respect to P?
(a) East (b) West
(c) North (d) South

Number Ranking Test   9

Learning Objectives : In this chapter, students will learn about:
- Number test
- Rank test

CHAPTER SUMMARY

Number Test

In these types of questions, a set group or series of numerals is given. We have to study the series and conditions given and answer the question carefully.

Example 1: In the series given below how many 6's are there which are preceded by 9 and followed by 7.

8 2 3 9 6 7 4 7 6 9 1 5 9 6 7 2 8 8 9 6 7 3.

    (a) 2   (b) 3
    (c) 4   (d) 5

Solution: (b)

8 2 3 9 6 7 4 7 6 9 1 5 9 6 7 2 8 8 9 6 7 3

Example 2: In the series given below, how many 2's are there which are in between two odd numbers.

6 4 2 3 5 2 7 6 2 4 3 5 2 9 4 7 2 5 3 2 8

    (a) 1   (b) 2
    (c) 3   (d) 4

Solution: (c)

6 4 2 3 5 2 7 6 2 4 3 5 2 9 4 7 2 5 3 2 8

Example 3: What is the difference between the sum of odd digits and the sum of even digits in the number 6 2 9 7 4 8 3 1 5 ?

    (a) 4   (b) 5
    (c) 3   (d) 7

Solution: (b)

Sum of odd digits = 9 + 7 + 3 + 1 + 5 = 25
Sum of even digits = 6 + 2 + 4 + 8 = 20
Difference = 25 − 20 = 5

Example 4: Find the difference of greatest and smallest number formed by the digits 7, 6, 8, 9.

    (a) 3187   (b) 3087
    (c) 2987   (d) 3078

Solution: (b)

Greatest number = 9876

Smallest number = 6789

Difference = 9876 − 6789

                   = 3087

Rank Test

These questions are based on the position or rank of a person from top or bottom or from left end and right end. We have to consider the direction given and answer carefully.

Example 5: Sudhir ranks 24th from the top and 35th from the bottom. How many boys are there?

    (a) 58   (b) 57
    (c) 59   (d) 61

Solution: (a)

There are 23 boys who have position higher than Sudhir and then Sudhir and 34 boys have ranks lower than Sudhir.

Total number of boys = 23 + 1 + 34

                       = 24 + 34 = 58

Example 6: In a class of 35 students Kuntal is placed seventh from the bottom. Nirala is placed ninth from the top. Pintu is exactly in between these two. What is Kuntal's position from Pintu?

   (a) 9th   (b) 10th
   (c) 11th   (d) 12th

Solution: (b)
No. of students between Kuntal and Nirala
$= 35 - (7 + 9)$
$= 35 - 16 = 19$
19 is an odd number.
So, there are 9 students between Kuntal and Pintu.
So, Kuntal's position $= 9 + 1 = 10$th

Example 7: Nitu ranks 5th in a class. Silu is 8th from the last. If Tinu is 6th after Nitu and just in the middle of Nitu and Silu, find the total no. of students in the class.

   (a) 24   (b) 25
   (c) 26   (d) 27

Solution: (a)

$\xleftrightarrow{4}$ Nitu $\xleftrightarrow{5}$ Tinu $\xleftrightarrow{5}$ Silu $\xleftrightarrow{7}$

Total no. of students
$= 4 + 1 + 5 + 1 + 5 + 1 + 7$
$= 5 + 6 + 6 + 7$
$= 24$

MULTIPLE CHOICE QUESTIONS

Direction (1 to 8): Study the given number series and answer the questions based on it.

5 7 8 9 7 6 5 3 4 2 6 8 9 7 5 2 4 6 2 9 7 6 4 7 8 9 7 6

1. How many 7s are preceded by 9 and followed by 6?
   (a) 1 (b) 2
   (c) 3 (d) 4

2. Which digits have equal frequency?
   (a) 2, 5, 8 (b) 2, 5, 6
   (c) 4, 5, 9 (d) 3, 4, 9

3. Which digit has highest frequency?
   (a) 5 (b) 6
   (c) 7 (d) 9

4. Which digit has lowest frequency?
   (a) 2 (b) 3
   (c) 4 (d) 5

5. Which digit occurs five times?
   (a) 4 (b) 5
   (c) 6 (d) 7

6. How many times an even number is preceded by an odd number?
   (a) 2 (b) 3
   (c) 4 (d) 6

7. How many times two consecutive digits are odd numbers?
   (a) 4 (b) 5
   (c) 6 (d) 7

8. How many times digit 9 occurs?
   (a) 2 (b) 3
   (c) 4 (d) 5

Direction (9 to 12): Study the following five numbers and answer the questions given below :

617, 325, 639, 841, 592

9. What will be the first digit of the second highest number after the positions of only the second and third digits within each number are interchanged?
   (a) 6 (b) 9
   (c) 3 (d) 8

10. What will be the last digit of the third number from bottom when they are arranged in descending order after reversing the position of the digits within each number?
    (a) 2 (b) 3
    (c) 5 (d) 6

11. What will be the middle digit of 2nd lowest number after the position of only the first and second digits within each number are interchanged?
    (a) 3 (b) 2
    (c) 5 (d) 6

12. What will be the first digit of the second number from top when they are arranged in descending order after reversing the position of digits within each number?
    (a) 3 (b) 5
    (c) 7 (d) 6

13. What will be the difference between the sum of odd digits and the sum of even digits in the number 98675321?
    (a) 6 (b) 7
    (c) 9 (d) 8

14. A number is greater than 5 but less than 8. Also it is greater than 6 but less than 10. What is that number?
    (a) 6 (b) 7
    (c) 8 (d) 9

15. Find the difference of largest number and smallest number formed by the digits 2, 3, 7, 9.
    (a) 7353 (b) 7363
    (c) 7373 (d) 6353

Direction (16 to 20): Answer the questions based on the set of numbers given below.

687, 469, 158, 273, 894

16. Which of the following will be last digit of the highest number after the position of the digits in each number is reversed?
    (a) 1 (b) 2
    (c) 4 (d) 6

Number Ranking Test

17. Which of the following is the first digit of the highest number when first and third digits in the given numbers are interchanged?
    (a) 9 (b) 8
    (c) 7 (d) 6

18. What will be the difference between the first digit of the highest number as well as that of the lowest number after the position of the first two digit in each number are reversed?
    (a) 1 (b) 2
    (c) 3 (d) 4

19. Which of the following is the last digit of the second highest number after the position of the digits in each number is reversed?
    (a) 1 (b) 4
    (c) 6 (d) 8

20. Which of the following is the second digit of the third number from the top when they are arranged in descending order, after the first digit in each number is changed to its next higher digit?
    (a) 2 (b) 4
    (c) 6 (d) 8

21. A class of students stand in a single line. Mukesh's position is 26th from both the ends. How many students are there in the class?
    (a) 50 (b) 51
    (c) 52 (d) 53

22. Sunil ranks 24th in a class of 67 students. What is his rank from the last?
    (a) 42th (b) 43th
    (c) 44th (d) 45th

23. Rohan is 12 ranks ahead of Ranjan in a class of 57. If Ranjan's rank is 23 from the last, what is Rohan's rank from the start?
    (a) 21st (b) 22nd
    (c) 23rd (d) 24th

24. Jatin is 17th from the right end in a row of 60 students. What is his position from left end?
    (a) 44th (b) 43rd
    (c) 42th (d) 41st

25. How many numbers from 21 to 100 are there which are exactly divisible by 7 but not by 3?
    (a) 6 (b) 7
    (c) 8 (d) 9

26. How many numbers from 11 to 100 are there which are exactly divisible by 8 but not by 6?
    (a) 8 (b) 7
    (c) 9 (d) 6

27. How many combination of two digit numbers having 6 can be made from the following numbers?
    5, 9, 6, 7, 1, 8
    (a) 9 (b) 10
    (c) 11 (d) 12

28. If the numbers from 11 to 100 which are exactly divisible by 6 are arranged in ascending order (minimum number being on the top) which would come at the ninth place from the top?
    (a) 54 (b) 60
    (c) 48 (d) 66

29. Sukesh and Rajesh are ranked 6th and 13th respectively from the top in a class of 71 students. What will be their respective position from the bottom in the class?
    (a) 65 and 59 (b) 66 and 58
    (c) 66 and 59 (d) 67 and 59

30. Sujata is 8 ranks ahead of Sunita who ranks 23rd in a class of 50 students. What is Sujata's rank from the last?
    (a) 33rd (b) 34th
    (c) 35th (d) 36th

Odd One Out   10

Learning Objectives : In this chapter, students will learn about:
- ✓ Solving figure based questions related to odd one out

CHAPTER SUMMARY

In these types of questions, five figures named 1, 2, 3, 4, 5 are given; four of these five figures have common features/characteristics and hence are similar in a certain way. One of the figures does not share common characteristics and hence does not match with other figures. You have to select the figure which does not belong to this group and this figure is your answer.

Example 1: Choose the figure which is different from the rest.

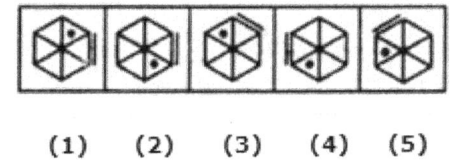

(1) (2) (3) (4) (5)

(a) 1   (b) 2
(c) 3   (d) 4
(e) 5

Solution: Option (b) is correct.

Explanation: In each one of the other figures, the small line segment lies one space ahead of the dot, in a CW direction.

Example 2: Choose the figure which is different from the rest.

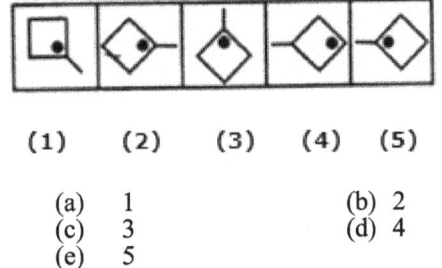

(1) (2) (3) (4) (5)

(a) 1   (b) 2
(c) 3   (d) 4
(e) 5

Solution: Option (d) is correct.

Explanation: In all other figures, the dot appears in the same corner of the square as the line outside it.

MULTIPLE CHOICE QUESTIONS

Direction (1 to 25): In each problem, out of the five figures marked (1), (2), (3), (4) and (5), four are similar in a certain manner. However, one figure is not like the other four.

1. Choose the figure which is different from the rest.

   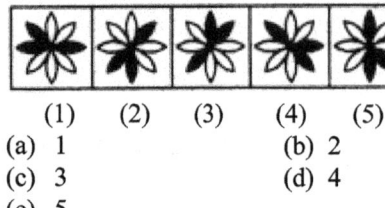

   (1)　(2)　(3)　(4)　(5)
   (a) 1　　　　(b) 2
   (c) 3　　　　(d) 4
   (e) 5

2. Choose the figure which is different from the rest.

   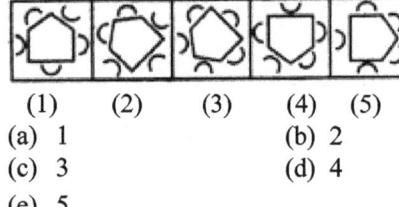

   (1)　(2)　(3)　(4)　(5)
   (a) 1　　　　(b) 2
   (c) 3　　　　(d) 4
   (e) 5

3. Choose the figure which is different from the rest.

   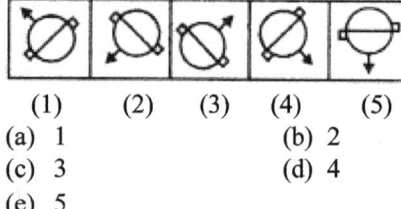

   (1)　(2)　(3)　(4)　(5)
   (a) 1　　　　(b) 2
   (c) 3　　　　(d) 4
   (e) 5

4. Choose the figure which is different from the rest.

   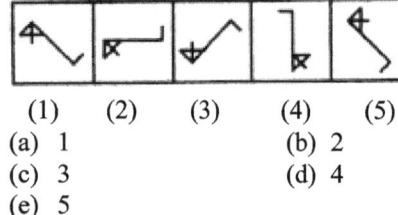

   (1)　(2)　(3)　(4)　(5)
   (a) 1　　　　(b) 2
   (c) 3　　　　(d) 4
   (e) 5

5. Choose the figure which is different from the rest.

   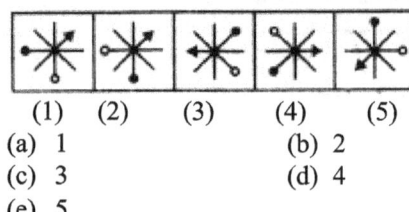

   (1)　(2)　(3)　(4)　(5)
   (a) 1　　　　(b) 2
   (c) 3　　　　(d) 4
   (e) 5

6. Choose the figure which is different from the rest.

   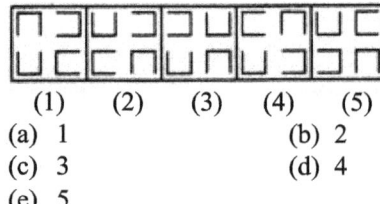

   (1)　(2)　(3)　(4)　(5)
   (a) 1　　　　(b) 2
   (c) 3　　　　(d) 4
   (e) 5

7. Choose the figure which is different from the rest.

   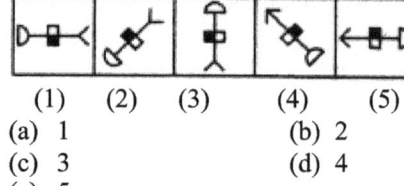

   (1)　(2)　(3)　(4)　(5)
   (a) 1　　　　(b) 2
   (c) 3　　　　(d) 4
   (e) 5

8. Choose the figure which is different from the rest.

   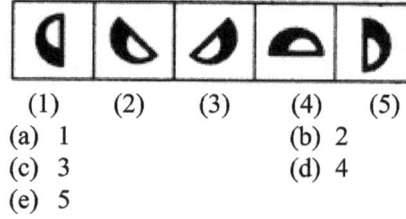

   (1)　(2)　(3)　(4)　(5)
   (a) 1　　　　(b) 2
   (c) 3　　　　(d) 4
   (e) 5

9. Choose the figure which is different from the rest.

   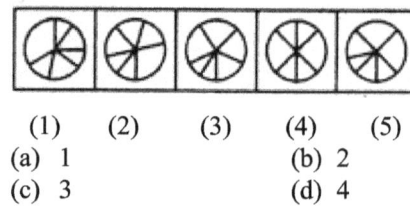

   (1)　(2)　(3)　(4)　(5)
   (a) 1　　　　(b) 2
   (c) 3　　　　(d) 4
   (e) 5

10. Choose the figure which is different from the rest.

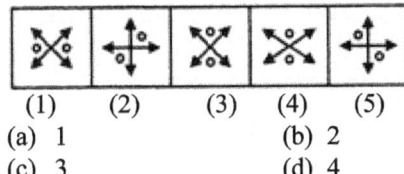

(1) (2) (3) (4) (5)
(a) 1 (b) 2
(c) 3 (d) 4
(e) 5

11. Choose the figure which is different from the rest.

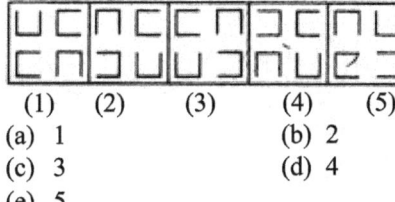

(1) (2) (3) (4) (5)
(a) 1 (b) 2
(c) 3 (d) 4
(e) 5

12. Choose the figure which is different from the rest.

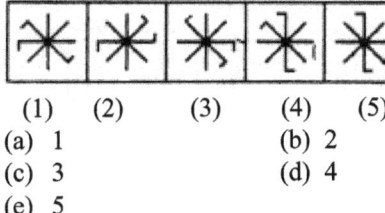

(1) (2) (3) (4) (5)
(a) 1 (b) 2
(c) 3 (d) 4
(e) 5

13. Choose the figure which is different from the rest.

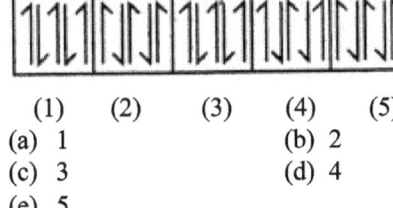

(1) (2) (3) (4) (5)
(a) 1 (b) 2
(c) 3 (d) 4
(e) 5

14. Choose the figure which is different from the rest.

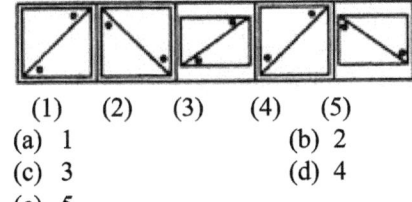

(1) (2) (3) (4) (5)
(a) 1 (b) 2
(c) 3 (d) 4
(e) 5

15. Choose the figure which is different from the rest.

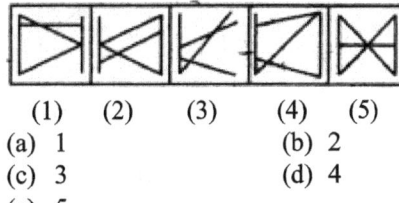

(1) (2) (3) (4) (5)
(a) 1 (b) 2
(c) 3 (d) 4
(e) 5

16. Choose the figure which is different from the rest.

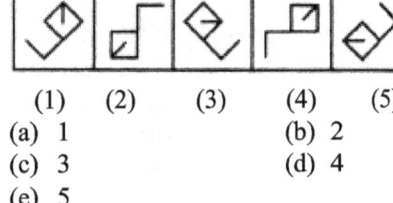

(1) (2) (3) (4) (5)
(a) 1 (b) 2
(c) 3 (d) 4
(e) 5

17. Choose the figure which is different from the rest.

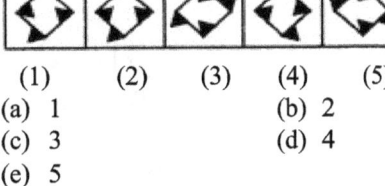

(1) (2) (3) (4) (5)
(a) 1 (b) 2
(c) 3 (d) 4
(e) 5

18. Choose the figure which is different from the rest.

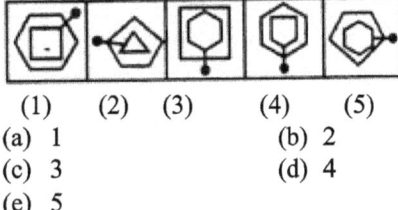

(1) (2) (3) (4) (5)
(a) 1 (b) 2
(c) 3 (d) 4
(e) 5

19. Choose the figure which is different from the rest.

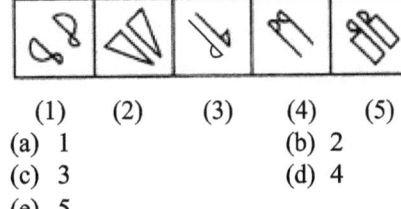

(1) (2) (3) (4) (5)
(a) 1 (b) 2
(c) 3 (d) 4
(e) 5

20. Choose the figure which is different from the rest.

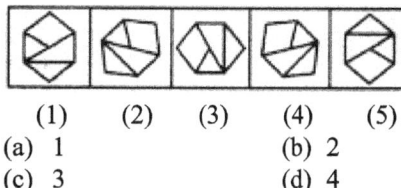

(1)	(2)	(3)	(4)	(5)

(a) 1 (b) 2
(c) 3 (d) 4
(e) 5

21. Choose the figure which is different from the rest.

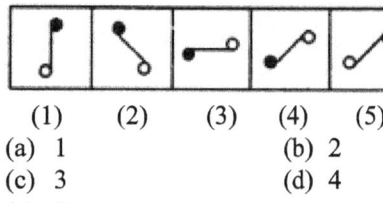

(1)	(2)	(3)	(4)	(5)

(a) 1 (b) 2
(c) 3 (d) 4
(e) 5

22. Choose the figure which is different from the rest.

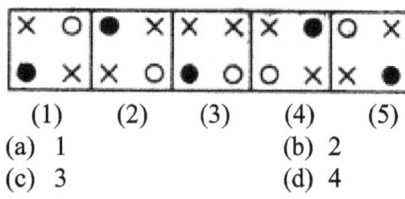

(1)	(2)	(3)	(4)	(5)

(a) 1 (b) 2
(c) 3 (d) 4
(e) 5

23. Choose the figure which is different from the rest.

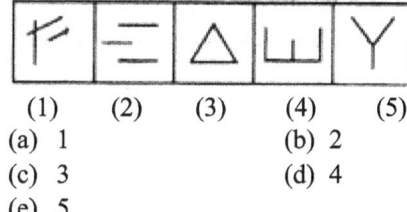

(1)	(2)	(3)	(4)	(5)

(a) 1 (b) 2
(c) 3 (d) 4
(e) 5

24. Choose the figure which is different from the rest.

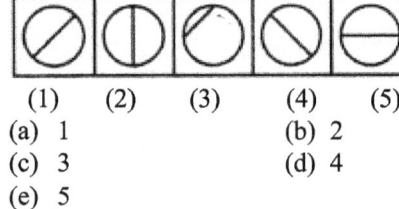

(1)	(2)	(3)	(4)	(5)

(a) 1 (b) 2
(c) 3 (d) 4
(e) 5

25. Choose the figure which is different from the rest.

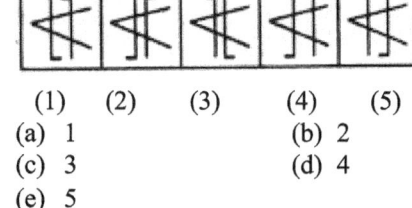

(1)	(2)	(3)	(4)	(5)

(a) 1 (b) 2
(c) 3 (d) 4
(e) 5

Dice 11

Learning Objectives: In this chapter, students will learn about:
- Solving questions related to Dice pattern

CHAPTER SUMMARY

Dice
Dice is a cube. In a cube there are 6 faces. Some important points are given below:

1. There are 6 faces in a cube - ABCG, GCDE, DEFH, BCDH, AGEF and ABHF.

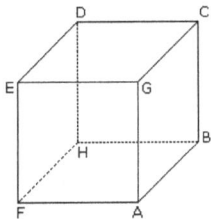

2. Always four faces are adjacent to one face.
3. Opposite of ABCG is DEFH and so on.
4. CDEG is the upper face of the cube.
5. ABHF is the bottom of the cube.

Important Rules
Rule No. 1.
Two opposite faces cannot be adjacent to one another.

Example 1: Two different positions of a dice are shown below. Which number will appear on the face opposite to the face with number 4?

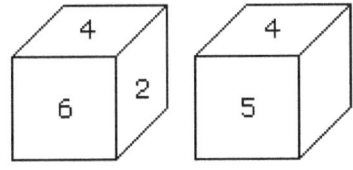

Solution: Faces with four numbers 6, 2, 5 and 3 are adjacent to the face with No. 4.

Hence the faces with no. 6, 2, 5 and 3 cannot be opposite to the face with no. 4.

Therefore the remaining face with no.1 will be the opposite of the face with no. 4.

Rule No. 2.
If two different positions of a dice are shown and one of the two common faces is in the same position, then the remaining faces will be opposite to each other.

Example 2: Two different positions of a dice are shown below.

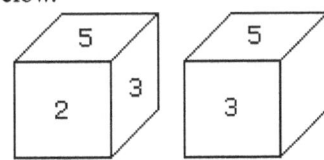

Solution: Here in both shown positions, two faces 5 and 3 are common.

The remaining faces are 2 and 4.

Hence, the number on the face opposite to the face with number 2 is 4.

Rule No. 3.
If in two different positions of a dice the position of a common face be the same, then each of the opposite faces of the remaining faces will be in the same position.

Example 3:

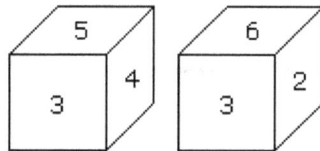

Solution: Here in both pictures positions of (3) is same.

Therefore, opposite of 5 is 6 and opposite of 4 is 2.

Rule No. 4.
If in two different positions of a dice, the position of the common face is not the same, then opposite face of the common face will be that which is not shown on any face in these two positions. Besides, the opposite faces of the remaining faces will not be the same.

Example 4:

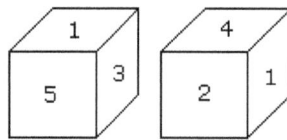

Solution: Here in two positions of a dice the face with number 1 is not in the same position.

The face with number 6 is not shown.

Hence, the face opposite to the face with number 1 is 6.

Besides the opposite face of 3 will be the face with number 2 and opposite face to face 5 will be the face with number 1.

Solved Examples

Example 5: Two positions of a dice are shown below. Which number will appear on the face opposite to the face with the number 5?

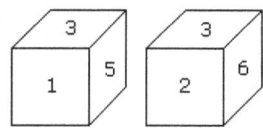

(a) 3 (b) 2
(c) 6 (d) 4

Solution: Option (c) is correct.

Explanation: According to the rule number (3), common faces with number 3 are in same positions. Hence, the number of the face opposite to face with number 5 will be 6.

Example 6: How many dots will be there on the face opposite to the face which contains 2 dots?

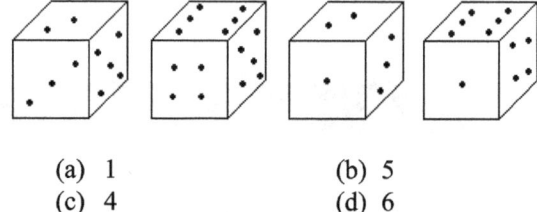

(a) 1 (b) 5
(c) 4 (d) 6

Solution: Option (d) is correct.

Explanation: In first two positions of the dice one common face containing 5 is same. Therefore according to rule number (3) the face opposite to the face which contains 2 dots will contain 6 dots.

Example 7: Two positions of a dice are shown below. When number '1' is on the top, what number will be at the bottom?

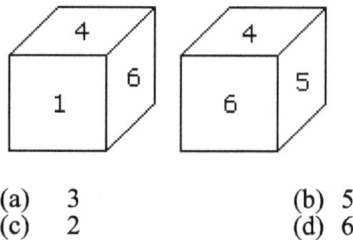

(a) 3 (b) 5
(c) 2 (d) 6

Solution: Option (b) is correct.

Explanation: According to the rule (2) when 'one' is at the top, then 5 will be at the bottom.

MULTIPLE CHOICE QUESTIONS

1. The positions of a cube are shown below, Which letter will be on the face opposite to face with 'A'?

   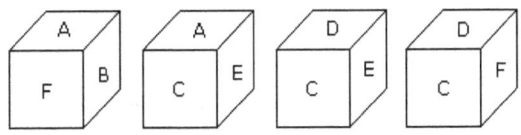

   (a) D (b) B
   (c) C (d) F

2. Two positions of a dice are shown below. When 3 dots are at the bottom, how many dots will be at the top?

   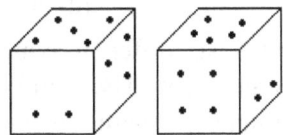

   (a) 2 (b) 5
   (c) 4 (d) 6

3. Observe the dots on the dice (one to six dots) in the following figures. How many dots are contained on the face opposite to the face containing four dots?

   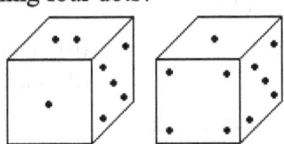

   (a) 2 (b) 3
   (c) 5 (d) 6

4. How many dots will be on the face opposite to the face which contains 3 dots?

   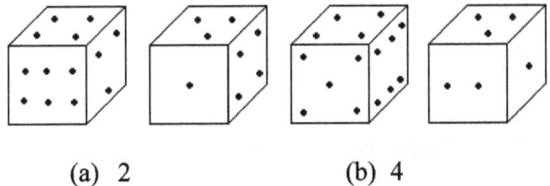

   (a) 2 (b) 4
   (c) 5 (d) 6

5. When the digit 5 is on the bottom, which number will be on its upper surface?

   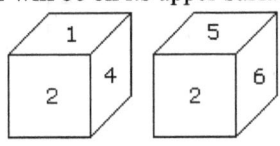

   (a) 1 (b) 3
   (c) 4 (d) 6

6. From the four positions of a dice given below, find the colour which is opposite to yellow?

   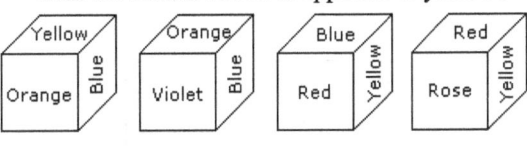

   (a) Violet (b) Red
   (c) Rose   (d) Blue

7. Two positions of a cubical block are shown. When 5 is at the top, which number will be at bottom?

   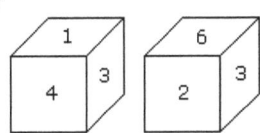

   (a) 1 (b) 2
   (c) 3 (d) 4

8. Here 4 positions of a cube are shown. Which sign will be opposite to '+'?

   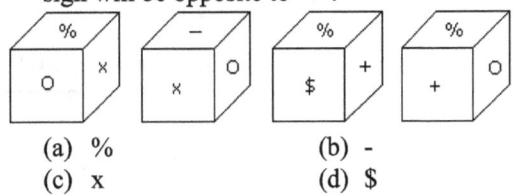

   (a) % (b) -
   (c) x (d) $

9. Two positions of a dice are shown below. How many dots will be on the top when 2 dots are at the bottom?

   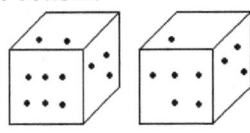

   (a) 6 (b) 5
   (c) 4 (d) 1

Dice

10. Here two positions of a dice are shown. If there are two dots in the bottom, then how many dots will be on the top?

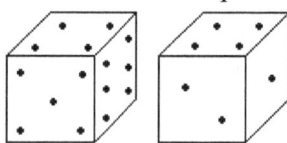

(a) 2 (b) 3
(c) 5 (d) 6

11. Two positions of a cube with its numbered surfaces are shown below. When the surface 4 touches the bottom, which surface will be on the top?

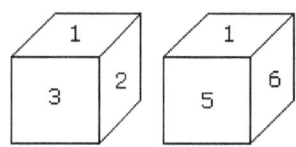

(a) 1 (b) 2
(c) 5 (d) 6

12. Two positions of a dice are shown below. When number '1' is on the top. What number will be at the bottom?

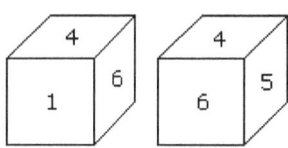

(a) 3 (b) 5
(c) 2 (d) 6

13. Which number is on the face opposite to 6?

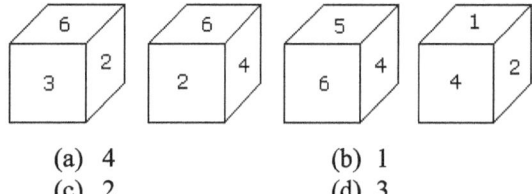

(a) 4 (b) 1
(c) 2 (d) 3

14. Six dice with upper faces erased are shown as:

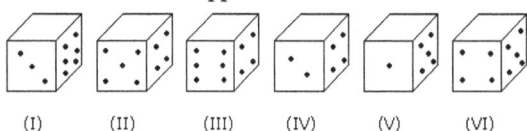

(I) (II) (III) (IV) (V) (VI)

The sum of the numbers of dots on the opposite face is 7.

If even numbered dice have even number of dots on their top faces, then what would be the total number of dots on the top faces of their dice?

(a) 12 (b) 14
(c) 18 (d) 24

15. How many dots will be on the face opposite to the face which contains 2 dots?

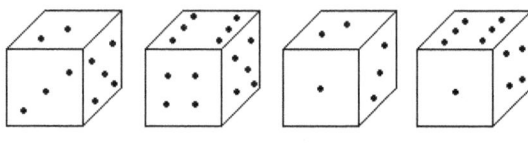

(a) 1 (b) 5
(c) 4 (d) 6

16. A cube has six different symbols drawn over its six faces. The symbols are dot, circle, triangle, square, cross and arrow. Three different positions of the cube are shown in figures X, Y, and Z. Which symbol is opposite the arrow?

(X) (Y) (Z)

(a) Circle (b) Triangle
(c) Dot (d) Cross

17. Given below are three different positions of a dice. Find the number of dots on the face opposite the face bearing 3 dots.

(i) (ii) (iii)

(a) 4
(b) 5
(c) 6
(d) Cannot be determined

18. Which number is on the face opposite 4, if the four different positions of a dice are as shown in the figure given below.

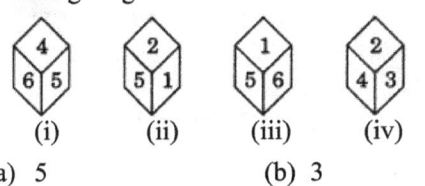

(a) 5 (b) 3
(c) 2 (d) 1

19. A cube has six different symbols drawn over its six faces. The symbols are dot, circle, triangle, square, cross and arrow. Three different positions of the cube are shown in figures X, Y, and Z.

Which symbol occurs at the bottom of fig. (Y)?

(X)　　　(Y)　　　(Z)

(a) Arrow (b) Triangle
(c) Circle (d) Dot

20. A dice is numbered from 1 to 6 in different ways.

If 1 is adjacent to 2, 4 and 6, then which of the following statements is necessarily true?
(a) 2 is opposite to 6
(b) 1 is adjacent to 3
(c) 3 is adjacent to 5
(d) 3 is opposite to 5

Mirror Images 12

Learning Objectives : In this chapter, students will learn about:
- ✓ Mirror images of letter
- ✓ Mirror images of number

CHAPTER SUMMARY

Mirror Image

The image of an object as seen in a mirror is called its mirror reflection or mirror image.

In a mirror image, the right part of an object appears at the left side and vice- versa, but the upper and lower parts remain the same. Observe the following mirror images:

Object	Mirror Image	Object Mirror Image	Object	Mirror Image

Lateral Inversion: In such an image, the right side of the object appears on the left side and vice - versa. A mirror - image is therefore said to be laterally inverted and the phenomenon is called Lateral Inversion.

Mirror Images of Capital Letters

Letters	Mirror Image	Letters	Mirror Image	Letters	Mirror Image
A	A	J	L	S	Ƨ
B	ꓭ	K	ꓘ	T	T
C	Ɔ	L	⅃	U	U
D	ꓷ	M	M	V	V
E	Ǝ	N	И	W	W
F	ꓞ	O	O	X	X
G	ꓨ	P	ꟼ	Y	Y
H	H	Q	Ọ	Z	Ƨ
I	I	R	Я		

Mirror Images of Small Letters

Letters	Mirror Image	Letters	Mirror Image	Letters	Mirror Image
a	ɒ	j	ᶑ	s	ƨ
b	d	k	ʞ	t	ƚ
c	ɔ	l	l	u	u
d	b	m	m	v	v
e	ɘ	n	n	w	w
f	ꞙ	o	o	x	x
g	ǫ	p	q	y	ʏ
h	ʜ	q	p	z	z
i	i	r	ɿ		

Mirror Images of Numbers

Letters	Mirror Image	Letters	Mirror Image	Letters	Mirror Image
1	1	4	ᔰ	7	٢
2	S	5	ट	8	8
3	Ɛ	6	ꓯ	9	ꓷ

MULTIPLE CHOICE QUESTIONS

Direction (1 to 15): In each of the following questions you are given a combination of alphabets and/or numbers followed by four alternatives (1), (2), (3) and (4).

1. Choose the alternative which closely resembles the mirror-image of the given combination.
   UTZFY6KH
   (1) HK9YFZTU (2) UTZFY9KH
   (3) HK6YFZTU (4) HK6YFZTU
   (a) 1 (b) 2
   (c) 3 (d) 4

2. Choose the alternative which closely resembles the mirror-image of the given combination.
   AN54WMG3
   (1) AN54WMG3 (2) 3GMW45NA
   (3) 3GMW45NA (4) 3GMW45NA
   (a) 1 (b) 2
   (c) 3 (d) 4

3. Choose the alternative which closely resembles the mirror-image of the given combination.
   SUPERVISOR
   (1) SUPERVISOR (2) SUPERVISOR
   (3) ROSIVREPUS (4) SUPERVIOSR
   (a) 1 (b) 2
   (c) 3 (d) 4

4. Choose the alternative which closely resembles the mirror-image of the given combination.
   MAGAZINE
   (1) MAGAZINE (2) ENIZAGAM
   (3) MAGAZINE (4) ENIZAGAM
   (a) 1 (b) 2
   (c) 3 (d) 4

5. Choose the alternative which closely resembles the mirror-image of the given combination.
   DL9CG4728
   (1) DL9CG4728 (2) 8274GC9LD
   (3) DL9CG4728 (4) 8274GC9LD
   (a) 1 (b) 2
   (c) 3 (d) 4

6. Choose the alternative which closely resembles the mirror-image of the given combination.
   PAINTED
   (1) PAINTED (2) PAINTED
   (3) PAINTED (4) PAINTED
   (a) 1 (b) 2
   (c) 3 (d) 4

7. Choose the alternative which closely resembles the mirror-image of the given combination.
   NATIONAL
   (1) NATIONAL (2) NATIONAL
   (3) NATIONAL (4) LANOITAN
   (a) 1 (b) 2
   (c) 3 (d) 4

8. Choose the alternative which closely resembles the mirror-image of the given combination.
   GEOGRAPHY
   (1) GEOGRAPHY (2) YHPARGOEG
   (3) GEOGRAPHY (4) GEOGRAPHY
   (a) 1 (b) 2
   (c) 3 (d) 4

9. Choose the alternative which closely resembles the mirror-image of the given combination.
   BR4AQ16HI
   (1) BR4AQ16HI (2) BR4AQ16HI
   (3) BR4AQ16HI (4) BR4AQ16HI
   (a) 1 (b) 2
   (c) 3 (d) 4

10. Choose the alternative which closely resembles the mirror-image of the given combination.
    247596
    (1) 695742 (2) 247596
    (3) 695742 (4) 247596
    (a) 1 (b) 2
    (c) 3 (d) 4

11. Choose the alternative which closely resembles the mirror-image of the given combination.
    NiCaRaGuA
    (1) AuGaRaCiN (2) AnGaRaCiN
    (3) AnGaRaCiN (4) AuGaRaCiN
    (a) 1 (b) 2
    (c) 3 (d) 4

Mirror Images 157

12. Choose the alternative which closely resembles the mirror-image of the given combination.
    COLONIAL
    (1) LAINOLOƆ   (2) ꓘAINOLOƆ
    (3) ΓAIꓕOΓOC   (4) ꓘAIꓕOꓕAꓕ
    (a) 1   (b) 2
    (c) 3   (d) 4

13. Choose the alternative which closely resembles the mirror-image of the given combination.
    BR4AQ16HI
    (1) IH6IQA4RB   (2) IH61QA4RB
    (3) IH6IQA4RB   (4) IH91QA4RB
    (a) 1   (b) 2
    (c) 3   (d) 4

14. Choose the alternative which closely resembles the mirror-image of the given combination.
    EMANATE
    (1) EMANATE   (2) ETANAME
    (3) ETANAME   (4) EATEMAN
    (a) 1   (b) 2
    (c) 3   (d) 4

15. Choose the alternative which closely resembles the mirror-image of the given combination.
    KALINGA261B
    (1) KALINGA261B   (2) B162AGNILAK
    (3) B261KALINGA   (4) KALINGA261B
    (a) 1   (b) 2
    (c) 3   (d) 4

Direction (16 to 30): In each of the following questions, choose the correct mirror image of the given image of the Fig.(X) from amongst the four alternatives (1), (2), (3) and (4) given along with it.

16. Choose the correct mirror image of the given figure (X) from amongst the four alternatives.

 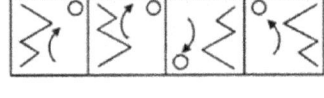

(a) 1   (b) 2
(c) 3   (d) 4

17. Choose the correct mirror image of the given figure (X) from amongst the four alternatives.

 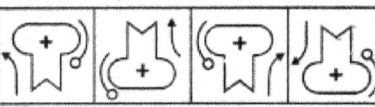

(X)   (1)   (2)   (3)   (4)
(a) 1   (b) 2
(c) 3   (d) 4

18. Choose the correct mirror image of the given figure (X) from amongst the four alternatives.

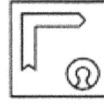 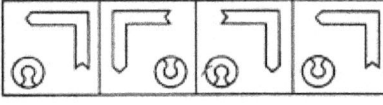

(X)   (1)   (2)   (3)   (4)
(a) 1   (b) 2
(c) 3   (d) 4

19. Choose the correct mirror image of the given figure (X) from amongst the four alternatives.

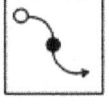 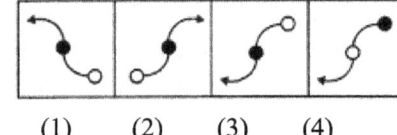

(X)   (1)   (2)   (3)   (4)
(a) 1   (b) 2
(c) 3   (d) 4

20. Choose the correct mirror image of the given figure (X) from amongst the four alternatives.

 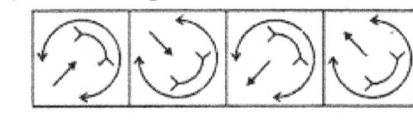

(X)   (1)   (2)   (3)   (4)
(a) 1   (b) 2
(c) 3   (d) 4

21. Choose the correct mirror image of the given figure (X) from amongst the four alternatives.

 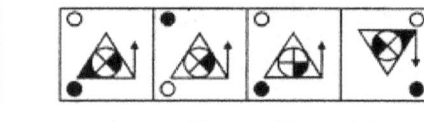

(X)   (1)   (2)   (3)   (4)
(a) 1   (b) 2
(c) 3   (d) 4

22. Choose the correct mirror image of the given figure (X) from amongst the four alternatives.

 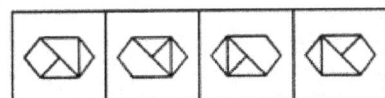

(X) (1) (2) (3) (4)
(a) 1 (b) 2
(c) 3 (d) 4

23. Choose the correct mirror image of the given figure (X) from amongst the four alternatives.

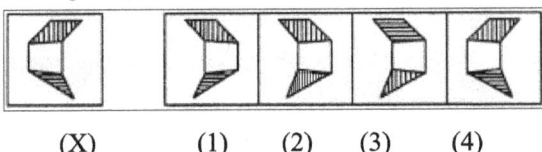

(X) (1) (2) (3) (4)
(a) 1 (b) 2
(c) 3 (d) 4

24. Choose the correct mirror image of the given figure (X) from amongst the four alternatives.

 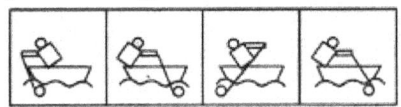

(X) (1) (2) (3) (4)
(a) 1 (b) 2
(c) 3 (d) 4

25. Choose the correct mirror image of the given figure (X) from amongst the four alternatives.

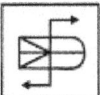 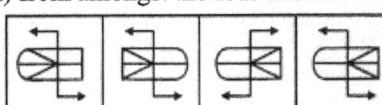

(X) (1) (2) (3) (4)
(a) 1 (b) 2
(c) 3 (d) 4

26. Choose the correct mirror image of the given figure (X) from amongst the four alternatives.

 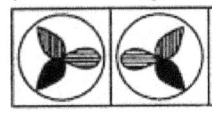 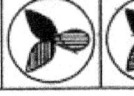 

(X) (1) (2) (3) (4)

(a) 1 (b) 2
(c) 3 (d) 4

27. Choose the correct mirror image of the given figure (X) from amongst the four alternatives.

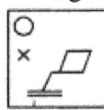 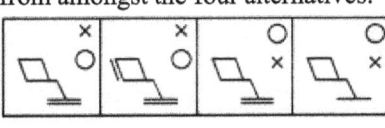

(X) (1) (2) (3) (4)
(a) 1 (b) 2
(c) 3 (d) 4

28. Choose the correct mirror image of the given figure (X) from amongst the four alternatives.

 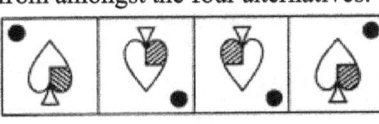

(X) (1) (2) (3) (4)
(a) 1 (b) 2
(c) 3 (d) 4

29. Choose the correct mirror image of the given figure (X) from amongst the four alternatives.

 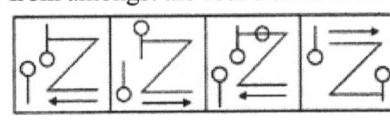

(X) (1) (2) (3) (4)
(a) 1 (b) 2
(c) 3 (d) 4

30. Choose the correct mirror image of the given figure (X) from amongst the four alternatives.

 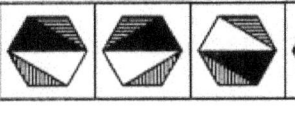

(X) (1) (2) (3) (4)
(a) 1 (b) 2
(c) 3 (d) 4

Mirror Images

Water Images — 13

Learning Objectives : In this chapter, students will learn about:
- ✓ Water images of letter
- ✓ Water images of number

CHAPTER SUMMARY

Water Image
The reflection of an object as seen in water is called its water image. It is the inverted image obtained by turning the object upside down.

Water Images of Capital Letters

Letters	A	B	C	D	E	F	G	H	I
Water Images	∀	B	C	D	E	ⱻ	ᑢ	H	I
Letters	J	K	L	M	N	O	P	Q	R
Water Images	ᒐ	K	Γ	W	И	O	ᑲ	Ό	ᖇ
Letters	S	T	U	V	W	X	Y	Z	--
Water Images	ƨ	⊥	∩	∧	M	X	⋏	Σ	--

Water Images of Small Letters

Letters	a	b	c	d	e	f	g	h	i
Water Images	ɐ	p	c	q	ǝ	ɟ	ɑ	ɥ	!
Letters	j	k	l	m	n	o	p	q	r
Water Images	!	ĸ	l	ɯ	u	o	b	d	ɾ
Letters	s	t	u	v	w	x	y	z	--
Water Images	ƨ	ɟ	n	ʌ	ʍ	x	λ	ƨ	--

Water Images of Numbers

Letters	0	1	2	3	4	5	6	7	8	9
Water Images	0	1	S	3	4	2	6	7	8	9

Notes :

- The letters whose water images remain unchanged are:
  C, D, E, H, I, K, O and X
- Certain words which have identical water images are:
  KICK, KID, CHIDE, HIKE, CODE, CHICK

Solved Examples

Example 1: Choose the correct water image of the given figure (X) from amongst the four alternatives.

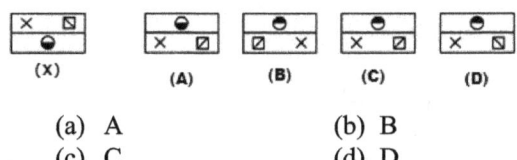

(a) A (b) B
(c) C (d) D

Solution: Option (c) is correct.

Example 2: Choose the correct water image of the given figure (X) from amongst the four alternatives.

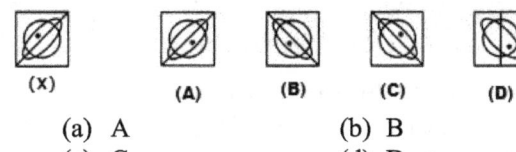

(a) A (b) B
(c) C (d) D

Solution: Option (b) is correct.

Example 3: Choose the alternative which closely resembles the water-image of the given combination.

TUceh96

(A) ୧ଟ୩ଠUT   (B) ୨୧ꟼecUT
(C) TUɔɘհ୨୧   (D) ꓕՈcehୡ୨

(a) A (b) B
(c) C (d) D

Solution: Option (d) is correct.

Example 4: Choose the alternative which closely resembles the water-image of the given combination.

XYZO48SX

(A) X284OƧYX   (B) XYƧO48SX
(C) X284OƧYX   (D) X284OƧYX

(a) A (b) B
(c) C (d) D

Solution: Option (b) is correct.

MULTIPLE CHOICE QUESTIONS

Direction (1 to 15): In each of the following questions, choose the water image of the Fig.(X) from amongst the four alternatives (A), (B), (C) and (D) given along with it.

1.
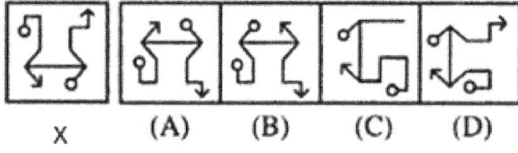
 (a) A (b) B
 (c) C (d) D

2.
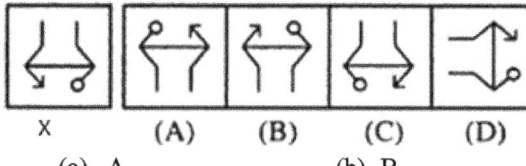
 (a) A (b) B
 (c) C (d) D

3.
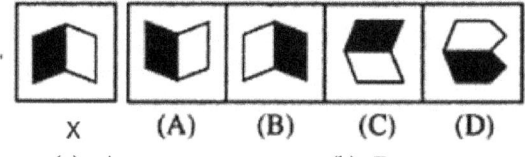
 (a) A (b) B
 (c) C (d) D

4.
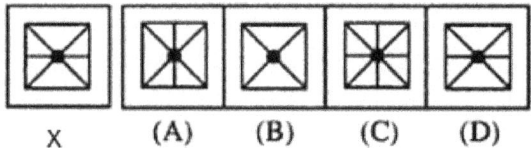
 (a) A (b) B
 (c) C (d) D

5.
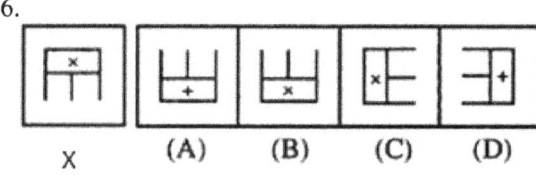
 (a) A (b) B
 (c) C (d) D

6.
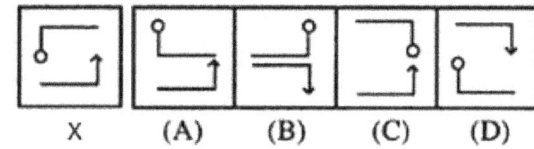
 (a) A (b) B
 (c) C (d) D

7.
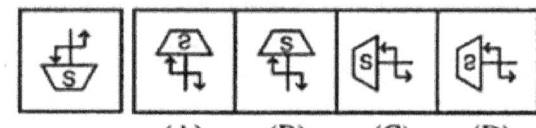
 (a) A (b) B
 (c) C (d) D

8.
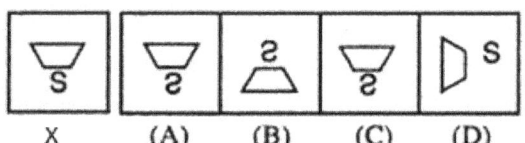
 (a) A (b) B
 (c) C (d) D

9.
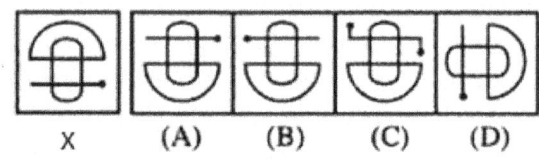
 (a) A (b) B
 (c) C (d) D

10.

11.

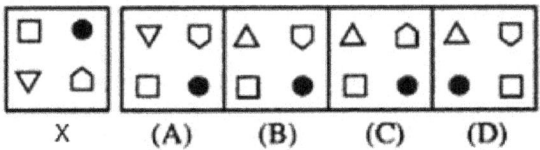

(a) A (b) B
(c) C (d) D

12.

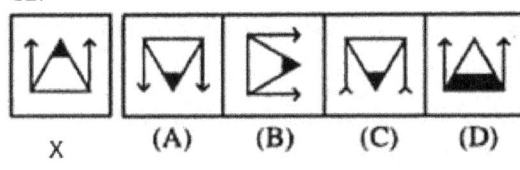

(a) A (b) B
(c) C (d) D

13.

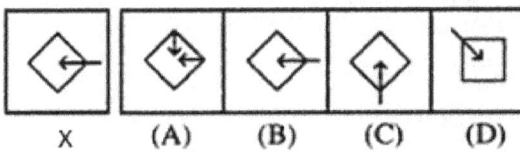

(a) A (b) B
(c) C (d) D

14.

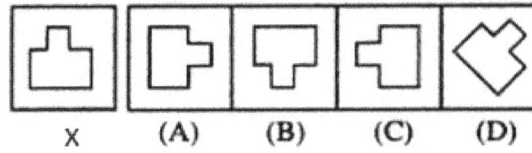

(a) A (b) B
(c) C (d) D

15.

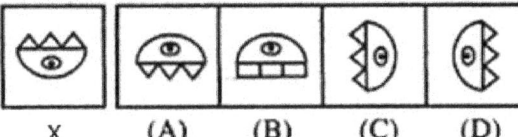

(a) A (b) B
(c) C (d) D

Direction (16 to 30): In each of the following questions, you are given a combination of alphabets and/or numbers followed by four alternatives (A), (B), (C) and (D).

16. Choose the alternative which closely resembles the water-image of the given combination.

    CDEF
    (A) CDEF̵ (B) CDEF
    (C) FEDC (D) FEDC (inverted)
    (a) A (b) B
    (c) C (d) D

17. Choose the alternative which closely resembles the water-image of the given combination.

    XYZ
    (A) XYZ (B) ZYX (inverted)
    (C) XZY (D) ZYX
    (a) A (b) B
    (c) C (d) D

18. Choose the alternative which closely resembles the water-image of the given combination.

    01234
    (A) 01534 (B) 43210
    (C) 01324 (D) 01534 (inverted)
    (a) A (b) B
    (c) C (d) D

19. Choose the alternative which closely resembles the water-image of the given combination.

    CHICK
    (A) CHICK (inverted) (B) KCIHC (inverted)
    (C) KCIHC (D) CHICK
    (a) A (b) B
    (c) C (d) D

20. Choose the alternative which closely resembles the water-image of the given combination.

    CODE
    (A) CODE (B) EDOC
    (C) CODE (inverted) (D) EDOC (inverted)
    (a) A (b) B
    (c) C (d) D

21. Choose the alternative which closely resembles the water-image of the given combination.

    HIKE

    (A) HIKE (B) EKIH
    (C) HIKE (mirrored vertically) (D) HIKE (mirrored vertically)

    (a) A (b) B
    (c) C (d) D

22. Choose the alternative which closely resembles the water-image of the given combination.

    CHIDE

    (A) CHIDE (mirrored) (B) CHIDE (mirrored)
    (C) EDIHC (D) CHIDE

    (a) A (b) B
    (c) C (d) D

23. Choose the alternative which closely resembles the water-image of the given combination.

    SUBHAM

    (A) SUBHAM (mirrored) (B) MAHBUS (mirrored)
    (C) SUBHAM (mirrored) (D) MAHBUS

    (a) A (b) B
    (c) C (d) D

24. Choose the alternative which closely resembles the water-image of the given combination.

    U4P15B7

    (A) U4P15B7 (mirrored) (B) U4P15B7 (mirrored variant)
    (C) U4P15B7 (mirrored) (D) U4P15B7

    (a) A (b) B
    (c) C (d) D

25. Choose the alternative which closely resembles the water-image of the given combination.

    96FSH52

    (A) 96FSH52 (mirrored) (B) 25HSF69
    (C) 96FSH52 (mirrored variant) (D) 25HSF69 variant

    (a) A (b) B
    (c) C (d) D

26. Choose the alternative which closely resembles the water-image of the given combination.

    US91Q4M5W3

    (A) US91Q4M5W3 (mirrored) (B) US91Q4M5W3 (mirrored)
    (C) US91Q4M5W3 (mirrored) (D) US91Q4M5W3 (mirrored)

    (a) A (b) B
    (c) C (d) D

27. Choose the alternative which closely resembles the water-image of the given combination.

    rise

    (A) rise (mirrored) (B) esir
    (C) rise (mirrored) (D) rise (inverted)

    (a) A (b) B
    (c) C (d) D

28. Choose the alternative which closely resembles the water-image of the given combination.

    BK50RP62

    (A) BK50RP62 (mirrored) (B) BK50RP62 (mirrored)
    (C) BK50RP62 (mirrored) (D) BK50RP62 (mirrored)

    (a) A (b) B
    (c) C (d) D

29. Choose the alternative which closely resembles the water-image of the given combination.

    NhRqSy

    (A) NhRqSy (mirrored) (B) NhRqSy (mirrored)
    (C) NhRqSy (mirrored) (D) NhRqSy (mirrored)

    (a) A (b) B
    (c) C (d) D

30. Choose the alternative which closely resembles the water-image of the given combination.

    MNOP

    (A) MNOP (mirrored) (B) PONM
    (C) MNOP (mirrored) (D) MNOP

    (a) A (b) B
    (c) C (d) D

Embedded Figures   14

Learning Objectives : In this chapter, students will learn about:
✓ Solving questions related to embedded figures

CHAPTER SUMMARY

Embedded Figure

A figure A is said to be embedded in figure B, if figure B contains figure A as its part. Many types of problems can be formed on embedded figures.

In such type of problems, we have a problem figure represented by X followed by four alternative figures A, B, C and D. One has to locate the correct alternative in which the figure X is embedded. The following examples will clarify.

Example 1:

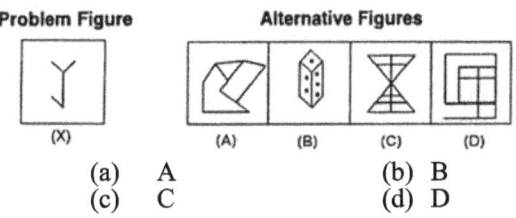

(a) A   (b) B
(c) C   (d) D

Solution: Option (b) is correct.

Explanation:

Example 2: Find out the alternative figure which contains figure (X) as its part.

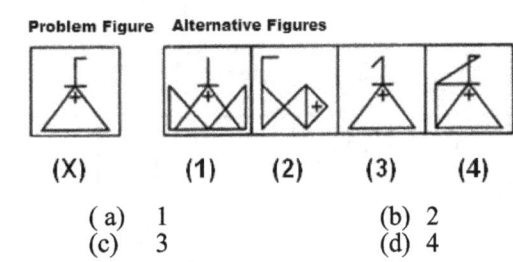

(a) 1   (b) 2
(c) 3   (d) 4

Solution: Option (d) is correct.

Explanation:

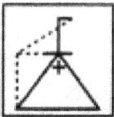

MULTIPLE CHOICE QUESTIONS

Direction (1 to 30): In each of the following questions, you are given a figure (X) followed by four alternative figures (A), (B), (C) and (D) such that figure (X) is embedded in one of them. Find out the alternative figure which contains figure (X) as its part.

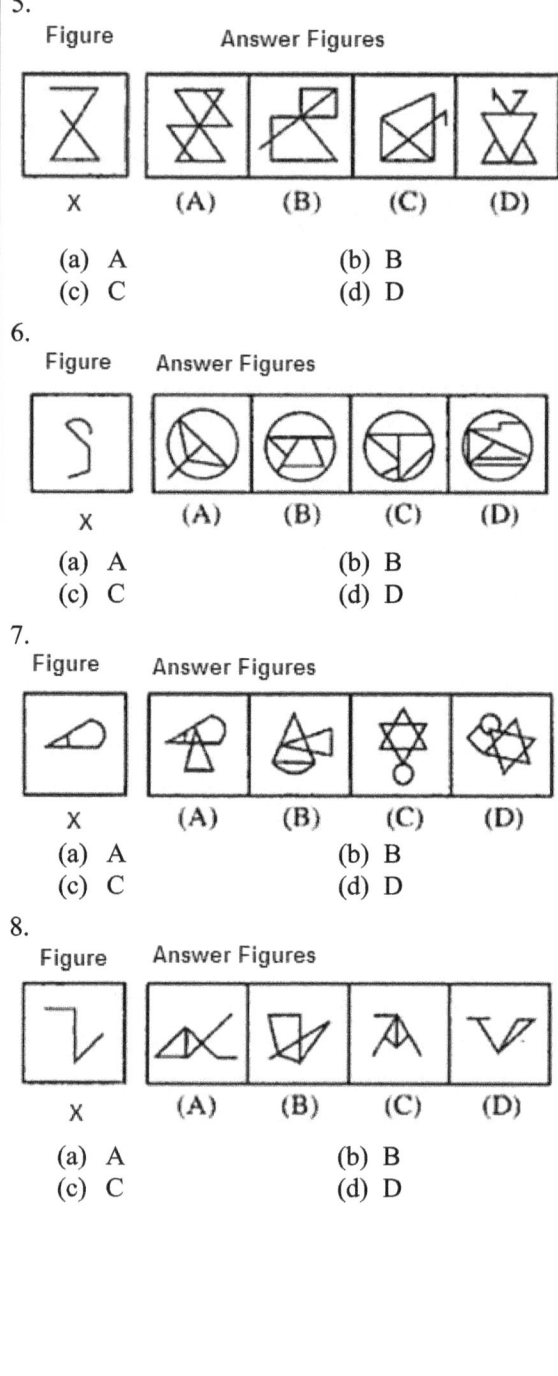

1.
   Figure   Answer Figures
   X   (A)   (B)   (C)   (D)
   (a) A   (b) B
   (c) C   (d) D

2.
   Figure   Answer Figures
   X   (A)   (B)   (C)   (D)
   (a) A   (b) B
   (c) C   (d) D

3.
   Figure   Answer Figures
   X   (A)   (B)   (C)   (D)
   (a) A   (b) B
   (c) C   (d) D

4.
   Figure   Answer Figures
   X   (A)   (B)   (C)   (D)
   (a) A   (b) B
   (c) C   (d) D

5.
   Figure   Answer Figures
   X   (A)   (B)   (C)   (D)
   (a) A   (b) B
   (c) C   (d) D

6.
   Figure   Answer Figures
   X   (A)   (B)   (C)   (D)
   (a) A   (b) B
   (c) C   (d) D

7.
   Figure   Answer Figures
   X   (A)   (B)   (C)   (D)
   (a) A   (b) B
   (c) C   (d) D

8.
   Figure   Answer Figures
   X   (A)   (B)   (C)   (D)
   (a) A   (b) B
   (c) C   (d) D

International Mathematics Olympiad – 7

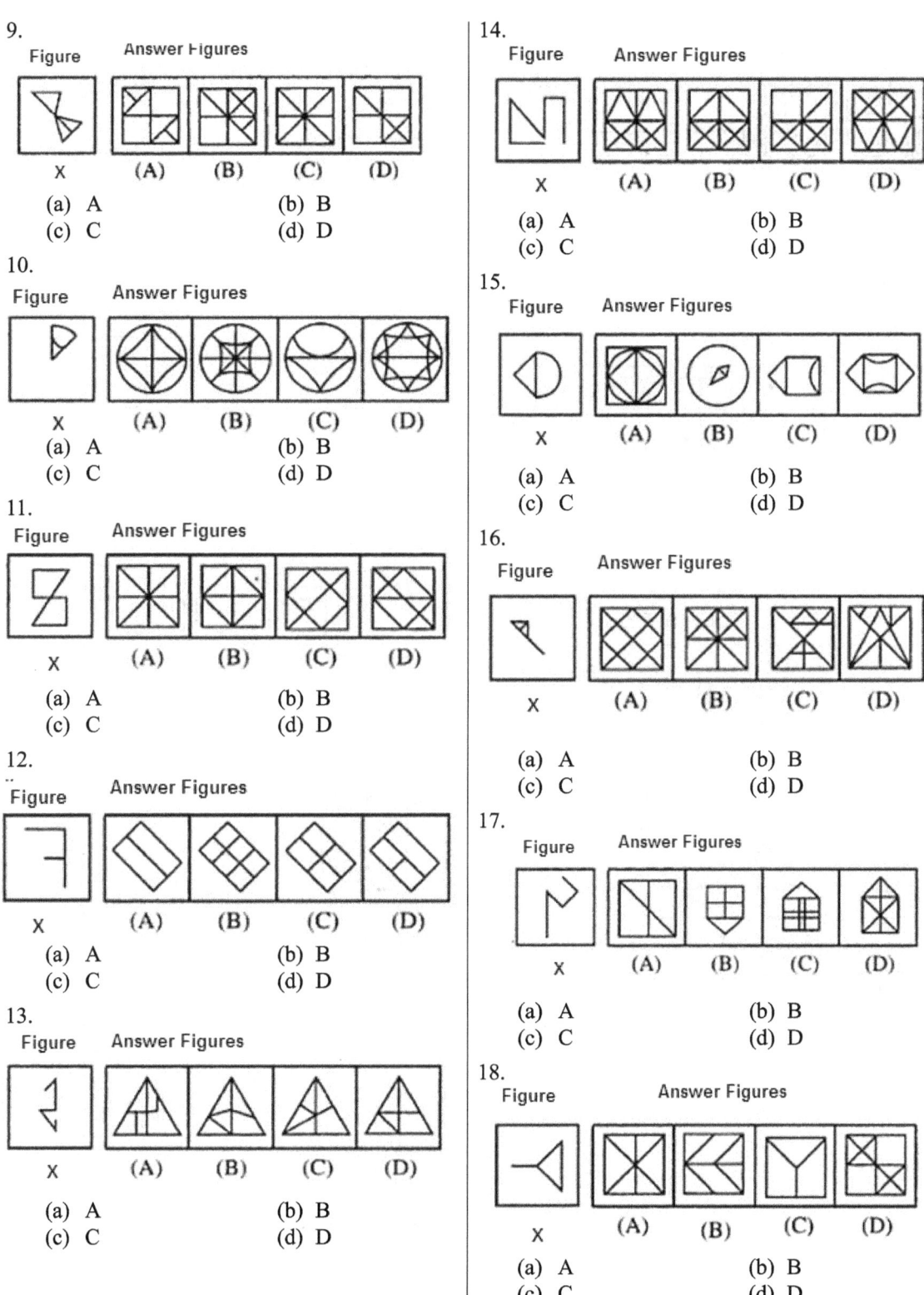

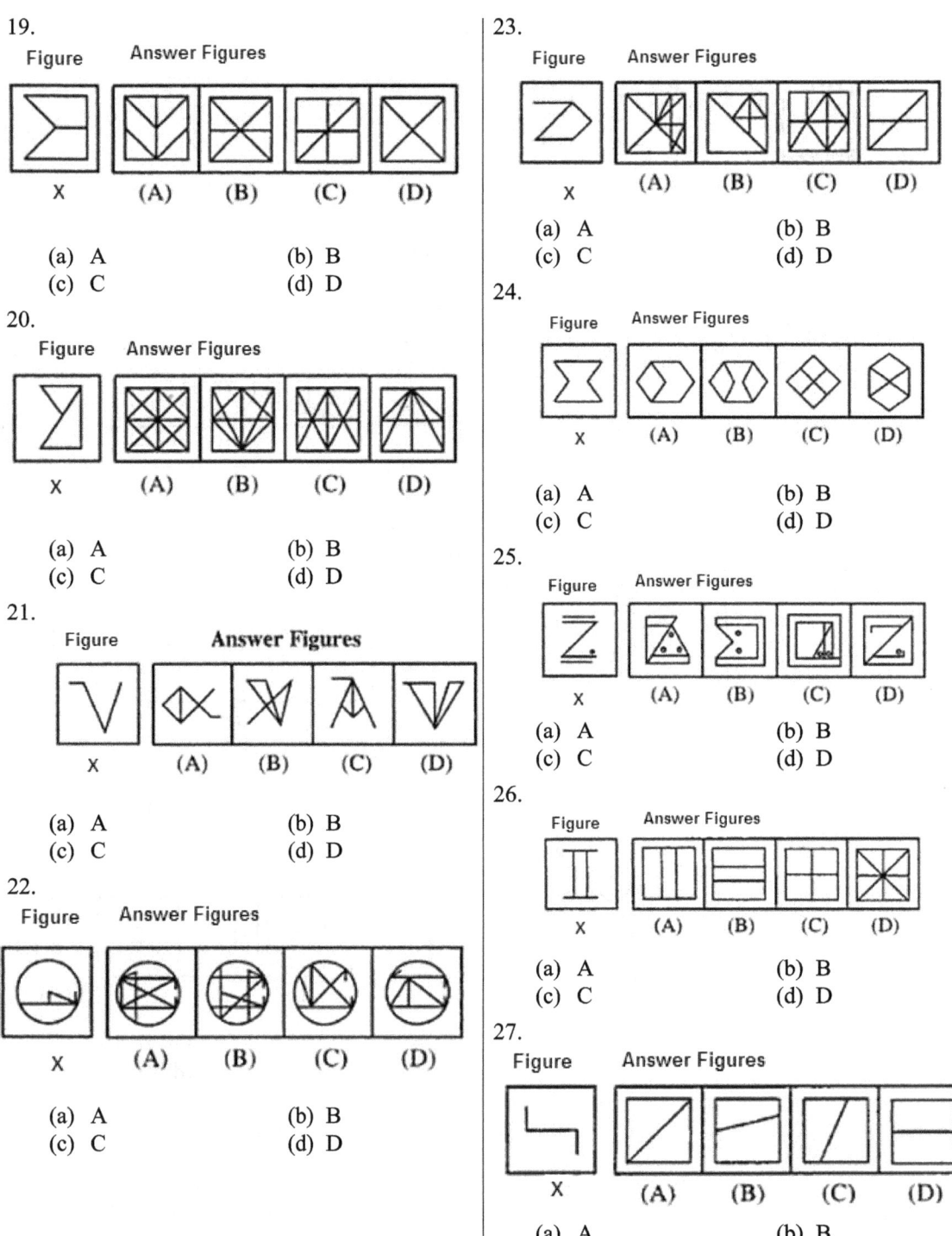

28.

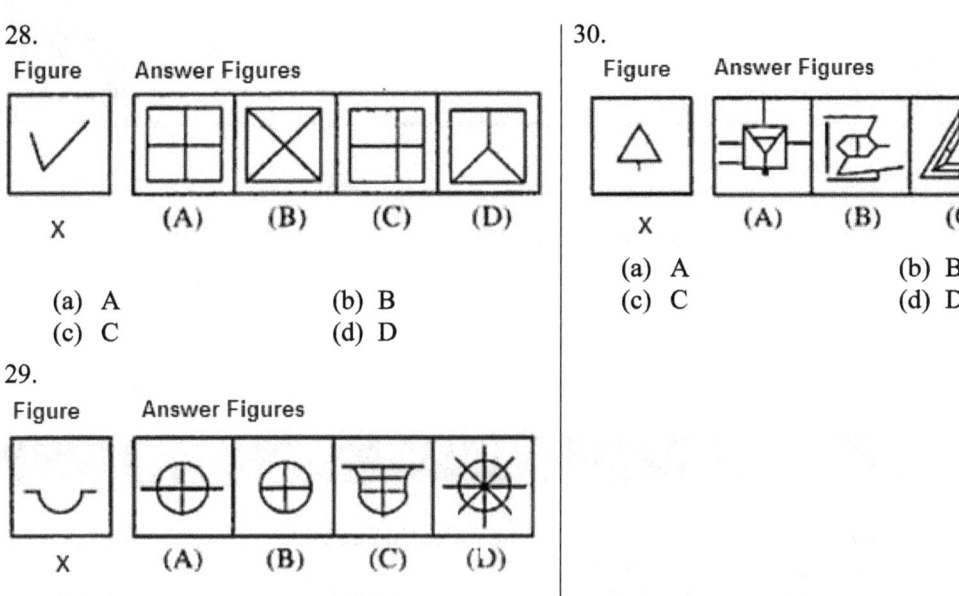

(a) A (b) B
(c) C (d) D

29.

(a) A (b) B
(c) C (d) D

30.

(a) A (b) B
(c) C (d) D

Embedded Figures

Venn Diagrams   15

Learning Objectives : In this chapter, students will learn about:
- ✓ Solving questions related to Venn diagram

CHAPTER SUMMARY

Venn diagrams are illustrations that are used in the branch of mathematics known as set theory. They are used to show the mathematical or logical relationship between different groups of things (sets). A Venn diagram shows all the logical relations between the sets.

The use of Venn diagram is made to test the aptitude of candidates regarding the relationship between some items of a group. A candidate can easily solve the problem if he/she has good understanding of the diagram.

Solved Examples

Example 1: If all the words are of different groups, then they will be shown by the diagram as given below.

Dog, Cow, Horse

Solution: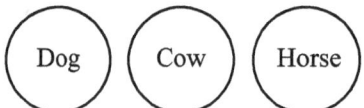

All these three are animals but of different groups, there is no relation between them. Hence they will be represented by three different circles.

Example 2: If the first word is related to second word and second word is related to third word. Then they will be shown by diagram as given below.

Unit, Tens, Hundreds

Solution: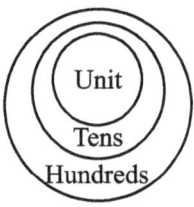

Ten units together make one Tens or in one tens a whole unit is available and ten tens together make one hundreds.

Example 3: If two different items are individually related to third item, they will be shown as below.

Pen, Pencil, Stationery

Solution: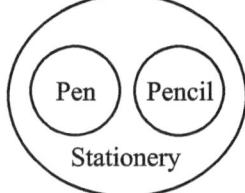

Example 4: If there is some relation between two items and these two items are completely related to a third item they will be shown as given below.

Women, Sisters, Mothers

Solution:

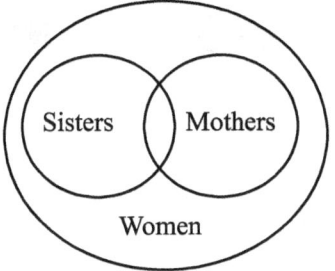

Some sisters may be mothers and vice-versa. Similarly some mothers may not be sisters and vice-versa. But all the sisters and all the mothers belong to the women group.

Example 5: Two items are related to a third item to some extent but not completely and first two items are totally different.

Students, Boys, Girls

Solution

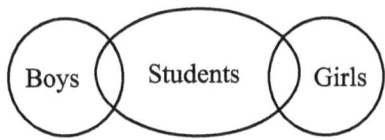

The boys and girls are different items while some boys may be students. Similarly among girls some may be students.

MULTIPLE CHOICE QUESTIONS

Direction (1 to 30): Each of these questions given below contains three elements. These elements may or may not have some inter linkage. Each group of elements may fit into one of these diagrams at (a), (b), (c), (d). You have to indicate the group of elements which correctly fits into the diagrams.

1. Which of the following diagrams indicates the best relation among Author, Lawyer and Singer?

2. Which of the following diagrams indicates the best relation among Factory, Product and Machinery?

3. Which of the following diagrams indicates the best relation among Women, Mothers and Engineers?

4. Which of the following diagrams indicates the best relation among Paper, Stationery and Ink?

5. Which of the following diagrams indicates the best relation among Teacher, Men and Women?

6. Which of the following diagrams indicates the best relation among Oil, Wick and Lamp?

7. Which of the following diagrams indicates the best relation among Football, Player and Field?

8. Which of the following diagrams indicates the best relation among Sweets, Rasgulla and Apple?

9. Which of the following diagrams indicates the best relation among Mammal, Cow and Bat?

10. Which of the following diagrams indicates the best relation among dogs, pet animals and animals?

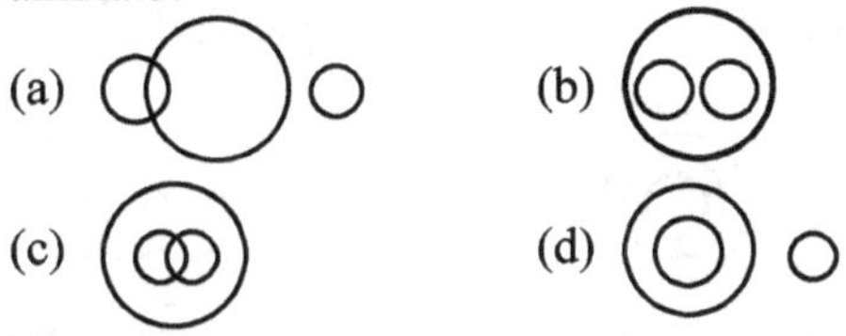

(a) (b) (c) (d)

11. Which of the following diagrams indicates the best relation among Sailor, Ship and Ocean?

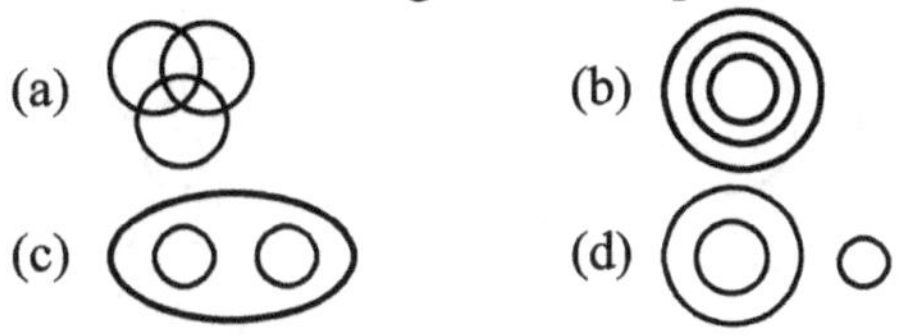

(a) (b) (c) (d)

12. Which of the following diagrams indicates the best relation among Gold, Metal and Zinc?

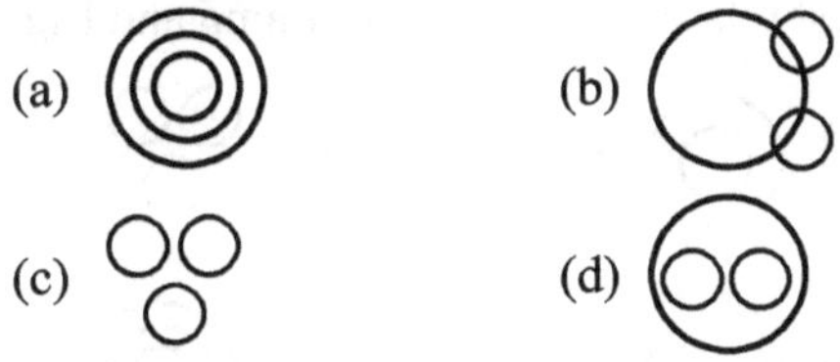

(a) (b) (c) (d)

13. Which of the following diagrams indicates the best relation among Professors, Doctors and Men?

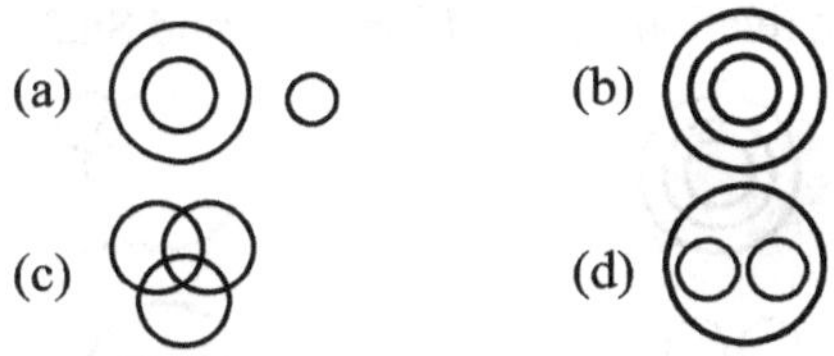

(a) (b) (c) (d)

14. Which of the following diagrams indicates the best relation among Ass, Pet and Horse?

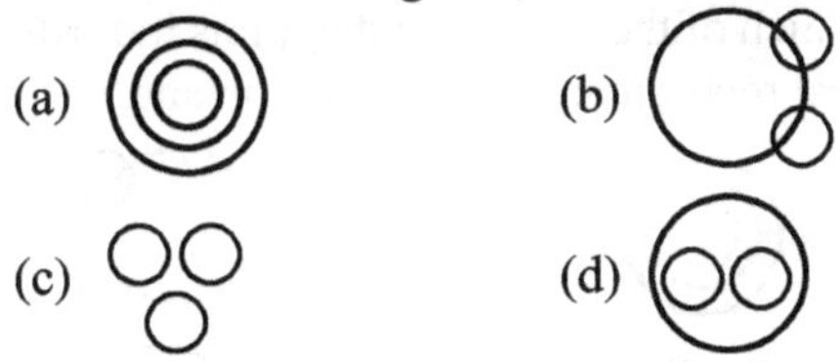

(a) (b) (c) (d)

15. Which of the following diagrams indicates the best relation among Page, Chapter and Book?

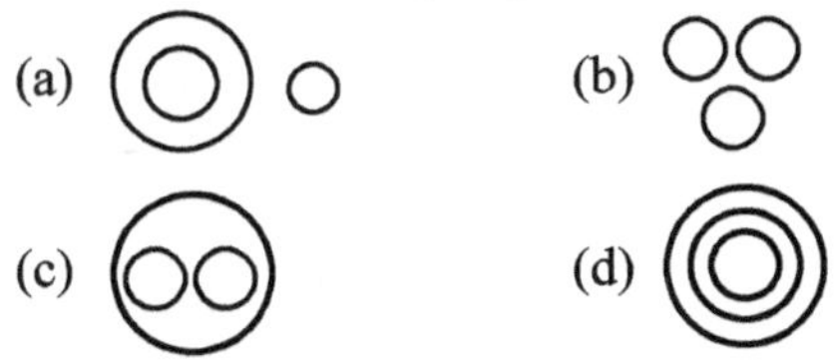

(a) (b) (c) (d)

16. Which of the following diagrams indicates the best relation among Parents, Mother and Father?

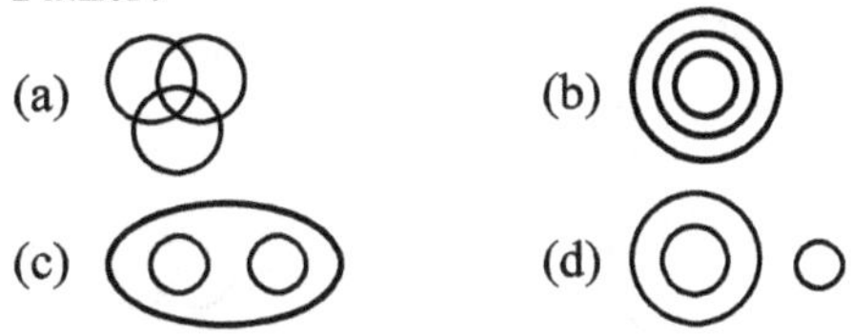

(a) (b) (c) (d)

17. Which of the following diagrams indicates the best relation among Men, Rodents and Living beings?

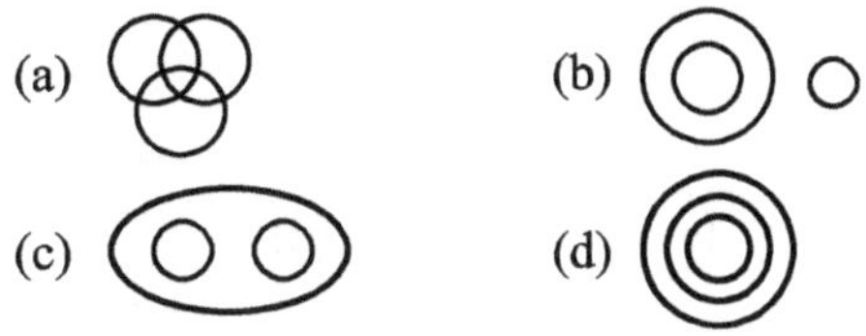

(a) (b) (c) (d)

18. Which of the following diagrams indicates the best relation among Elephants, Wolves and Animals?

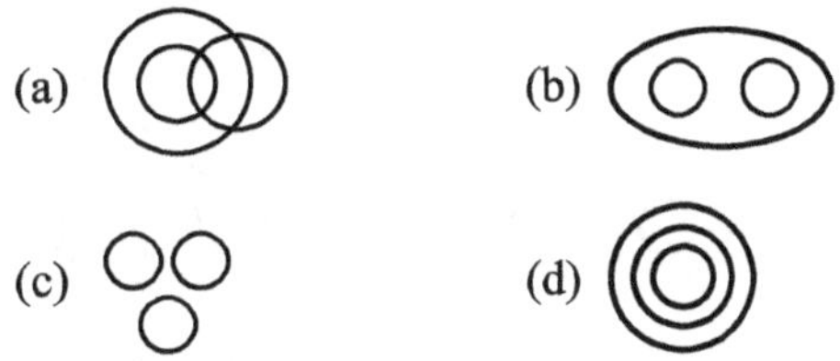

(a) (b) (c) (d)

19. Which of the following diagrams indicates the best relation among Furniture, Chairs and Tables?

(a) (b) (c) (d)

20. Which of the following diagrams indicates the best relation among Elephant, Carnivorous and Tiger?

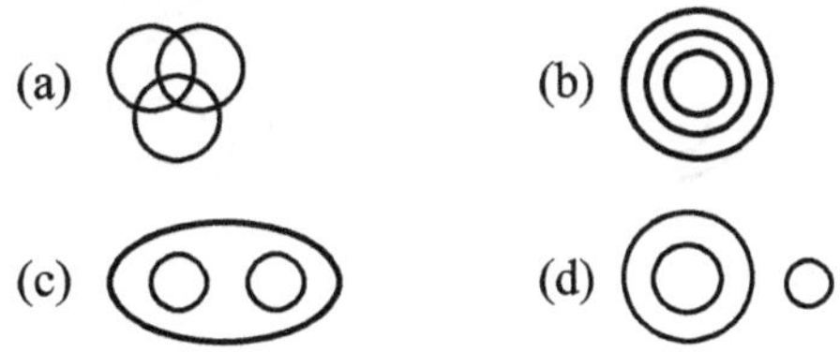

(a) (b) (c) (d)

Venn Diagrams

21. Which of the following diagrams indicates the best relation among Class, Blackboard and School?
    (a) (b) (c) (d)

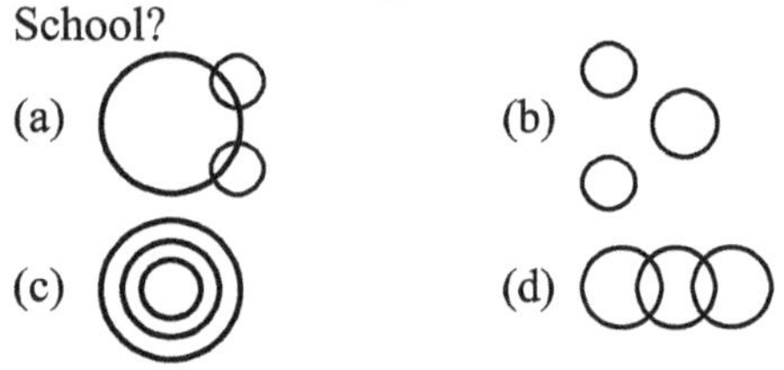

22. Which of the following diagrams indicates the best relation among Rabi-Crop, Paddy and Wheat?
    (a) (b) (c) (d)

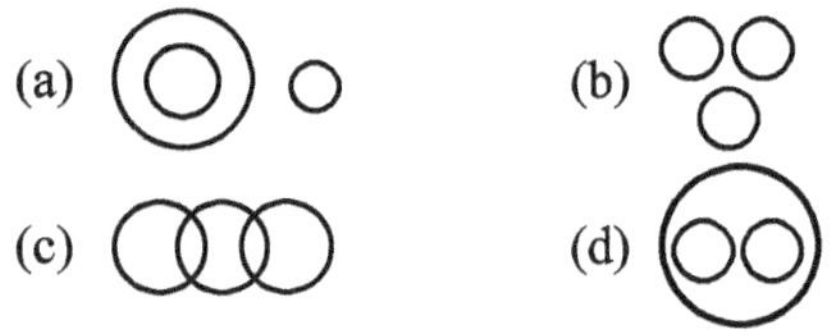

23. Which of the following diagrams indicates the best relation among Hospital, Nurse and Patient?
    (a) (b) (c) (d)

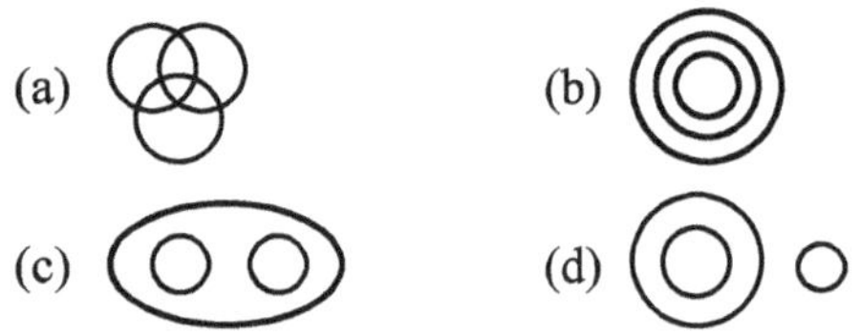

24. Which of the following diagrams indicates the best relation among tree, cat and metal?
    (a) (b) (c) (d)

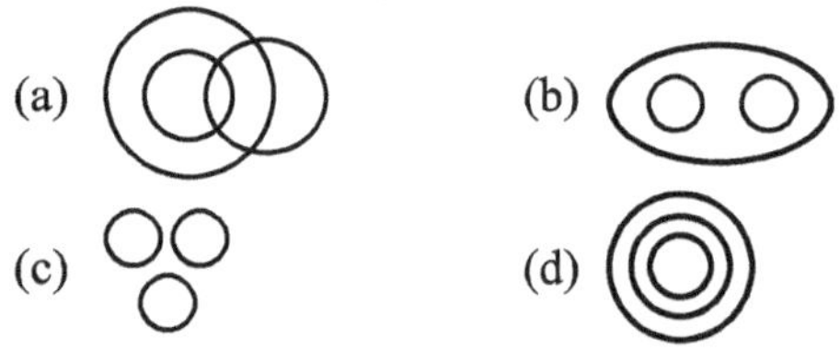

25. Which of the following diagrams indicates the best relation among Teacher, Writer and Musician?
    (a) (b) (c) (d)

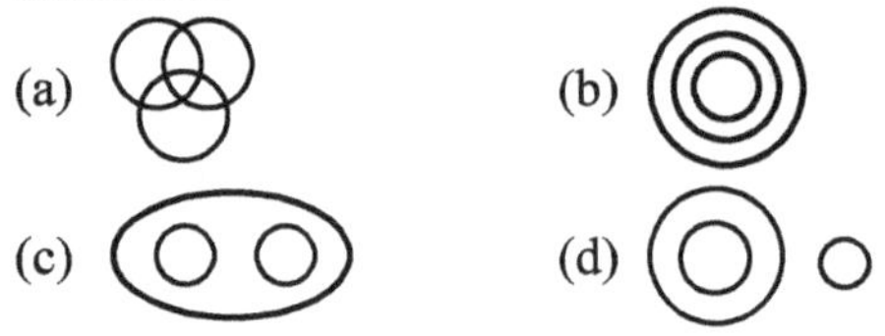

26. Which of the following diagrams indicates the best relation among Iron, Lead and Nitrogen?
    (a) (b) (c) (d)

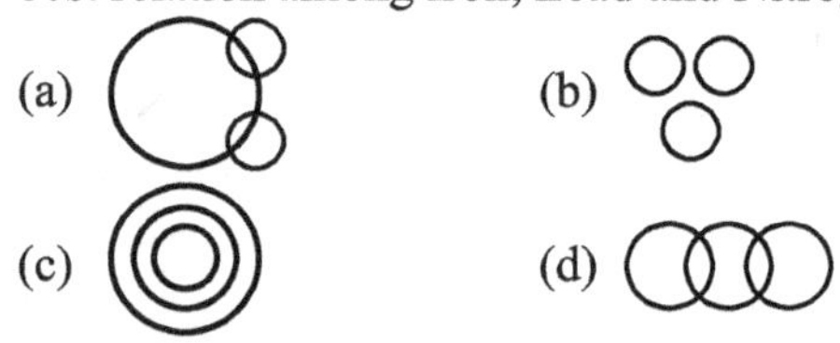

27. Which of the following diagrams indicates the best relation among Examination, Questions and Practice?
    (a) (b) (c) (d)

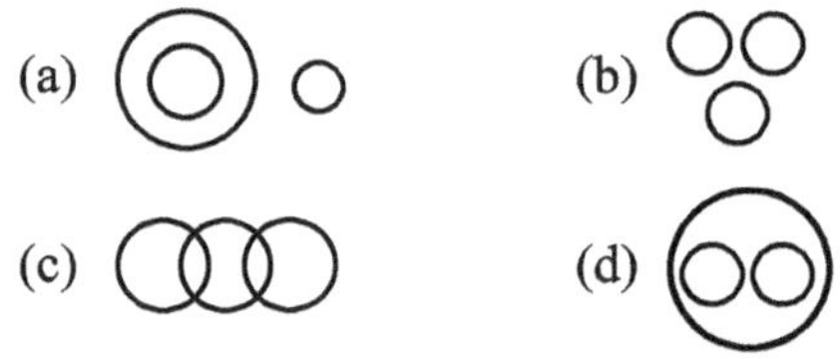

28. Which of the following diagrams indicates the best relation among Bulb, Lamp and Light?
    (a) (b) (c) (d)

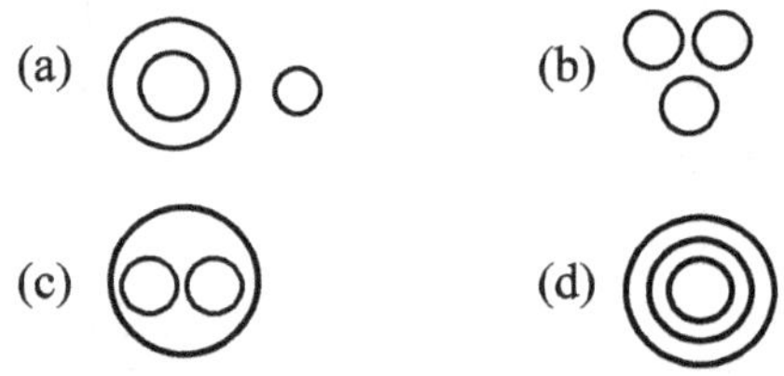

29. Which of the following diagrams indicates the best relation among Lion, Dog and Snake?
    (a) (b) (c) (d)

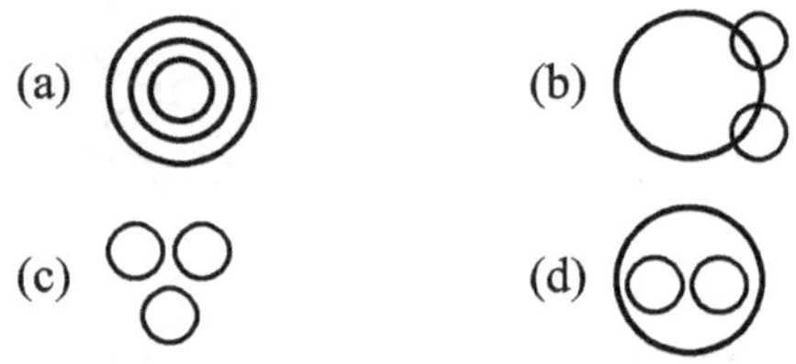

30. Which of the following diagrams indicates the best relation among Moon, Sun and Earth?
    (a) (b) (c) (d)

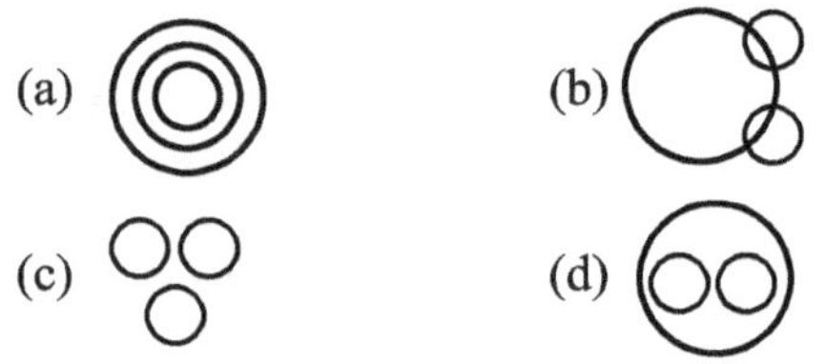

Direction (31 to 34): Study the following figure and answer the questions given below.

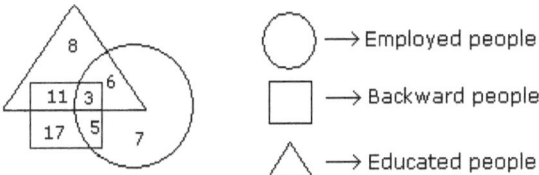

31. How many educated people are employed?
    (a) 9 (b) 18
    (c) 20 (d) 15
32. How many backward people are educated?
    (a) 9 (b) 28
    (c) 14 (d) 6
33. How many backward uneducated people are employed?
    (a) 14 (b) 5
    (c) 7 (d) 11
34. How many backward people are not educated?
    (a) 3 (b) 14
    (c) 22 (d) 25

Direction (35 to 38): Study the following figure and answer the questions given below.

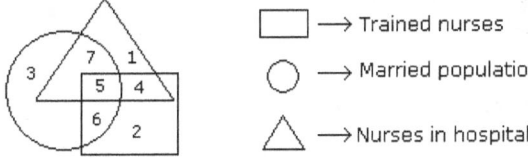

35. If the hospital management requires only married trained nurses for operation theatre, which number of diagram should be chosen by it?
    (a) 7 (b) 4
    (c) 5 (d) 6
36. By which number, married but untrained nurses in the hospital are represented?
    (a) 4 (b) 6
    (c) 7 (d) 5
37. By which number is unmarried trained nurses who are not in hospitals represented?
    (a) 6 (b) 5
    (c) 2 (d) 1
38. What is represented by the number 7?
    (a) Married nurses in the hospital
    (b) Trained nurses
    (c) Unmarried trained nurses
    (d) Married trained nurses

Direction (39 to 40): Study the following figure and answer the questions given below.

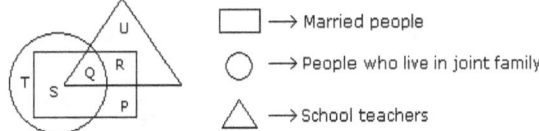

39. By which letter is the married teachers who live in joint family represented?
    (a) R (b) Q
    (c) S (d) P
40. By which letter is the married people who live in joint family but are not school teachers represented?
    (a) R (b) U
    (c) S (d) P

Venn Diagrams

SECTION 3
ACHIEVERS' SECTION

Some Thoughtful Questions

1. Complete the following multiplication table:

   Second number

First number	x	−4	−3	−2	−1	0	1	2	3	4
	−4									
	−3									
	−2									
	−1									
	0									
	1									
	2									
	3									
	4									

   Is the multiplication table symmetrical about the diagonal joining the upper left corner to the lower right corner?

   Answer:

   Second number

First number	x	−4	−3	−2	−1	0	1	2	3	4
	−4	16	12	8	4	0	−4	−8	−12	−16
	−3	12	9	6	3	0	−3	−6	−9	−12
	−2	8	6	4	2	0	−2	−4	−6	−8
	−1	4	3	2	1	0	−1	−2	−3	−4
	0	0	0	0	0	0	0	0	0	0
	1	−4	−3	−2	−1	0	1	2	3	4
	2	−8	−6	−4	−2	0	2	4	6	8
	3	−12	−9	−6	−3	0	3	6	9	12
	4	−16	−12	−8	−4	0	4	8	12	16

   From the table it is clear that, the table is symmetrical about the diagonal joining the upper left corner to the lower right corner.

2. The temperature at 12 noon was 10°C above zero. If it decreases at the rate of 2°C per hour until midnight, at what time would the temperature be 8°C below zero? What would be the temperature at midnight?

Answer:

From the question, it is given,

The temperature at the beginning, i.e., at 12 noon = 10°C

Rate of change of temperature = – 2°C per hour

Then,

Temperature at 1 PM = 10 + (–2) = 10 – 2 = 8°C
Temperature at 2 PM = 8 + (–2) = 8 – 2 = 6°C
Temperature at 3 PM = 6 + (–2) = 6 – 2 = 4°C
Temperature at 4 PM = 4 + (–2) = 4 – 2 = 2°C
Temperature at 5 PM = 2 + (–2) = 2 – 2 = 0°C
Temperature at 6 PM = 0 + (–2) = 0 – 2 = –2°C
Temperature at 7 PM = –2 + (–2) = –2 –2 = –4°C
Temperature at 8 PM = –4 + (–2) = –4 – 2 = –6°C
Temperature at 9 PM = –6 + (–2) = –6 – 2 = –8°C

∴ At 9 PM, the temperature will be 8°C below zero.

Then,

The temperature at midnight, i.e., at 12 AM

Change in temperature in 12 hours = –2°C × 12 = – 24°C

So, at midnight temperature will be = 10 + (–24)

= – 14°C

So, at midnight, the temperature will be 14°C below 0

3. In mid-day meal scheme $\left(\dfrac{3}{10}\right)$ liter of milk is given to each student of a primary school. If 30 liters of milk is distributed every day in the school, how many students are there in the school?

Answer:

Given $\left(\dfrac{3}{10}\right)$ liter of milk is given to each student

Number of student given $\left(\dfrac{3}{10}\right)$ liter of milk = 1

Number of students giving 1 liter of milk = $\left(\dfrac{10}{3}\right)$

Numbers of students giving 30 liters of milk = $\left(\dfrac{10}{3}\right) \times 30 = 100$ students

Read the bar graph, which shows the number of books sold by a bookstore during five consecutive years, and answer the following questions.

(i) About how many books were sold in 1989, 1990 and 1992?

(ii) In which year was about 475 books and 225 books sold?

(iii) In which years were fewer than 250 books sold?
(iv) Can you explain how you would estimate the number of books sold in 1989?

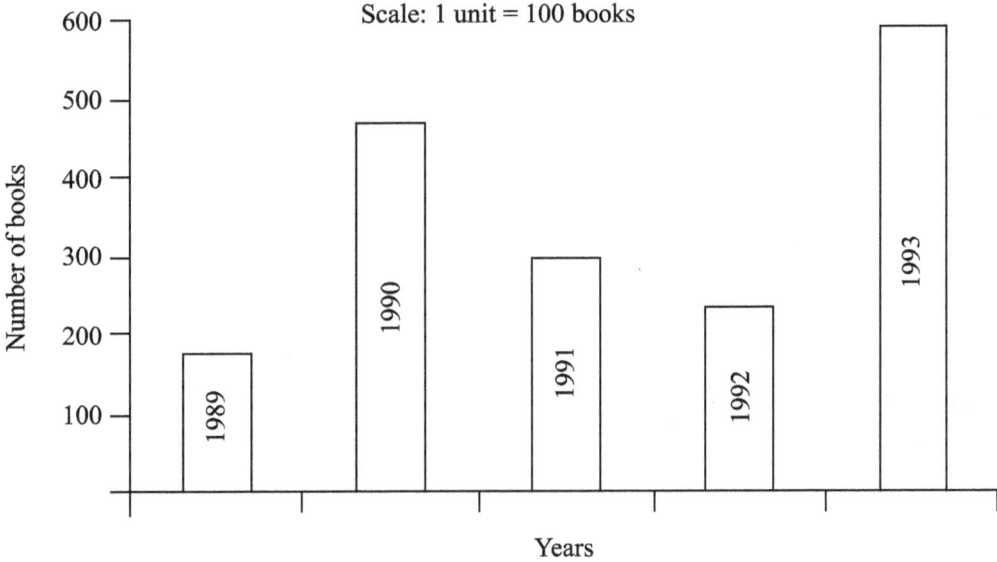

Answer:
(i) By observing the bar graph,
   175 books were sold in the year 1989.
   475 books were sold in the year 1990.
   225 books were sold in the year 1992.
(ii) By observing the bar graph,
   475 books were sold in the year 1990.
   225 books were sold in the year 1992.
(iii) By observing the bar graph,
   In the years 1989 and 1992, the number of books sold was less than 250.
(iv) By observing the bar graph, we can conclude that
   The number of books sold in the year 1989 is about 1 and $\frac{3}{4}$ th part of 1 cm.
   WKT, Scale is taken as 1 cm = 100 books
   $= 100 + \left(\frac{3}{4} \times 100\right)$
   $= 100 + (3 \times 25)$
   $= 100 + 75 = 175$

4. Shikha is 3 years younger to her brother Ravish. If the sum of their ages 37 years, what are their present age?

   Answer:
   Let the present age of Shikha be x years.
   Therefore, the present age of Shikha's brother Ravish = $(x + 3)$ years.
   So, sum of their ages = $x + (x + 3)$

Some Thoughtful Questions

$\Rightarrow x + (x + 3) = 37$

$\Rightarrow 2x + 3 = 37$

Subtracting 3 from both sides, we get

$\Rightarrow 2x + 3 - 3 = 37 - 3$

$\Rightarrow 2x = 34$

Dividing both sides by 2, we get

$\Rightarrow \dfrac{2x}{2} = \dfrac{34}{2}$

$\Rightarrow x = 17$

Therefore, the present age of Shikha = 17 years,

And the present age of Ravish = $x + 3 = 17 + 3 = 20$ years.

5. Fill in the blanks:

English Alphabet Letter	Line Symmetry	Number of Lines of Symmetry	Rotational symmetry	Order of rotational symmetry
Z	Nil	0	Yes	2
S	–	–	–	–
H	Yes	–	Yes	–
O	Yes	–	Yes	–
E	Yes	–	–	–
N	–	–	Yes	–
C	–	–	–	–

Answer:

English Alphabet Letter	Line Symmetry	Number of Lines of Symmetry	Rotational symmetry	Order of rotational symmetry
Z	Nil	0	Yes	2
S	Nil	0	Yes	2
H	Yes	2	Yes	2
O	Yes	4	Yes	2
E	Yes	1	No	0
N	Nil	0	Yes	2
C	Yes	1	No	0

Model Test Paper 1

1. What is the next number in the given sequence 5, 6, 10, 19, 35, ?
   (a) 60 (b) 64
   (c) 70 (d) 72

2. ACE, JLN, SUW, PRT, DEG, IKM. In the given pattern of letters, which is wrong?
   (a) JLN (b) DEG
   (c) IKM (d) None of these

3. Engineer is related to Machine in the same way, Doctor is related to.
   (a) Medicine (b) Hospital
   (c) Disease (d) Body

4. In a certain code TRAINS is coded as RTIASN. How will MASTER be coded in that code?
   (a) AMTSRE (b) AMSTER
   (c) MATSRE (d) None of these

5. Which of the following is wrong?
   (a) 49(68)32 (b) 62(52)49
   (c) 78(32)69 (d) 37(56)23

6. If INK is coded as 91411; DOG is coded as 4157 then what is the code for FOX?
   (a) 61522 (b) 61524
   (c) 61423 (d) 61523

7. How many 7's are there in the given series which are preceded by 9 and followed by 6?
   7897653428972459297647
   (a) 2 (b) 3
   (c) 4 (d) 5

8. Rajesh ranks 9th from the top and 35th from the bottom in a class. How many students are there in the class?
   (a) 41 (b) 42
   (c) 43 (d) 44

9. If L stands for +, M stands for –, N stands for ×, P stands for ÷ then 14N10L42P2M8 = ?
   (a) 153 (b) 155
   (c) 156 (d) 157

10. By interchanging two signs the given equation becomes correct. Find the correct option?
    $121 \div 11 - 3 \times 13 + 2 = 22$
    (a) – & × (b) – & ÷
    (c) ÷ & – (d) + & –

11.
    9   12   18
    8 ⓪ 6   11 ② 7   25 ⓵ 12
    5   4   11
    (a) 6 (b) 7
    (c) 8 (d) 9

12. A is uncle of B who is the daughter of C and C is the daughter-in-law of P. How is A related to P?
    (a) Son (b) Brother
    (c) Son-in-law (d) None of these

13. If 7 * 1 = 64; 3 * 9 = 144 then what is the value of 7 * 6?
    (a) 169 (b) 196
    (c) 144 (d) 256

14. Rohan in 8th from top and on 47th position from bottom in a class. How many students are there in the class?
    (a) 53 (b) 54
    (c) 55 (d) 56

15. If A stands for +, B stands for –, C stands for ÷ and D stands for × then what is the value of 49C7D4B32A4?
    (a) 0 (b) 1
    (c) 2 (d) 3

Model Test Paper

16. Choose the Odd One Out
    (a) Volume : Litre
    (b) Length : Metre
    (c) Pressure : Barometer
    (d) Time : Seconds

17. Igloo : Ice : : Marquee : ?
    (a) Silk   (b) Satin
    (c) Canvas   (d) Buckram

18. In a code language if SUGAR is coded as ZNMDB and TEA is coded as FLD. How would you code GRATE in the same code language?
    (a) BNDFL   (b) MBDFL
    (c) FLDZB   (d) LDZMN

19. How many 5s are there in the following sequence which are immediately followed by 3 but not immediately preceded by 7?
    8 9 5 3 2 5 3 8 5 5 6 8 7 3 3 5 7 7 5 3 6 5 3 3 5 7 3 8
    (a) 1   (b) 2
    (c) 3   (d) 4

20. Choose the correct one that will belong to the group of Potato, Carrot, Raddish
    (a) Tomato   (b) Spinach
    (c) Sesame   (d) Groundnut

21. 25 of $\frac{3}{5} \div 1\frac{2}{3} + 3$ of $\frac{1}{3} - 10 = ?$
    (a) 0   (b) 1
    (c) $\frac{1}{2}$ (d) $\frac{1}{3}$

22. $0.01 + 2 \times 1.02 \div 0.2 - 0.5 = ?$
    (a) 9.07   (b) 9.71
    (c) 9.27   (d) None of these

23. One U.S. Dollar equals 0.623 British pounds. How many pounds will Shankar receive in exchange for $252?
    (a) 153.996   (b) 152.96
    (c) 154.96   (d) 156.996

24. $\frac{5° + 6° + 7° - 12°}{5° + 6° + 7°} = ?$
    (a) 2   (b) ½
    (c) 3   (d) 1/3

25. If $6^x = 216$ then find the value of x^2 ?
    (a) 3   (b) 9
    (c) 27   (d) 1

26. The side of an equilateral triangle is $7x + 3$. What is its perimeter?
    (a) $21x + 27$ (b) $21x - 3$
    (c) $21x$ (d) $21x + 9$

27. What must be added to $-4a^3 + 7a^2 - 3a + 1$ to get zero?
    (a) $4a^3 + 7a^2 - 3a + 1$
    (b) $-4a^3 + 7a^2 - 3a + 1$
    (c) $4a^3 - 7a^2 + 3a - 1$
    (d) None of these

28. What is the degree of the algebraic expression $3x^3 - 4x^2y^2 + 3y$?
    (a) 1   (b) 2
    (c) 3   (d) 4

29. The sum of three consecutive integers is 36. What is the smallest number?
    (a) 11   (b) 12
    (c) 13   (d) None of these

30. In an isosceles triangle the base angles are equal to 50°. What is the vertex angle?
    (a) 70°   (b) 80°
    (c) 90°   (d) None of these

31. If 12 men can repair a road in 16 days. How long will it take for 8 men to repair it?
    (a) 12 days   (b) 16 days
    (c) 24 days   (d) 36 days

32. If the angles of a triangle are in the ratio 1 : 2 : 3 then the triangle is
    (a) a right triangle
    (b) a scalene acute triangle
    (c) an acute triangle
    (d) an obtuse triangle

33. If 4, x, 9 are in continued proportion then what is the value of x?
    (a) 6   (b) 8
    (c) 7   (d) 9

34. In an examination, a student must get 40% marks to pass. A student gets 96 marks out of 400. How many more marks should he had got to pass the examination?
    (a) 54   (b) 64
    (c) 74   (d) 84

35. The selling price of 10 pencils is equal to cost price of 11 pencils. What is the profit percent?
    (a) 10%   (b) $10\frac{1}{9}$%
    (c) $11\frac{1}{9}$%   (d) None of these

36. In what time will a sum of money put at 15% simple interest triple itself?
    (a) $13\frac{1}{3}$ years   (b) 12 years
    (c) 20 year   (d) None of these

37. Find the value of x if $\left(\frac{3}{7}\right)^{15} \div \left(\frac{3}{7}\right)^x = \frac{27}{343}$
    (a) 10   (b) 11
    (c) 12   (d) 14

38. What is value of m if
    $\frac{m-3}{5} + 7 = \frac{2m+1}{3}$
    (a) 12   (b) 14
    (c) 13   (d) 17

39. In the given figure DE ∥ AB, ∠DEC = 45° and ∠EDC = 35°. what is the value of x and y?

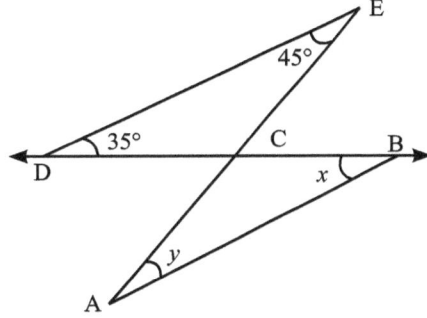

    (a) 35°, 45°   (b) 45°, 35°
    (c) 55°, 35°   (d) None of these

40. Which triplets of numbers cannot possibly represent the sides of a right triangle?
    (a) 15, 20, 25   (b) 8, 9, 10
    (c) 16, 20, 12   (d) 2.5, 6.5, 6

41. In △ABC, which of the following is correct?
    (a) AB + BC > AC   (b) AC + BC = AB
    (c) BC > AB + AC   (d) None of these

42. The perimeter of a triangle is 900m. What is the largest side of the triangle if the sides are in the ratio 5 : 7 : 8?
    (a) 225 m   (b) 315 m
    (c) 360 m   (d) None of these

43. The inner and outer circumference of a circular ring are 44 cm and 88 cm. Find the width of the ring?
    (a) 3 cm   (b) 6 cm
    (c) 7 cm   (d) 8 cm

44. What is the height of a parallelogram if the base is 48 cm and the area is 360 cm^2?
    (a) 7.5 cm   (b) 8 cm
    (c) 8.5 cm   (d) 9 cm

45. A small metallic washer is of 7 mm radius with a hole of 3.5 mm radius. What is the area of the washer?
    (a) 115.5 mm^2 (B) 128 mm^2
    (c) 110.5 mm^2 (d) None of these

46. What is the median of the following data.

    14, 11, 7, 21, 12, 9, 18

    (a) 11 (b) 12
    (c) 14 (d) 9

47. While throwing a dice, what is the probability of getting an odd number?

    (a) 1 (b) $\frac{1}{2}$
    (c) $\frac{1}{3}$ (d) $\frac{1}{4}$

48. A father is 32 years of age. At present, his son is 8 year old. In how many years will the father be three times as old as his son?

    (a) 3 years (b) 4 years
    (c) 5 years (d) 6 years

49. If AB ∥ CD, what is the value of x?

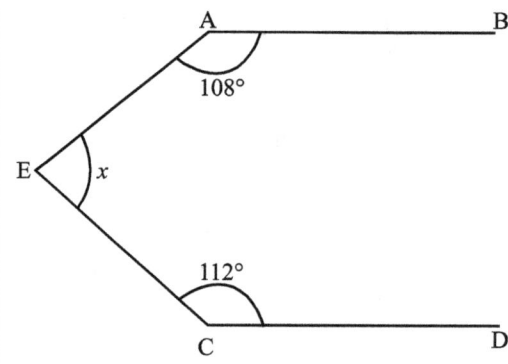

    (a) 140° (b) 120°
    (c) 90° (d) 110°

50. If a man's wages is increased by 10% and afterward decreased by 10% then the total change in wage in percent is:

    (a) 9 % (b) 10%
    (c) 1% (d) 2%

Model Test Paper 2

1. Sum of two integers is 32. If one of the integer is −32, then the other is:
   (a) 64
   (b) 32
   (c) −32
   (d) −64

2. The smallest possible decimal fraction upto three decimal places is:
   (a) 0.001
   (b) 0.011
   (c) 0.101
   (d) 0.111

3. Find the value of the expression given by $(2/3)^2 \times (3/4)^2 \times (4/9)^0$.
   (a) 116
   (b) 14
   (c) 18
   (d) 29

4. Find the value of $a^2 + b^2 + c^2 - ab - bc - ca$, if $a = 1, b = 2$ and $c = 3$.
   (a) 2
   (b) 1
   (c) 3
   (d) 7

5. The ratio of 700 g to 6 kg is:
   (a) 7 : 6
   (b) 7 : 60
   (c) 6 : 13
   (d) 6 : 11

6. 1/2 is what percent of 1/3 ?
   (a) 4 %
   (b) 150 %
   (c) 2 %
   (d) 1200 %

7. If selling price of 10 note books is same as cost price of 5 note books then find the loss %.
   (a) 20%
   (b) 30%
   (c) 40%
   (d) 50%

8. Find the simple interest on Rs. 5, 000 for 2 years at 8 % per annum.
   (a) Rs. 800
   (b) Rs. 900
   (c) Rs. 850
   (d) Rs. 875

9. Find the area of rectangle, whose length is 1.5 m and breadth is 30 cm.
   (a) 45 cm^2
   (b) 450 cm^2
   (c) 4500 cm^2
   (d) 455 cm^2

10. At a particular place temperature of the weekdays is shown in the table given below. Find the difference between highest and the lowest temperature.

Day	Temperature °C
Monday	−20°C
Tuesday	−5°C
Wednesday	15°C
Thursday	10°C
Friday	−15°C
Saturday	−12°C
Sunday	14°C

    (a) 35°C
    (b) −25°C
    (c) −35°C
    (d) 20°C

11. Order the following rational numbers from least to greatest. −4, 6, 9, 0, −19, −8, 8, 2,
    (a) 0, 2, 4, −4, 6, 8, −8, −19
    (b) −4, −8, −19, 0, 2, 4, 6, 8
    (c) −19, −8, −4, 0, 2, 6, 8, 9
    (d) −19, −8, −4, 0, 4, 6, 8, 9

12. Simplify : $(a + b - c)^2 + (a - b - c)^2$
    (a) $a^2 + b2 + c^2 - 2ca$
    (b) $2a^2 + b2 + c^2 - 2ca$
    (c) $2(a^2 + b2 + c^2 - 2ca)$
    (d) $2(a^2 - b^2 + c^2 - 2ca)$

13. If $x: 8 :: 3 : 2$ then the value of x is :
    (a) 14
    (b) 12
    (c) 15
    (d) 10

14. In an examination, 96 % of the candidates passed and 100 failed. How many candidates appeared?
    (a) 2500
    (b) 2700
    (c) 2750
    (d) 2900

15. A bicycle was purchased for Rs. 1800 and sold for Rs. 2000. Find the gain percent.
    (a) 13%
    (b) 11.11%
    (c) 15%
    (d) 18%

16. From the following table find the values of p, q and r.

Scores	Tally Mark	Frequency
0	II	r
1	I	1
25	I	1
34	p	3
67	II	2
71	I	q
73	I	1

   (a) $p \to$ III, $q = 2$ and $r = 2$
   (b) $p \to$ III, $q = 1$ and $r = 1$
   (c) $p \to$ II, $q = 1$ and $r = 2$
   (d) $p \to$ III, $q = 1$ and $r = 2$

17. The diagrammatic representation with the help of pictures is called:
   (a) Cartogram (b) Pie chart
   (c) Pictogram (d) Bar chart

18. Which of the following cannot be the sides of a right angled triangle?
   (a) 3 cm, 4 cm and 5 cm
   (b) 6 cm, 8 cm and 10 cm
   (c) 6 cm, 9 cm and 12 cm
   (d) 5 cm, 12 cm and 13 cm

19. Which one of the following is equal to $25x^2 + 4y^2 + 20xy$?
   (a) $(5x + 2y)^2$ (b) $(5x - 2y)^2$
   (c) $(x + 2y)^2$ (d) $(9x + 3y)^2$

20. Find the supplement of an angle which is 5 times of its complement.
   (a) 150° (b) 105°
   (c) 130° (d) 60°

21. If $4A = 5B$ and $6B = 7C$, then A : C is equal to:
   (a) 35 : 24 (b) 8 : 9
   (c) 24 : 35 (d) 14 : 15

22. The marked price of an article is Rs. 540 and the shopkeeper allows a successive discount of 15% and 20% on it. Find the selling price of the article.
   (a) Rs. 367.20 (b) Rs. 351.00
   (c) Rs. 351.20 (d) Rs. 351.67

23. Which shall come next in the series given below?
   6, 12, 20, 30, ?
   (a) 40 (b) 42
   (c) 52 (d) 48

24. Find the mean proportional between 16 and 81.
   (a) 24 (b) 32
   (c) 36 (d) 42

25. Taking today as zero on the number line if the day before yesterday is 24 February 2016, what is the day, 6 days after tomorrow?
   (a) Thursday (b) Friday
   (c) Saturday (d) Wednesday

26. Find the value of $4xy(x - y) - 6x^2(y - y^2) - 3y^2(2x^2 - x) + 2xy(x - y)$ for $x = 5$ and $y = 13$.
   (a) −1955 (b) 2535
   (c) −2535 (d) 1955

27. The denominator of a rational number is greater than its numerator by 6. If the numerator is increased by 5 and the denominator is decreased by 3 then the number obtained is 5/4. Find the rational number.
   (a) 5/11 (b) 13/19
   (c) 11/17 (d) 7/13

28. A sum of money doubles itself in 10 years at simple interest. In how many years would it triple itself?
   (a) 10 (b) 15
   (c) 20 (d) 25

29. What is the total number of candidates who appeared in an examination, if 31% has failed and the number of passed candidates are 247 more than the number of failed candidates?
   (a) 650 (b) 750
   (c) 800 (d) 900

30. The price of pure mustard oil is Rs. 100 per litre. A shopkeeper adulterates it with some other types of oils at Rs. 50 per litre. He sells the mixture at the rate of Rs. 96 per litre so as to gain 20 % on the whole transaction. The ratio in which he mixed the two oils is:
   (a) 1 : 2 (b) 2 : 3
   (c) 3 : 2 (d) 1 : 4

31. If the simple interest on a certain sum for 3 years at the rate of 8% per annum is half of the compound interest on Rs. 4000 for 2 years at the rate of 10% per annum, then the sum for simple interest is:
    (a) Rs. 1230 (b) Rs. 1250
    (c) Rs. 1730 (d) Rs. 1750

32. Veer performs his project work on a number of students who like soft drinks of different flavors in a school. After collecting the data he wants to know the most flavored soft drink which is liked by most of the students. Which central tendency makes his wish true?
    (a) Mean (b) Row data
    (c) Median (d) Mode

33. The first, second and third class fares between New Delhi and Chandigarh were in the ratio 10 : 8 : 3 and the number of the first, second and third class passengers between the two stations was in the ratio 3 : 4 : 10. If the total sales of tickets is Rs. 161000 per day, find the money obtained by the sales of second class tickets.
    (a) Rs. 58000 (b) Rs. 56000
    (c) Rs. 48700 (d) Rs. 32200

34. The interior angle of a regular polygon exceeds its exterior angle by 108°. The number of sides of the polygon is
    (a) 14 (b) 12
    (c) 10 (d) 16

35. The variable x varies directly as y and varies inversely as z. When $x = 8$, $y = 12$, then $z = 3$. What is x when $z = 6$ and $y = 24$?
    (a) 2 (b) 4
    (c) 8 (d) 12

36. Two blends of a commodity costing Rs. 35 and Rs. 40 kg respectively are mixed in the ratio 2 : 3 by weight. If one-fifth of the mixture is sold at Rs. 46 per kg and the remaining at the rate of Rs. 55 per kg, then the profit percent is
    (a) 20 (b) 30
    (c) 40 (d) 50

37. A and B can do a given piece of work in 8 days, B and C can do the same work in 12 days and A, B, C can complete it in 6 days. The number of days required to finish the work by A and C is
    (a) 16 (b) 12
    (c) 8 (d) 24

38. Height of a certain flag pole is 60 feet. Grease is applied to the pole. A monkey attempts to climb the pole. It climbs 5 feet every second but slips down 2ft the next second. When will the monkey reach the top of the flag pole?
    (a) 48 seconds (b) 39 seconds
    (c) 30 seconds (d) 29 seconds

39. Anita and Geeta are experts in dance and music. Seeta and Geeta are experts in music and painting. Anita and Neeta are experts in debate and dance. Neeta and Seeta are experts in painting and debate. Who is/are not expert in painting?
    (a) Anita only (b) Seeta only
    (c) Anita and Geeta (d) Neeta only

40. Replace the question mark with the correct number.

15	225	30
7	70	20
3	?	8

    (a) 12 (b) 16
    (c) 24 (d) 70

41. If 'MANGO' is coded as 50 and 'ORANGE' is coded as 60, then what is the code for PINEAPPLE'?
    (a) 84 (b) 85
    (c) 90 (d) 94

42. Find the missing term in the following sequence. ACH, FAI, JYK, MWN, _____.
    (a) PVS (b) OUR
    (c) PTQ (d) OTS

43. Six members of a family A, B, C, D, E and F are travelling together. B is the son of C but C is not the mother of B. A and C are a married couple. E is the brother of C. D is the daughter of A. F is the brother of B. How many male members are there in the family?
    (a) 1 (b) 2
    (c) 3 (d) 4

44. Select the set of letters missing in the following series. bdabcdbdabcd_dabcdb_abcdbd_
    (a) bcd (b) bda
    (c) dbc (d) cda

45. Choose the item which is not similar to the other items.
    (a) 8, 24 (b) 7, 22
    (c) 5, 16 (d) 14, 43

46. Find the wrong number in the given series. 142, 119, 100, 83, 65, 59, 52
    (a) 119 (b) 100
    (c) 83   (d) 65

47. Mr. Prakash and Mr. Prem each bought the same motorcycle using a 10% off coupon. Mr. Prakash's cashier took 10% off the price and then added 8.5% sales tax whereas Mr. Prem's cashier first added the sales tax and then took 10% off the total price. The amount Mr. Prakash paid is
    (a) same as the amount Mr. Prem paid.
    (b) greater by Rs. 850 from the amount Mr. Prem paid.
    (c) lesser by Rs. 550 from the amount Mr. Prem paid.
    (d) greater by Rs. 85 from the amount Mr. Prem paid.

48. Three glasses of equal volume contains acid mixed with water. The ratios of acid and water in the three glasses are 2 : 3, 3 : 4 and 4 : 5 respectively. The contents of these glasses are poured in a larger vessel. The ratio of acid and water in the large vessel is
    (a) 407 : 560 (b) 411 : 564
    (c) 417 : 564 (d) 401 : 544

49. If $x + y = 6$ and $x^3 + y^3 = 72$, then the value of xy is:
    (a) 12 (b) 8
    (c) 6   (d) 9

50. The area of the parallelogram whose length is 30 cm, width is 20 cm and one diagonal is 40 cm, is
    (a) $100\sqrt{15}$ cm^2 (b) $150\sqrt{15}$ cm^2
    (c) $200\sqrt{15}$ cm^2 (d) $300\sqrt{15}$ cm^2

Answer Keys

Scan the QR Code to see the Hints and Solutions

Access Content Online on Dropbox: https://www.dropbox.com/scl/fi/1ytekiwscpktjdl0dbu9o/IMO-5-Math-Olympiad-Hints-Solution-Dropbox.pdf?rlkey=qnw9lcelb5g1yg523pl02tthz&dl=0

SECTION 1: MATHEMATICAL REASONING

1. INTEGERS

Answer Key

1. (a)	2. (a)	3. (a)	4. (c)	5. (d)	6. (a)	7. (b)	8. (c)	9. (b)	10. (c)
11. (a)	12. (b)	13. (d)	14. (d)	15. (a)	16. (c)	17. (b)	18. (c)	19. (b)	20. (d)
21. (a)	22. (a)	23. (b)	24. (a)	25. (b)	26. (c)	27. (c)	28. (d)	29. (b)	30. (b)

HOTS

| 1. (d) | 2. (b) | 3. (c) | 4. (b) | 5. (d) |

2. FRACTIONS AND DECIMALS

Answer Key

1. (b)	2. (c)	3. (c)	4. (b)	5. (b)	6. (a)	7. (d)	8. (c)	9. (b)	10. (c)
11. (d)	12. (a)	13. (c)	14. (d)	15. (a)	16. (c)	17. (b)	18. (c)	19. (c)	20. (c)
21. (d)	22. (a)	23. (d)	24. (a)	25. (a)	26. (b)	27. (b)	28. (c)	29. (c)	30. (a)

HOTS

| 1. (a) | 2. (b) | 3. (d) | 4. (b) | 5. (d) |

3. RATIONAL NUMBERS

Answer Key

1. (b)	2. (c)	3. (a)	4. (b)	5. (c)	6. (d)	7. (b)	8. (d)	9. (b)	10. (b)
11. (b)	12. (c)	13. (a)	14. (d)	15. (c)	16. (a)	17. (b)	18. (d)	19. (a)	20. (a)
21. (c)	22. (b)	23. (b)	24. (a)	25. (b)	26. (a)	27. (c)	28. (c)	29. (d)	30. (b)

HOTS

| 1. (a) | 2. (b) | 3. (c) | 4. (a) | 5. (a) |

4. EXPONENTS AND POWERS

Answer Key

1. (b)	2. (b)	3. (d)	4. (a)	5. (b)	6. (b)	7. (b)	8. (c)	9. (a)	10. (c)
11. (d)	12. (d)	13. (a)	14. (b)	15. (d)	16. (c)	17. (a)	18. (c)	19. (c)	20. (b)
21. (c)	22. (d)	23. (c)	24. (b)	25. (c)	26. (d)	27. (d)	28. (b)	29. (c)	30. (b)

HOTS

1. (c)	2. (d)	3. (a)	4. (c)	5. (b)

5. RATIO AND PERCENTAGE

Answer Key

1. (b)	2. (c)	3. (d)	4. (c)	5. (d)	6. (a)	7. (d)	8. (d)	9. (d)	10. (a)
11. (a)	12. (b)	13. (c)	14. (a)	15. (b)	16. (a)	17. (b)	18. (c)	19. (a)	20. (d)
21. (a)	22. (c)	23. (b)	24. (d)	25. (c)					

HOTS

1. (d)	2. (d)	3. (b)	4. (c)	5. (a)

6. PROFIT AND LOSS

Answer Key

1. (b)	2. (b)	3. (b)	4. (b)	5. (c)	6. (a)	7. (c)	8. (c)	9. (c)	10. (d)
11. (d)	12. (c)	13. (a)	14. (b)	15. (b)	16. (b)	17. (b)	18. (c)	19. (d)	20. (c)
21. (c)	22. (d)	23. (a)	24. (c)	25. (d)	26. (d)	27. (d)	28 (c)	29. (b)	30. (a)

HOTS

1. (a)	2. (d)	3. (b)	4. (d)	5. (a)	6. (a)	7. (a)	8. (c)	9. (a)	10. (a)

7. SIMPLE AND COMPOUND INTEREST

Answer Key

1. (a)	2. (a)	3. (a)	4. (c)	5. (b)	6. (d)	7. (b)	8. (c)	9. (b)	10. (d)
11. (b)	12. (b)	13. (c)	14. (a)	15. (a)	16. (b)	17. (a)	18. (b)	19. (d)	20. (c)
21. (a)	22. (d)	23. (c)	24. (d)	25. (d)	26. (c)	27. (a)	28. (c)	29. (c)	30. (b)

HOTS

| 1. (b) | 2. (b) | 3. (a) | 4. (a) | 5. (d) | | |

8. ALGEBRAIC EXPRESSIONS

Answer Key

1. (b)	2. (a)	3. (d)	4. (a)	5. (b)	6. (c)	7. (a)	8. (a)	9. (b)	10. (d)
11. (b)	12. (a)	13. (b)	14. (b)	15. (a)	16. (c)	17. (d)	18. (b)	19. (a)	20. (b)
21. (a)	22. (b)	23. (a)	24. (c)	25. (a)	26. (a)	27. (b)	28. (c)	29. (d)	30. (a)

HOTS

| 1. (a) | 2. (a) | 3. (a) | 4. (b) | 5. (c) |

9. LINEAR EQUATIONS IN ONE VARIABLE

Answer Key

1. (c)	2. (b)	3. (b)	4. (a)	5. (b)	6. (d)	7. (c)	8. (c)	9. (a)	10. (b)
11. (c)	12. (d)	13. (d)	14. (a)	15. (a)	16. (d)	17. (b)	18. (a)	19. (b)	20. (b)
21. (c)	22. (c)	23. (b)	24. (c)	25. (d)					

HOTS

| 1. (a) | 2. (a) | 3. (a) | 4. (c) | 5. (d) |

10. LINES AND ANGLES

Answer Key

| 1. (c) | 2. (a) | 3. (a) | 4. (b) | 5. (c) | 6. (c) | 7. (b) | 8. (b) | 9. (b) | 10 (b) |
| 11. (a) | 12. (c) | 13. (b) | 14. (c) | 15. (b) | 16. (c) | 17. (b) | 18. (a) | 19. (a) | 20. (c) |

HOTS

| 1. (a) | 2. (c) | 3. (a) | 4. (b) | 5. (c) |

11. TRIANGLES

Answer Key

1. (b)	2. (a)	3. (d)	4. (a)	5. (c)	6. (d)	7. (b)	8. (c)	9. (d)	10 (b)
11. (b)	12. (c)	13. (a)	14. (b)	15. (c)	16. (b)	17. (d)	18. (b)	19. (d)	20. (b)
21. (a)	22. (a)	23. (c)	24. (d)	25. (a)					

HOTS

1. (c)	2. (b)	3. (a)	4. (a)	5. (c)

12. DATA HANDLING

Answer Key

1. (c)	2. (a)	3. (b)	4. (c)	5. (c)	6. (b)	7. (a)	8. (b)	9. (b)	10. (c)
11. (b)	12. (c)	13. (c)	14. (c)	15. (c)	16. (b)	17. (c)	18. (b)	19. (c)	20. (d)
21. (a)	22. (d)	23. (b)	24. (b)	25. (c)	26. (d)	27. (b)	28. (c)	29. (b)	30. (d)

HOTS

1. (a)	2. (c)	3. (a)	4. (a)	5. (c)

13. ELEMENTARY MENSURATION

Answer Key

1. (b)	2. (d)	3. (b)	4. (c)	5. (b)	6. (c)	7. (d)	8. (c)	9. (b)	10. (a)
11. (d)	12. (b)	13. (d)	14. (d)	15. (c)	16. (c)	17. (d)	18. (a)	19. (d)	20. (c)
21. (a)	22. (b)	23. (d)	24. (d)	25. (a)	26. (c)	27. (a)	28 (b)	29. (b)	30. (b)

HOTS

1. (c)	2. (d)	3. (a)	4. (d)	5. (c)	6. (a)	7. (b)	8. (d)	9. (d)	10. (c)
11. (d)	12. (c)	13. (d)	14. (a)	15. (c)					

14. VISUALIZING SOLID SHAPES

Answer Key

1. (a)	2. (b)	3. (c)	4. (a)	5. (b)	6. (b)	7. (b)	8. (c)	9. (a)	10. (b)
11. (b)	12. (b)	13. (c)	14. (c)	15. (c)	16. (c)	17. (d)	18. (c)	19. (d)	20. (c)
21. (d)	22. (b)	23. (c)	24. (d)	25. (b)	26. (c)	27. (c)	28. (c)	29. (c)	30. (a)
31. (d)	32. (c)	33. (d)	34. (b)	35. (c)	36. (c)	37. (d)	38. (d)	39. (b)	40. (a)

HOTS

| 1. (d) | 2. (c) | 3. (d) | 4. (d) | 5. (b) |

15. MATHEMATICAL REASONING

Answer Key

1. (b)	2. (d)	3. (c)	4. (d)	5. (b)	6. (a)	7. (c)	8. (c)	9. (c)	10 (c)
11. (a)	12. (c)	13. (d)	14. (b)	15. (c)	16. (b)	17. (b)	18. (d)	19. (a)	20. (c)
21. (a)	22. (b)	23. (a)	24. (b)	25. (a)					

HOTS

| 1. (b) | 2. (c) | 3. (d) | 4. (b) | 5. (a) | 6. (c) | 7. (c) | 8. (c) | 9. (c) | 10. (d) |
| 11. (b) | 12. (c) | 13. (b) | 14. (a) | 15. (d) | | | | | |

SECTION 2: LOGICAL REASONING

1. PATTERN

Answer Key

1. (c)	2. (a)	3. (b)	4. (b)	5. (c)	6. (c)	7. (d)	8. (a)	9. (c)	10 (b)
11. (b)	12. (b)	13. (b)	14. (c)	15. (d)	16. (a)	17. (b)	18. (c)	19. (a)	20. (b)
21. (b)	22. (c)	23. (c)	24. (b)	25. (d)	26. (b)	27. (b)	28. (a)	29. (b)	30. (c)

2. NUMBER SERIES

Answer Key

1. (a)	2. (d)	3. (c)	4. (a)	5. (b)	6. (a)	7. (d)	8. (a)	9. (c)	10. (c)
11. (a)	12. (b)	13. (b)	14. (b)	15. (d)	16. (d)	17. (d)	18. (a)	19. (b)	20. (d)
21. (c)	22. (a)	23. (b)	24. (c)	25. (b)					

3. ALPHABETICAL SERIES

Answer Key

1. (a)	2. (c)	3. (c)	4. (a)	5. (a)	6. (b)	7. (a)	8. (b)	9. (b)	10. (c)
11. (a)	12. (d).	13. (c)	14. (a)	15. (c)	16. (d)	17. (b)	18. (b)	19. (a)	20. (c)
21. (d)	22. (c)	23. (c)	24. (a)	25. (d)					

4. ODD ONE OUT

Answer Key

1. (d)	2. (d)	3. (a)	4. (b)	5. (b)	6. (d)	7. (a)	8. (d)	9. (b)	10. (d)
11. (c)	12. (d)	13. (d)	14. (c)	15. (d)	16. (c)	17. (b)	18. (d)	19. (d)	20. (d)
21. (c)	22. (d)	23. (b)	24. (d)	25. (c)	26. (a)	27. (d)	28. (c)	29. (a)	30. (c)
31. (c)	32. (b)	33. (d)	34. (d)	35. (b)	36. (c)	37. (b)	38. (c)	39. (d)	40. (a)
41. (d)	42. (c)	43. (d)	44. (a)	45. (d)	46. (b)	47. (d)	48. (a)	49. (c)	50. (b)
51. (c)	52. (d)	53. (a)	54. (d)	55. (b)	56. (a)	57. (d)	58. (d)	59. (b)	60. (b)

5. CODING DECODING

Answer Key

1. (a)	2. (a)	3. (c)	4. (c)	5. (c)	6. (b)	7. (a)	8. (c)	9. (b)	10 (c)
11. (b)	12. (b)	13. (c)	14. (a)	15. (b)	16. (d)	17. (b)	18. (a)	19. (c)	20. (d)
21. (a)	22. (c)	23. (d)	24. (d)	25. (c)	26. (d)	27. (a)	28. (d)	29. (a)	30. (a)

6. ALPHABET TEST

Answer Key

1. (c)	2. (a)	3. (d)	4. (a)	5. (b)	6. (b)	7. (a)	8. (c)	9. (d)	10 (d)
11. (d)	12. (c)	13. (b)	14. (d)	15. (b)	16. (c)	17. (b)	18. (a)	19. (d)	20. (c)
21. (a)	22. (d)	23. (b)	24. (d)	25. (b)	26. (a)	27. (c)	28. (d)	29. (b)	30. (a)

7. BLOOD RELATION TEST

Answer Key

1. (d)	2. (a)	3. (c)	4. (b)	5. (b)	6. (c)	7. (a)	8. (d)	9. (a)	10. (b)
11. (b)	12. (b)	13. (b)	14. (d)	15. (b)	16. (d)	17. (d)	18. (d)	19. (a)	20. (a)
21. (b)	22. (b)	23. (b)	24. (d)	25. (b)	26. (a)	27. (b)	28. (d)	29. (c)	30. (c)

8. DIRECTION SENSE TEST

Answer Key

1. (c)	2. (a)	3. (c)	4. (c)	5. (b)	6. (a)	7. (b)	8. (b)	9. (a)	10. (b)
11. (b)	12. (b)	13. (c)	14. (a)	15. (c)	16. (a)	17. (c)	18. (b)	19. (a)	20. (c)
21. (b)	22. (b)	23. (d)	24. (b)	25. (c)					

9. NUMBER RANKING TEST

Answer Key

1. (c)	2. (a)	3. (c)	4. (b)	5. (c)	6. (d)	7. (d)	8. (c)	9. (a)	10 (b)
11. (a)	12. (c)	13. (c)	14. (b)	15. (a)	16. (c)	17. (a)	18. (d)	19. (a)	20. (c)
21. (b)	22. (c)	23. (c)	24. (a)	25. (c)	26. (b)	27. (c)	28. (b)	29. (c)	30. (d)

10. ODD ONE OUT

Answer Key

1. (a)	2. (b)	3. (a)	4. (d)	5. (a)	6. (c)	7. (b)	8. (b)	9. (d)	10. (d)
11. (a)	12. (c)	13. (d)	14. (d)	15. (c)	16. (c)	17. (d)	18. (d)	19. (c)	20. (d)
21. (e)	22. (c)	23. (d)	24. (c)	25. (d)					

11. DICE

Answer Key

1. (a)	2. (c)	3. (a)	4. (c)	5. (a)	6. (a)	7. (c)	8. (c)	9. (c)	10. (c)
11. (a)	12. (b)	13. (b)	14. (c)	15. (d)	16. (b)	17. (c)	18. (d)	19. (c)	20. (c)

12. MIRROR IMAGES

Answer Key

1. (d)	2. (b)	3. (a)	4. (d)	5. (c)	6. (b)	7. (b)	8. (a)	9. (a)	10. (d)
11. (d)	12. (d)	13. (a)	14. (b)	15. (d)	16. (c)	17 (d)	18. (a)	19. (c)	20. (b)
21. (a)	22. (d)	23. (a)	24. (d)	25. (d)	26. (c)	27. (c)	28 (a)	29. (c)	30. (d)

13. WATER IMAGES

Answer Key

1. (c)	2. (a)	3. (b)	4. (a)	5. (d)	6. (b)	7. (d)	8. (a)	9. (b)	10. (a)
11. (b)	12. (a)	13. (b)	14. (b)	15. (a)	16. (a)	17. (b)	18. (d)	19. (d)	20. (a)
21. (a)	22. (d)	23. (c)	24. (c)	25. (c)	26. (d)	27. (a)	28. (b)	29. (d)	30. (c)

14. EMBEDDED FIGURES

Answer Key

1. (c)	2. (c)	3. (a)	4. (a)	5. (a)	6. (c)	7. (a)	8. (b)	9. (d)	10. (a)
11. (a)	12. (c)	13. (d)	14. (d)	15. (a)	16. (b)	17. (d)	18. (b)	19. (b)	20. (a)
21. (b)	22. (d)	23. (c)	24. (b)	25. (d)	26. (a)	27. (d)	28. (b)	29. (a)	30. (c)

15. VENN DIAGRAMS

Answer Key

1. (b)	2. (d)	3. (a)	4. (a)	5. (d)	6. (d)	7. (c)	8. (a)	9. (b)	10. (c)
11. (b)	12. (d)	13. (c)	14. (d)	15. (d)	16. (c)	17. (c)	18. (b)	19. (c)	20. (d)
21. (c)	22. (a)	23. (c)	24. (c)	25. (a)	26. (b)	27. (c)	28. (c)	29. (c)	30. (c)
31. (a)	32. (c)	33. (b)	34. (c)	35. (c)	36. (c)	37. (c)	38. (a)	39. (b)	40. (c)

MODEL TEST PAPER – 1

Answer Key

1. (a)	2. (b)	3. (c)	4. (a)	5. (c)	6. (b)	7. (a)	8. (c)	9. (a)	10. (a)
11. (c)	12. (a)	13. (a)	14. (b)	15. (a)	16. (c)	17. (c)	18. (b)	19. (c)	20. (d)
21. (a)	22. (b)	23. (d)	24. (d)	25. (b)	26. (d)	27. (c)	28. (d)	29. (a)	30. (b)
31. (c)	32. (a)	33. (a)	34. (b)	35. (a)	36. (a)	37. (c)	38. (c)	39. (a)	40. (b)
41. (a)	42. (c)	43. (c)	44. (a)	45. (a)	46. (b)	47. (b)	48. (b)	49. (a)	50. (c)

MODEL TEST PAPER – 2

Answer Key

1. (a)	2. (a)	3. (b)	4. (c)	5. (b)	6. (b)	7. (d)	8. (a)	9. (c)	10. (a)
11. (c)	12. (c)	13. (b)	14. (a)	15. (b)	16. (d)	17. (c)	18. (c)	19. (b)	20. (b)
21. (a)	22. (a)	23. (b)	24. (c)	25. (b)	26. (c)	27. (a)	28. (c)	29. (a)	30. (c)
31. (d)	32. (d)	33. (b)	34. (c)	35. (c)	36. (c)	37. (c)	38. (b)	39. (a)	40. (a)
41. (d)	42. (b)	43. (d)	44. (b)	45. (a)	46. (d)	47. (a)	48. (d)	49. (b)	50. (b)

Appendix

There are different organizations that conduct these examinations and covering all of them is not needed as the focus should be to understand the main type of exams conducted. They are similar for these organizations with the difference being the change in name of the exam.

\multicolumn{3}{c}{SCIENCE OLYMPIAD FOUNDATION (SOF)}		
S. No.	Name of Exam	Grade
1.	National Science Olympiad (NSO)	Class 1-10
2.	National Cyber Olympiad (NCO)	Class 1-10
3.	International Mathematics Olympiad (IMO)	Class 1-10
4.	International English Olympiad (IEO)	Class 1-10
5.	International Commerce Olympiad (ICO)	Class 1-10
6.	International General Knowledge Olympiad (IGKO)	Class 1-10
7.	International Social Studies Olympiad (ISSO)	Class 1-10
\multicolumn{3}{c}{INDIAN TALENT OLYMPIAD (ITO)}		
S. No.	Name of Exam	Grade
1.	International Science Olympiad (ISO)	Class 1-12
2.	International Math Olympiad (IMO)	Class 1-12
3.	English International Olympiad (EIO)	Class 1-12
4.	General Knowledge International Olympiad (GKIO)	Class 1-12
5.	International Computer Olympiad (ICO)	Class 1-12
6.	International Drawing Olympiad (IDO)	Class 1-12
7.	National Essay Olympiad (NESO)	Class 1-12
8.	National Social Studies Olympiad (NSSO)	Class 1-12
\multicolumn{3}{c}{EDUHEAL FOUNDATION}		
S. No.	Name of Exam	Grade
1.	Eduheal International Cyber Olympiad (ICO)	Class 1-12
2.	Eduheal International English Olympiad (IEO)	Class 1-12
3.	National Interactive Math Olympiad (NIMO)	Class 1-12
4.	National Interactive Science Olympiad (NISO)	Class 1-12
5.	International General Knowledge Olympiad (IGO)	Class 1-12
6.	National Space Science Olympiad (NSSO)	Class 1-12

HUMMING BIRD EDUCATION

S. No.	Name of Exam	Grade
1.	Humming Bird Commerce Competency Olympiad (HCC)	Class 1-12
2.	Humming Bird Cyber Olympiad (HCO)	Class 1-12
3.	Humming Bird English Olympiad (HEO)	Class 1-12
4.	Humming Bird General Knowledge Olympiad (HGO)	Class 1-12
5.	Humming Bird Hindi Olympiad (HHO)	Class 1-12
6.	Humming Bird Mathematics Olympiad (HMO)	Class 1-12
7.	Humming Bird Science Olympiad (HSO)	Class 1-12
8.	Humming Bird Aptitude and Reasoning Olympiad (ARO)	Class 1-12
9.	Humming Bird Spelling Competition (Spell BEE)	Class 1-12
10.	Humming Bird Language Olympiad	Class 1-12

INTERNATIONAL ASSESSMENTS FOR INDIAN SCHOOLS (IAIS) (MACMILLAN AND EEA COLLABORATION)

S. No.	Name of Exam	Grade
1.	IAIS Maths Olympiad	Class 3-12
2.	IAIS ScienceOlympiad	Class 3-12
3.	IAIS English Olympiad	Class 3-12
4.	IAIS Digital Technologies Olympiad	Class 3-12

SILVERZONE FOUNDATION

S. No.	Name of Exam	Grade
1.	International Informatics Olympiad	Class 1-12
2.	International Olympiad of Mathematics	Class 1-12
3.	International Olympiad of Science	Class 1-12

UNIFIED COUNCIL

S. No.	Name of Exam	Grade
1.	Unified Council Cyber Exam	Class 1-12
2.	Unified International English Olympiad.	Class 1-12
3.	Unified International Mathematics Olympiad (UIMO)	Class 1-12

UNICUS

S. No.	Name of Exam	Grade
1.	Unicus Non-Routine Mathematics Olympiad (UNRMO)	Class 1-11
2.	Unicus Mathematics Olympiad (UMO)	Class 1-11

3.	Unicus Science Olympiad (USO)	Class 1-11
4.	Unicus English Olympiad (UEO)	Class 1-11
5.	Unicus Cyber Olympiad (UCO)	Class 1-11
6.	Unicus General knowledge Olympiad (UGKO)	Class 1-11
7.	Unicus Critical Thinking Olympiad (UCTO)	Class 1-11
CREST (ONLINE MODE)		
S. No.	**Name of Exam**	**Grade**
1.	Mathematics (CMO)	Classes KG-10
2.	Science (CSO)	Classes KG-10
3.	English (CEO)	Classes KG-10
4.	Computer (CCO)	Classes 1-10
5.	Reasoning (CRO)	Classes 1-10
6.	Spell Bee Summer (CSB)	Classes 1-8
7.	Spell Bee Winter (CSBW)	Classes 1-8
8.	Mental Maths (MMO)	Classes 1-12
9.	Green Warrior Olympiad (GWO)	Classes 1-12

HOW TO APPLY?

Anyone willing to participate in the Olympiad exam can follow these steps to apply for the exam:

- ☞ Log in to the official website of the conducting organization.
- ☞ Find the Registration Option to register
- ☞ Fill up the details such as Student Name, Parent Name, School Name, Class, Postal Address, E-mail Address, Password, etc.
- ☞ Select the subjects you want to apply for. Pay the necessary registration fees and you are done.
- ☞ You will receive necessary details on your email id.

There are no minimum marks required by the Olympiad conducting organizations to apply for the exam.

AWARDS

Based on the organization rules, students as well as schools participating in these exams are awarded with several recognitions based on the marks they score.

www.ingramcontent.com/pod-product-compliance
Lightning Source LLC
Chambersburg PA
CBHW081919170426
43200CB00014B/2762